The 12 questions Thaddeus raises are the right que
today's troubled world. Read with an open mind. Risk
along into false answers that lead to only more injusti

JOHN PERKINS, president, The John and Ve.
Perkins Foundation; author of *One Blood*

As an African American pastor of a predominately African American church, I'm
often asked what book I would recommend on the controversial topic of social justice.
Thaddeus Williams has written my top recommendation. Thoroughly biblical, well-
reasoned, and deeply charitable, this balanced book is a beacon of gospel light to every
believer desiring to confront injustice armed with the truth of the Word. There are few
issues of our day more important for Christians to get right than this one, and we owe
Dr. Williams a debt of gratitude for his courage and skill applied to the production of
this excellent work.

ANTHONY D. KIDD, pastor of preaching,
Community of Faith Bible Church, South Gate, California

This is the most important book I have recommended in over twenty years. I have known
Professor Williams for many years as a graduate student, friend, and faculty colleague.
He is recognized as a person who walks what he talks. Thus, he brings biblical rigor,
fidelity, cultural sensitivity, and concern to the topics in this book. It is now the go-to
resource for clear, biblical thinking about social justice. I know of no other evangelical
book with such rigor, insight, biblical fidelity, ethical maturity, and breadth of coverage
as this one. This is the book for you!

J. P. MORELAND, distinguished professor of philosophy,
Talbot School of Theology; author of *Finding Quiet*

If you are a Christian concerned about oppression, injustice, racism, and other moral
ills that plague our culture, there may not be a more important book you read this year.
Secular ideologies offer solutions to age-old problems that may act like temporary fixes,
but only the Christian worldview can provide a robust and deeply satisfying action
plan. *Confronting Injustice without Compromising Truth* is *the* definitive guide to help
Christians "do justice, and to love kindness, and to walk humbly with your God . . ."
as Micah 6:8 puts it, while not sacrificing one iota of biblical truth.

ALISA CHILDERS, blogger and podcast host at
www.alisachilders.com, author of *Another Gospel?*

Confronting Injustice without Compromising Truth is the book I've been waiting for! This is the book that explains and analyzes the social justice movement—that treats it fairly and evaluates it critically. This is the book that prioritizes the gospel as the foundation for any true justice. This is the book that helps Christians understand why they must emphasize social justice, but why they must emphasize the right kind of social justice. This is the book I highly recommend.

> **TIM CHALLIES,** blogger at www.challies.com,
> author of *Do More Better*

Williams shows us how to think *from* the Christian faith, rather than allowing the categories and concerns of the day to rule the way Christians talk about race, politics, and inequality. This well-written, highly engaging book deserves careful consideration by every thoughtful Christian concerned about the issues of our time—not least because it allows Scripture to question some of our key assumptions about these issues, while also providing alternative ways to think about and engage them as kingdom citizens.

> **UCHE ANIZOR,** associate professor of theology,
> Biola University; author of *How to Read Theology*

Simply outstanding. Williams is fair-minded to Christians on both sides of the political spectrum while not shying away from what needs to be said. This urgently needed guide brings clarity to one of the greatest confusions Christians have in today's culture: discerning the difference between notions of justice rooted in a Christian worldview and those rooted in a godless secularism. Make no mistake—there's a critical difference, and it's one that's dangerously deceiving a great number in the church.

> **NATASHA CRAIN,** blogger at www.christianmomthoughts.com;
> author of *Talking with Your Kids about Jesus*

In our tribalized social-media age, the loudest voices are the ones that tend to get a hearing. But I'm thankful for the thoughtful voices that speak with wisdom to some of the most contentious issues we face today. Thaddeus Williams tackles them all—racism, sexuality, socialism, abortion, critical theory, identity politics—and argues that social justice, while not the gospel, isn't optional for Christians. Justified people seek to be a just people. But Williams also reminds us that not everything branded "social justice"—the increasingly superficial, knee-jerk activism of our day is truly biblical. Whatever your starting point in this conversation, here's a book that will help inform, equip, and serve the church.

> **IVAN MESA,** editor, the Gospel Coalition

Are you concerned about social justice and the church? If so, Thaddeus Williams's contribution to the discussion is a must-read. As an academic committed to justice concerns, I'm thankful for Williams's approach. He's unequivocal yet charitable and proves to be percipient and discerning as he unpacks his subject with care achieving the often elusive combination of necessary depth and broad accessibility. Join him and his cadre of diverse contributors as they address arguably the most significant issue facing today's church.

PAT SAWYER, professor of education and cultural studies,
University of North Carolina at Greensboro

Thaddeus, without a doubt, distributed some much-needed truth to the issue of how the social justice argument is contrary to gospel truth. His section on "Sinners or Systems" was a breath of fresh air to a critical thinker like myself. I recommend this work to anyone who desires to stand on the side of the truth rather than speculations when it pertains to how we apply the Word of God in today's cultural climate.

JAMAL BANDY, host, the *Prescribed Truth* podcast

Wherever one finds oneself in the debate related to Christians and social justice, this important work by Thaddeus Williams and friends will offer wise guidance to these challenging issues. Williams is to be commended for his courage in offering this road map for his readers. Anyone who wishes to engage in the debate regarding social justice in the days ahead will find *Confronting Injustice without Compromising Truth* an essential prerequisite to that discussion.

DAVID S. DOCKERY, president, International Alliance
for Christian Education; theologian-in-residence,
Southwestern Baptist Theological Seminary

As a parent, teacher, and Christ-follower, my heart has been so troubled by the way many Christians have been drawn into false notions of social justice. Williams's book provides the kind of courageous, clear, truth-telling that can help bring sanity and unifying, gospel-centered love and justice to hurting people, fragmented churches, and a hostile world. This book provides direction for those who would seek to do justice in a way that honors God and truly loves others without resorting to us-versus-them dichotomies that tear people apart.

LAURA ROSENKRANZ, mother, teacher

"Social Justice"—the very term too often quickly divides the room, resulting in rancor, uncivility, and broken relationships. This work will change that. Williams's bold contribution displays devotion to loving both God and neighbor with fidelity. Traveling beyond bogus binaries, pietistic proof-texting, and poisonous partisanship, Williams instead probes today's complex issues with riveting penetration, yet gracious patience so this crucial conversation can be continued, not censored.

> **JEFFERY J. VENTRELLA,** senior counsel, senior vice president of
> academic affairs and training, Alliance Defending Freedom

Thaddeus Williams tackles the emotional topic of social justice in a way that is simultaneously personable, compassionate, and biblically faithful. Thaddeus doesn't try to "Christianize" secular social justice ideology with a few Bible verses taken out of context. Rather, he works toward a faithful presentation of the biblical data. As a theologian working on justice questions, I am grateful for this contribution to this field.

> **KRISTA BONTRAGER,** theologian at Theology Mom,
> cohost of *All the Things* podcast

In the task of fulfilling a biblical vision for humanity, we must heed the cry of our generation. This book calls us to conform our minds to the truth that informs justice. With its source in God, justice must flow through the human heart in order for it to be actualized in our world. *Confronting Injustice without Compromising Truth* attempts to clear the way to let justice roll down as waters.

> **JACOB DANIEL,** founder, The Heritage Counsel

Williams offers a needed correction to some of the excesses in today's modern social justice movement. He does so without denying the existence of many of the problems such movements hope to address. The addition of *Confronting Injustice without Compromising Truth* to our personal libraries will help us to move closer to a holistic approach to issues tied to social justice.

> **GEORGE YANCEY,** professor of sociology,
> Baylor University; author of *Beyond Racial Gridlock*

Thaddeus Williams raises a number of good questions about justice—how the Bible defines it, what actions promote it, and what philosophies and ideologies might undermine it. There's plenty here to challenge your presuppositions and assumptions—all with the goal of being more faithful to Scripture and clear-eyed regarding today's possibilities and pitfalls for doing justice in society.

> **TREVIN WAX,** senior vice president for theology and communications,
> LifeWay Christian Resources; author of *Rethink Your Self*

CONFRONTING
INJUSTICE
WITHOUT
COMPROMISING
TRUTH

CONFRONTING INJUSTICE

WITHOUT COMPROMISING

TRUTH

12 QUESTIONS CHRISTIANS SHOULD ASK ABOUT SOCIAL JUSTICE

THADDEUS J. WILLIAMS

WITH THE VOICES OF SURESH BUDHAPRITHI, EDDIE BYUN,
FREDDY CARDOZA, BECKET COOK, BELLA DANUSIAR,
MONIQUE DUSON, MICHELLE LEE-BARNEWALL, OJO OKOYE,
EDWIN RAMIREZ, SAMUEL SEY, NEIL SHENVI, AND WALT SOBCHAK

ZONDERVAN
ACADEMIC

ZONDERVAN ACADEMIC

Confronting Injustice without Compromising Truth
Copyright © 2020 by Thaddeus Williams

Requests for information should be addressed to:
Zondervan, *3900 Sparks Dr. SE, Grand Rapids, Michigan 49546*

Zondervan titles may be purchased in bulk for educational, business, fundraising, or sales promotional use. For information, please email SpecialMarkets@Zondervan.com.

ISBN 978-0-310-11948-7 (softcover)

ISBN 978-0-310-11949-4 (ebook)

ISBN 978-0-310-11950-0 (audio)

Library of Congress Cataloging-in-Publication Data

Names: Williams, Thaddeus J., author.
Title: Confronting injustice without compromising truth : 12 questions Christians should ask about social justice / Thaddeus J Williams ...
Description: Grand Rapids : Zondervan, [2020] | "... with the voices of Suresh Budhaprithi, Eddie Byun, Freddy Cardoza, Becket Cook, Bella Danusiar, Monique Duson, Michelle Lee-Barnewall, Ojo Okoye, Edwin Ramirez, Samuel Sey, Neil Shenvi, and Walt Sobchak."
Identifiers: LCCN 2020037890 (print) | LCCN 2020037891 (ebook) | ISBN 9780310119487 (paperback) | ISBN 9780310119494 (ebook)
Subjects: LCSH: Social justice--Religious aspects--Christianity. | Christianity and justice.
Classification: LCC BR115.J8 W55 2020 (print) | LCC BR115.J8 (ebook) | DDC 261.8--dc23
LC record available at https://lccn.loc.gov/2020037890
LC ebook record available at https://lccn.loc.gov/2020037891

Cover design and art: Thaddeus Williams

Printed in the United States of America

20 21 22 23 24 25 26 27 28 29 30 /LSC/ 15 14 13 12 11 10 9 8 7 6 5 4 3 2 1

To Gracie, Dutch, Jalula, and Henny
May you each grow "to do justice, and to love kindness,
and to walk humbly with your God" (Micah 6:8)

Contents

Part 3: Sinners or Systems? Three Questions about Social Justice and Salvation

Part 4: Truth or Tribes Thinking? Three Questions about Social Justice and Knowledge

Foreword

I was born on a Mississippi cotton plantation in 1930. My mother died of nutrition deficiency when I was just seven months old. My big brother, a World War II veteran, was gunned down by a town marshal when I was seventeen years old. As a civil rights activist, I was jailed and beaten nearly to death by police. They tortured me without mercy, stuck a fork up my nose and down my throat, then made me mop up my own blood. I have known injustice.

It would have been the easiest thing in the world for me to answer hate with hate. But God had another plan for my life, a redemptive plan. Jesus saved me. He saved me from my sin. He saved me from what could have easily become a life of hatred and resentment. He saved me by his amazing grace. And it's by that same grace that I have spent the last sixty years with my wife, Vera Mae, confronting injustice. We have literally poured blood, sweat, and tears into the causes of civil rights, multiethnic reconciliation, community development, building good relationships between urban communities and the police, education, teaching the gospel, and wholistic ministry. I have labored not by my strength but "by his strength that works powerfully in me," as Paul said. And God has been faithful.

Through my sixty years of working for justice, I offer four admonishments to the next generation of justice seekers.

First, *start with God!* God is bigger than we can imagine. We have to align ourselves with his purpose, his will, his mission to let justice roll down, and bring forgiveness and love to everyone on earth. The problem of injustice is a God-sized problem. If we don't start with him first, whatever we're seeking, it ain't justice.

Second*, be one in Christ!* Christian brothers and sisters—black, white, brown, rich, and poor—we are family. We are one blood. We are adopted by the same Father, saved by the same Son, filled with the same Spirit. In John 17 Jesus prays for everyone who would believe in him, that people from every tongue, tribe, and nation would be one. That oneness is how the world will know who Jesus is. If we give a foothold to any kind of tribalism that could tear down that unity, then we aren't bringing God's justice.

Third, *preach the gospel!* The gospel of Jesus's incarnation, his perfect life, his death as our substitute, and his triumph over sin and death is good news for everyone. It is multicultural good news. In the blood of Jesus, we are able to truly see ourselves as one race, one blood. We've got to stop playing the race game. Christ alone can break down the barriers of prejudice and hate we all struggle with. There is no power greater than God's love expressed in Jesus. That's where we all find real human dignity. If we replace the gospel with this or that man-made political agenda, then we ain't doing biblical justice.

Fourth and finally, *teach truth!* Without truth, there can be no justice. And what is the ultimate standard of truth? It is not our feelings. It is not popular opinion. It is not what presidents or politicians say. God's Word is the standard of truth. If we're trying harder to align with the rising opinions of our day than with the Bible, then we ain't doing real justice.

Those four marks of my sixty years in ministry are exactly what this book is about and why I wholeheartedly stand behind it. Dr. Thaddeus Williams and his twelve coauthors are important voices for helping us pursue the kind of justice that starts with God, champions our oneness in Christ, declares the gospel, and refuses to compromise truth.

We are in the midst of a great upheaval. There is much confusion, much anger, and much injustice. Sadly, many Christian brothers and sisters are trying to fight this fight with man-made solutions. These solutions promise justice but deliver division and idolatry. They become false gospels. Thankfully, in these trying times, new conversations are happening, and the right questions are beginning to be asked. I believe the twelve questions Thaddeus raises in the book are the right questions we should all be asking in today's troubled world.

So I encourage you, read with an open mind. Risk a change of heart. Dare to reach across the divides of our day. Venture beyond anger and hurt into grace and forgiveness. Don't get swept along into false answers that lead only to more injustice. Love one another. Confront injustice without compromising truth—healing, unifying, biblical truth! May this book be a guide to do exactly that, for God's glory and the good of every tongue, tribe, and nation.

John M. Perkins
President Emeritus
John and Vera Mae Perkins Foundation
Jackson, Mississippi
Author of *One Blood, Let Justice Roll Down,* and *With Justice for All*

Why Write about the Most Explosive, Polarizing, and Mentally Exhausting Issues of Our Day?

My wife and I muse together over the fact that we are the last generation on earth to know life without the internet. I didn't hear the first dying robot-cat squeals of a dial-up modem until I was fourteen. That is not the only major culture shift I am old enough to have lived through. I came of age in the 1990s. It was the heyday of not only Britney Spears, grunge rock, and *Seinfeld* but also moral relativism in America. It was the "not that innocent" age of "come as you are" and "not that there's anything wrong with that." The only real sin was calling anything "sin." "Don't judge!" was the creed of the era (other than the actual band Creed, which, of course, it is always okay to judge).

Since then we have watched a culture that prided itself in its nonjudgmentalism turn into one of the most judgmental societies in history. Just this morning my news feed blew up with bristling judgments against every Christian who has yet to publicly voice their outrage about a headline that dropped less than twenty-four hours ago. If you happened to be off the grid hiking or at grandma's house, then too bad. "Your silence is deafening." You've been outed as the misanthrope you are before a digital jury of millions. "Make sweeping moral indictments of people you barely know" has replaced "Don't judge" as the anthem of our era. Some have branded our age the age of feeling or the age of authenticity. Another contender could be the age of the gavel.

Of course, there have always been judgmental mobs through history. But it took a lot of work. How do we get a critical mass of people assembled in the same physical space? How do we get someone with enough rabble-rousing charisma to rile everyone up? Who'll bring the pitchforks? Who's painting the banners? Who's supplying the torches? Nowadays, anyone can stir up a judgmental mob with a few thumb taps on a glowing box while sipping a flat white in an air-conditioned coffee shop.

Let's be honest. Our ubiquitous judgmentalism is not sustainable. It's exhausting. With the trifecta of cell phones, the internet, and social media, horrible incidents scroll into our consciousness from all over the world every day. It's enough to make us envy the Amish. Except it isn't Jedediah's busted wagon or Zeke's bum horse that troubles our minds. We are bombarded with the worst of humanity around the globe faster than any generation in history. As technology has made the world smaller—small enough to fit into a rectangle in our pockets—it has made our awareness of how fallen our world is exponentially bigger. There is plenty to be morally outraged about, plenty of people voicing their outrage, and plenty of those willing to voice their moral outrage at others, either for not having enough or for having the wrong kind of outrage. It's really quite outrageous.

Why, then, would I write a book about the powder-keg issues that blow up our devices daily? Why write about "social justice," given all the land mines buried in that word combination? I was recently asked a version of that question on a podcast. My response, given my character flaw of excessive sarcasm, was, "Mostly for the fame and popularity." I am well aware that questioning the sacred orthodoxies of the Left and the Right will not score me any popularity points. It will likely earn me the ire of online mobs. Why *did* I write this book?

To be blunt, I have all the answers. I have managed to solve all society's complex problems so decisively that social media can again become what it was meant to be—a place where we share cat videos, epic fails, and glamourous filtered selfies instead of yelling at each other about politics all day. (Apologies, there's that sarcasm again.) I don't pretend to have all the answers, and my many blind spots will be seen by readers and critics alike. So let's try this again.

Did I write this for the sheer joy of it? Nothing, after all, sparks more fuzzy feel-good tingles than researching injustice every day for years. Wrong again. This was easily the most soul-taxing work I have ever written. But it *had* to be written, despite several prayerful pleas for a heavenly green light to call it quits.

One last try. It was not to win the approval of online inquisitors (because I won't) or because I have it all figured out (because I don't) or because it was fun (because it wasn't). I wrote this book because I care about God, I care about his church, I care about the gospel, and I care about true justice (though I am zero for four in caring as much as I should). Not all, but much of what is branded "social justice" these days is a threat to all four of those things I hold dear.

Even though I question popular versions of social justice, I have zero interest in justifying racism or any other sinful "ism." I have zero interest in protecting my power and privilege. I have zero interest in the kind of individualistic, head-in-the-clouds Christianity that plugs its ears to the oppressed. I care about bringing Christians together in the pursuit of more authentic worship, a more unified church, a clearer gospel, and more justice in the world. If you also care about advancing the kind of social justice that glorifies God first, draws people into Christ-centered community, and champions the good news of saving grace while working against real oppression, then this book is for you. If you don't care about those things, then you are to a better world what Creed was to rock and roll.

Thaddeus Williams
Biola University
La Mirada, California

What Is "Social Justice"?

Every age of church history has its controversies. If we hopped into a DeLorean and set our digital clock to the '50s of the first century, one big question was, "What do we do with the Judaizers telling everyone that circumcision is essential to a right relationship with God?" If we punched in to the early fourth century, a big question was, "How should we think about the deity of Jesus?" If we hit eighty-eight miles per hour and flashed to the early 1500s, we would grapple with whether salvation comes by God's grace alone or whether we could gaze at sacred relics and purchase indulgences to expedite our entry through the pearly gates.

I am convinced that social justice is one of the most epic and age-defining controversies facing the twenty-first-century church. In the twentieth century you would encounter the term *social justice* while auditing a sociology course or perhaps joining the chapter of a local activists' group. Now it is in our coffee shops, our ads for soda, shoes, and shaving cream, our fast food establishments, our Super Bowls, our internet browsers, our blockbuster movies, our kindergarten curricula, our Twitter feeds, our national media, and our pulpits. It's everywhere.

Whether we see this as progress or as something pernicious hangs on questions that seem to have nothing to do with social justice controversies. Who is God? What does it mean to be human? Why does the church exist? When did the world go wrong and how can it be put right? To be a Christian who thinks seriously about social justice in the twenty-first century is to simultaneously face all the big questions that our brothers and sisters have faced for the last two thousand years of church history. Few see the deeper issues at stake.

Truly Execute Justice

Social justice is not optional for the Christian. (What justice isn't social, for that matter? God designed us as social creatures, made for community, not loners designed to live on deserted islands or staring solo at glowing screens all day. All injustice affects others, so talking about justice that isn't social is like

1

talking about water that isn't wet or a square with no right angles.) The Bible is crystal clear:

God does not suggest, He commands that we do justice.

> Do justice and righteousness, and deliver from the hand of the oppressor him who has been robbed.[1]

> What does the LORD require of you
> but to do justice, and to love kindness,
>   and to walk humbly with your God?[2]

> Is not this the fast that I choose:
>   to loose the bonds of wickedness,
>   to undo the straps of yoke,
> to let the oppressed go free,
>   and break every yoke?[3]

Doing justice brings a brightness and blessing into our lives.

> Then shall your light break forth like the dawn,
>   and your healing shall spring up speedily. . . .
> If you pour yourself out for the hungry
>   and satisfy the desire of the afflicted,
> then shall your light rise in the darkness
>   and your gloom be as the noonday.[4]

Defending the cause of the poor and needy is what it means to know God.

> He judged the cause of the poor and needy;
>   then it was well.
> Is not this to know me?
>   declares the LORD.[5]

Apathy toward the oppressed can hinder our prayers and sever our connection with God.

> When you spread out your hands,
>   I will hide my eyes from you;

even though you make many prayers,
>   I will not listen;
>   your hands are full of blood. . . .
> Cease to do evil,
>   learn to do good;
> seek justice,
>   correct oppression;
> bring justice to the fatherless,
>   plead the widow's cause.[6]

"Seek justice"[7] is a clarion call of Scripture, and those who plug their ears to that call are simply not living by the Book. But the Bible's call to seek justice is not a call to superficial, knee-jerk activism. We aren't commanded to merely execute justice but to *"truly* execute justice."[8] That presupposes there are *untrue* ways to execute justice, ways of trying to make the world a better place that aren't in sync with reality and end up unleashing more havoc in the universe. The God who commands us to seek justice is the same God who commands us to "test everything" and "hold fast to what is good."[9]

> The oppressed deserve more than our good intentions. We must love them not merely with our hearts and hands, but with our heads too.

Jesus launched his public ministry in a synagogue, declaring his mission to "proclaim good news to the poor . . . liberty to the captives and recovering of sight to the blind, to set at liberty those who are oppressed."[10] But Jesus did not seek justice at the level of headlines and hearsay. One of the marks of the Messiah is that "he shall not judge by what his eyes see, or decide disputes by what his ears hear, but with righteousness he shall judge the poor, and decide with equity for the meek of the earth."[11] When he encountered a group in protest over what they saw as the gross injustice of Sabbath day violations, he called out their unwarranted moral outrage, their failure to get at the real issues: "Do not judge by appearances, but judge with right judgment."[12]

Paul prayed that the Philippians' love would "abound more and more, with knowledge and all discernment."[13] He told the Romans not to conform to the world but to renew their minds, that by testing they "may discern what is the will of God, what is good and acceptable and perfect."[14] He commands us to "take every thought captive to obey Christ."[15] That includes the way we think about social justice. We can't separate the Bible's commands to do justice from its commands to be discerning. The oppressed deserve more than our good intentions. We must love them not merely with our hearts and hands but with our heads too. This includes carefully distinguishing true social justice from its counterfeits.

Social Justice A and B

We won't get far unless we stop to ask, "What do we mean when we say 'social justice'?" What are we to make of this potentially explosive combination of thirteen letters? "I put on my prospector's helmet and mined the literature for an agreed-upon definition of social justice," says one popular journalist. "What I found," he laments, "was one deposit after another of fool's gold. From labor unions to countless universities to gay rights groups to even the American Nazi Party, everyone insisted they were champions of social justice."[16]

Perhaps we could use *social justice* to describe what our ancient brothers and sisters did to rescue and adopt the precious little image-bearers who had been discarded like trash at the dumps outside many Roman cities. The same two words could describe William Wilberforce's and the Clapham Sect's efforts to topple slavery in the UK, along with Frederick Douglass, Harriet Tubman, and others in the US. *Social justice* could describe Sophie Scholl's and the White Rose Society's work or Dietrich Bonhoeffer's and the Confessing Church's efforts to subvert Hitler's Third Reich. It could also describe Abraham Kuyper's vision, not of an individualistic pietism but of a robust Christianity that seeks to express the lordship of Jesus over "every square inch" of life and society.

Nowadays, the same word combination could even describe Christian efforts to abolish human trafficking, work with the inner-city poor, invest in microloans to help the destitute in the developing world, build hospitals and orphanages, upend racism, and protect the unborn. Let us call this broad swath of biblically compatible justice-seeking "Social Justice A."

When many brothers and sisters hear the words *social* and *justice* put together, that's the kind of stuff they think about. They aren't wrong. But for many brothers and sisters, the identical configuration of thirteen letters is packed with altogether non-Christian and often explicitly anti-Christian meanings. They aren't wrong either.

In the last few years, *social justice* has taken on an extremely charged political meaning. It became a waving banner over movements like Antifa, which sees physical violence against those who think differently as "both ethically justifiable and strategically effective" and celebrates its underreported "righteous beatings." Social justice is the banner waved by a disproportionate ratio of professors in universities around the nation where the "oppressor vs. oppressed" narrative of Antonio Gramsci and the Frankfurt School, the deconstructionism of Michel Foucault and Jacques Derrida, and the gender and queer theory of Judith Butler have been injected into the very definition of the term. This ideological definition of social justice has been enshrined in many minds not as *a* way but as *the* way to think about justice.

Social justice is also the banner over movements with a stated mission to "disrupt the western-prescribed nuclear family structure,"[17] movements on college campuses that have resorted to violence to silence opposing voices, and movements that seek to shut down the Little Sisters of the Poor and Christian universities who will not bow to their orthodoxy. In other words, if we paint Christians who sound the call for biblical discernment about social justice as a bunch of culturally tone-deaf curmudgeons, then it is we who are tone-deaf to the current cultural moment. We are naive to the meanings that have been baked into many minds with the word combination of *social* and *justice*. Let us call this second kind of justice-seeking "Social Justice B," the kind of social justice that, for reasons we will explore, conflicts with a biblical view of reality.[18]

Hopefully, Christians across the political spectrum can unite around the fact that not everything *branded* social justice *is* social justice. When Antifa and the American Nazi Party both consider themselves bastions of social justice, most can agree that there are forms of "social justice" that go too far. Let's call the kind of justice we should seek "Social Justice A" and the kinds we should not "Social Justice B." Where, then, are the boundaries? Where can we march forward together with interlocked arms and biblically faithful hearts? And where might a vision of justice cross the line and lure us away from "the faith once and for all entrusted to God's holy people"?[19] Those are critical questions we must ask if the church is to pierce the political atmosphere of our age without bursting into fragments and flames.

Madness Machines

It is especially easy in our day, even in the church, to think *we* are for justice while *they* are against justice. This certainly helps us feel better about ourselves. But it's not that simple. The point is brilliantly made in the HBO comedy series *Flight of the Conchords*. Murray Hewitt, band manager for a struggling folk parody duo from New Zealand, tries to convince the band to avoid getting political. He cautions them against writing any more songs on the divisive issue of canine epilepsy. Murray argues, "If you were to record a song that was anti-AIDS, for example, then you'd end up alienating all those people that are pro-AIDS."[20] A ten-second straw poll around the New Zealand consulate reveals the obvious. No one, it turns out, is pro-AIDS.

We don't need a Gallup poll to tell us that basically no one identifies as pro-injustice. Yet ask half of America to describe the other half, and the majority would see the other half as pro-injustice. So what gives?

It all comes down to the issues behind the issues. The transgender debate isn't about pronouns. The same-sex marriage debate isn't about cakes. The abortion debate isn't about clumps of cells and coat hangers. The poverty debate isn't about greedy capitalists versus the commies. People on both sides of those controversies believe they are fighting for justice. Peel away the layers of each controversy and, at the onion's core, you'll find different answers to some of life's deepest questions.

Picture a big chrome box covered with buttons and blinking lights. In one end goes the question. What is economic justice? What is racial justice? What is social justice? And so on. Like a vending machine feeds on your dollar bill, this machine eats up your question. After some whizzing and buzzing, bits of paper spit out the other side. With red ink on tiny white fortune cookie rectangles come the answers: "Socialism is justice; get mad about capitalism" or perhaps "Socialism is injustice; get mad about socialism," and so on.

Each of us has a machine like that deep in our consciousness, an apparatus of fundamental convictions that signals what constitutes justice versus what we should get mad about. Philosophers call it our worldview. A worldview is not what we might *say* we believe in a street survey or online quiz. It's what we truly believe and act from in our core about who we are, where we came from, and where humanity is headed.

What philosophers call a "worldview," I will call a "madness machine." In goes the questions: "That baker declined to bake a cake for a gay couple's wedding. Should I be mad?" "That person makes a lot more money than that other person. Should I be mad?" "Those scientists want to genetically engineer a superior breed of humanity. Should I be mad?" Answers to such questions never poof into existence in a vacuum. They emerge from an intricate, often subconscious, network of beliefs and convictions, from a madness machine that yields conclusions about what in our news feeds should incur our wrath.

The question, again, is not who is pro-injustice. That's a self-serving and simplistic way to see it. No one stands on the corner waving a "Boo Justice!" protest sign. Our answers are a product of our underlying worldviews. Different madness machines churn out different political conclusions. Of course, that does not make justice relative. Certain worldviews are more calibrated toward human flourishing than others. Before the civil rights movement brought about greater racial justice in the 1960s, it had already gotten certain aspects of human nature profoundly right. Martin Luther King Jr.'s "Letter from a Birmingham Jail," for example, understood "the dignity and worth of human personality," that human rights are "God-given," that "all men are created equal," that man is neverthe-less haunted by "tragic sinfulness," but that we should be like Jesus Christ, "an extremist for love, truth, and goodness."[21] Some worldviews are more broken. They spit out answers that claim to be about justice, but unwittingly hurt people by misunderstanding what makes people *people*. Before communist experiments in economic justice went wrong in the twentieth century, communism had already gone wrong on human nature, denying the reality of sin in every human heart, reducing people to *homo economicus*, and blaming all evil on systems.[22]

If we, as a culture and as a church, can't have the hard conversations about enduring questions—What are humans for? What is our place in the universe? Are we fallen? How do we flourish?—then it is unlikely we will rise above the self-righteousness of our political tribes. There is simply no worldview-neutral way to think about or act out justice.

12 Questions: An Overview

The problem is not with the quest for social justice. The problem is what hap-pens when that quest is undertaken from a framework that is not compatible with the Bible. Today many Christians accept conclusions that are generated from madness machines that are wired with very different presuppositions about reality than those we find in Scripture. We shirk God's commands and hurt his image-bearers when we unwittingly allow unbiblical worldview assumptions to shape our approach to justice. Now is the time to show the watching world just how true, good, and beautiful justice becomes when we are driven by the Creator and his Word rather than cultural fads.

This book is about helping Christians better discern between Social Justice A and Social Justice B. Part 1, "Jehovah or Jezebel?," asks three questions about worship that will help us better seek justice without losing sight of the godhood of God. Part 2, "Unity or Uproar?" asks three questions about community that will help us better seek justice without becoming bitter and divisive. Part 3, "Sinners or Systems?" asks three questions about salvation that will help us better seek justice without losing the gospel. In Part 4, "Truth or Tribes Thinking?" asks three questions about knowledge to help us seek justice with-out losing our minds and sacrificing truth on the altar of ideology.

Each of the twelve questions posed through these chapters concludes with a personal story from one of my coauthors, dear brothers and sisters who have found liberation from bad ideas through Jesus—liberation from white supremacy, identity politics, and other ideologies of rage and division. Each chapter offers questions for personal reflection or small group discussion. These twelve chapters are followed by several appendixes that shed light on specific controversies for interested readers, including abortion, racism, socialism, sexuality, and other social justice questions.

The "Newman Effect"

Conversations about social justice in our polarized age tend to generate more heat than light because of a phenomenon we may call the "Newman effect." In 2018 Canadian psychology professor Jordan Peterson joined Channel Four host Cathy Newman to discuss gender inequality in what became one of the most viral interviews of the twenty-first century. The lively exchange sparked the "So you're saying" meme, based on Newman's repeated use of that phrase to interpret Peterson's statements in the most unflattering and inflammatory light possible.

> So you're saying that anyone who believes in equality . . . should basically give up, because it ain't gonna happen . . .
>
> You're saying that's fine. The patriarchal system is just fine . . .
>
> You're saying that women aren't intelligent enough to run these top companies . . .
>
> You're saying that trans activists could lead to the deaths of millions of people . . .
>
> You're saying that we should organize our societies along the lines of the lobsters . . .[23]

Professor Peterson wasn't saying any of that. But because his perspective did not fit neatly into the black-and-white boxes of our day, anything that seemed out of sync with Newman's perspective was taken in the most extreme, cartoonish, and damning way possible.

The truth is, we are all Cathy Newmans now, and that has become a serious existential threat to the unity of the church. "Racism is still a problem."

"So you're saying we should abandon the gospel and embrace neo-Marxism!" "Black lives matter." "So you're saying all lives don't matter?" "The fact that 70 percent of black children are born without married parents in the home should matter to us!" "So you're saying you're a racist, blaming the victim, and saying the black community's problems are completely their own fault!" "Marriage is a complementary union between a male and a female." "So you're saying you hate gay people." "During the COVID-19 pandemic, we should shelter in place to protect the most vulnerable." "So you're saying you are anti-freedom and want us all to bow to tyranny!" "We should reopen the economy to help those whose livelihoods and mental health are being devastated by quarantine." "So you're saying you want the virus to spread and more people to die!" The list could go on and on.

This is what conversations about important questions have reduced to in our day and age. The only way someone could possibly disagree with me is if they are a bad person, a sworn enemy of justice. And so we tar-and-feather any dissonant idea with the worst ideologies we can imagine. The result is rampant self-righteousness, a loss of humble self-criticism, widespread confirmation bias, a loss of real listening required to reach nuanced truths, and pervasive partisanship, a loss of real community that requires us to give charity and the benefit of the doubt to others. The Newman effect has become a true meme, not just in the popular sense of a witty graphic shared on social media but also in the more technical sense of a kind of "thought contagion," an idea or phenomenon that transmits person-to-person throughout culture.[24]

Given the Newman effect, each of the four parts of this book will end with a brief section called "So You're Saying," in which I address some of the most predictable misreads of what my coauthors and I are actually saying.

Four Essential Disclaimers

I offer four more important disclaimers. First, some may think what I have branded Social Justice A is just a clever way of pushing right-wing politics. Let me be clear. *Social Justice A—the kind of justice that flows from Scripture—is not synonymous with the Republican Party or its policies.* This book is about social justice, which is a banner waved mostly by the political left. That fact should not be taken as if I am baptizing the right. There are plenty of problems and antigospel tendencies on the right too, some of which will come to light in this book. I preach and teach against those often. Yet no book can be about everything. Since this book is about social justice—a label adopted mostly by those on the left—that will be our focus.

My friend and colleague Rick Langer talks often about what he brands "hermit crab theology." A hermit crab does not have its own shell. It finds some other shell to call home and crams itself inside. Hermit crab theology takes Jesus and jams him inside the preexisting shell of some extrabiblical ideology. This book offers reasons we should never cram Jesus into leftist ideology, and I would say the same thing about the right. Why? Because Jesus is too big to fit into the gnarled, cracked shells of any man-made political party.

Second, some may think I am building a straw man of Social Justice B, cherry-picking worrisome quotes from radicals to weave an ominous picture of a helpful movement in the church. Surely Christians aren't really buying into the bad ideas as you present them! I assure you, the doctrines of Social Justice B I present are doctrines I have read or heard face-to-face from people who identify as Christians, including many leaders and influencers, with increasing frequency. *If you find any of the Social Justice B doctrines objectionable or not representative of how you approach social justice, then I say, "Fantastic!" We have found yet one more area where we can march together toward justice.* Again, one of my driving motives behind this book is to spur more unity in the church over the splintering questions of social justice. That includes showing where ideas marketed as "social justice" cross the line from Christian truth into a danger zone of bad ideas that hurt people.

Third, *this book should not be used as a billy club to bash brothers or sisters who disagree with us.* We must actively resist a bad habit that is so easily formed in cyberspace today. A Christian brother or sister posts about the reality of racism. The lazy, predictable, and utterly unfruitful response would be to instantly assume the worst—they must be a social justice warrior snowflake, brainwashed by far left identity politics! A brother or sister comments that this or that event may not, in fact, be as racist, sexist, or homophobic as the media would have us believe. Again, it is easy to write them off as far right bigots, stone-hearted to the plight of the oppressed. This easy and wide road of writing off those who challenge our perspectives leads us post-by-post into an echo chamber in which we can no longer smell our own smugness and self-righteousness because they become the daily air we breathe.

This leads to a fourth and final disclaimer from the pen of Francis Schaeffer: "I need to remind myself constantly that this is not a game I am playing. If I begin to enjoy it as a kind of intellectual exercise, then I am cruel and can expect no real spiritual results. As I push the man off his false balance, he must be able to feel that I care for him. Otherwise I will end up only destroying him and the cruelty and ugliness of it all will destroy me as well."[25]

Schaeffer, who spent his career engaging culture, was known to weep often for a generation held captive by bad ideas. In doing so, Schaeffer followed in Paul's footsteps, the apostle who said "with tears" that many "walk as enemies of the cross of Christ."[26] Schaeffer and Paul imitated Jesus, who saw people "harassed and helpless, like sheep without a shepherd" and wept over Jerusalem.[27]

We are talking about ideas that have real consequences for real people. Let me be clear: this book takes aim at *ideas*, not *people*. It takes aim only at certain ideas because they hurt people we are called to love. Please don't take anything said here as an attack on *you as a person*. Please don't use anything said here to attack *other people*. If we play by the rules of our current cultural moment, then our study will be little more than a self-righteous exercise in dehumanizing those we disagree with—expanding the chasm between a tribalized "us" and a demonized "them." It is easy to be tickled by this or that problem in someone else's ideology. It requires supernatural help to be genuinely concerned that fellow image-bearers, made to know and enjoy God, have been taken in by bad ideas.

God, help us do something radically countercultural—help us love, with tears if necessary, those we disagree with. Amen.

PART 1

JEHOVAH OR JEZEBEL?

■ ■ ■

Three Questions about
Social Justice and Worship

You shall have no other gods before me.

−Exodus 20:3

Today almost everything is considered a matter of injustice, everything, of course, except the *main* thing. There is talk of economic injustice, reproductive injustice, racial injustice, and even, according to yesterday's headlines, facial injustice (based on a recent university policy that threatens expulsion for "mean" facial expressions).[1] What no one seems to be talking about—though it is at the bedrock of all other injustice—is *worship*. Theistic justice—bowing down to something that is worth bowing down to—is not *a* justice issue; it is *the* justice issue from which all other justice blooms.

Justice has been defined for millennia as giving others what is due them. Let's test that definition with a little exercise that will help us fine-tune our injustice detecting skills. In the following snapshots from Latin American history, see whether you can name, as precisely as possible, the injustices that occurred. In what ways were others not given what was due them? Fair warning: injustice is not pretty.

The year was 1519. While Martin Luther was busy launching the Protestant Reformation in Europe, a Spanish conquistador named Hernán Cortés landed in what is now Mexico City. Back then it was called Tenochtitlan, capital of the Aztec Empire, one of the five most populous cities on the planet. Towering over the city skyline stood Templo Mayor, a pyramid base with two peaks—a red shrine for the sun god, Huitzilopochtli, and a blue shrine for the water god, Tlaloc.

At the sun god shrine, which today has a scaled-down model in Disney World's Epcot, tens of thousands had their hearts cut from their chests with flint knives. Hearts were set on fire and held up to the sky as an offering to Huitzilopochtli. Heads were removed for public display on a massive skull rack called the Huey Tzompantli, showcasing the skulls of as many as sixty thousand victims. Bodies were kicked down the 180-foot pyramid staircase to cannibals waiting below.

On the water god shrine of Templo Mayor, archeologists have found children's remains and evidence that the young Aztecs were brutalized before their ritualistic murders. Why? Because children's tears were believed to have sacred powers to please Tlaloc. I warned you that injustice is not pretty.

When Cortés and his conquistadors entered the city in November 1519, they brought with them new injustices. A Franciscan priest narrates: "Fear prevailed. . . . There was terror. . . . And the Spanish walked everywhere. . . . They took all, all that they saw which they saw to be good. . . . They took it all."[2] Within two bloody years Cortés and his troops had seized full control of the Aztec capital. The conquistadors quickly implemented a system called *encomienda*. *Encomienda* meant Spanish rulers had not just land but also, more importantly, the *people* on the land granted (or "encommended") to them as property over which they claimed total sovereignty.[3]

What happened next was exactly what tends to happen when fallen humans play God and pretend to be sovereign lords over one another: theft, oppression, rape, exploitation, fraud, murder. In short, social injustice is first and foremost a matter of misplaced worship.

These grim snapshots raise three questions about social justice and worship:

Does our vision of social justice take the godhood of God seriously?
Does it acknowledge the image of God in everyone, regardless of size, shade, sex, or status?
Does it make a false god out of the self, the state, or social acceptance?

Chapter 1

The God Question

Does our vision of social justice take
seriously the godhood of God?

We find an explanation of what occurred in Tenochtitlan in a two-thousand-year-old letter written from the opposite side of the globe. Both the Aztecs and the conquistadors did "what ought not to be done. They were filled with all manner of unrighteousness, evil, covetousness, malice. They are full of envy, murder, strife, deceit, maliciousness."[1]

Those words were written nearly 1,500 years before Cortés set foot in Tenochtitlan. They were written nearly seven thousand miles from the blood-drenched steps of Templo Mayor. They are words Paul the apostle wrote in the opening paragraphs of his famous letter to Rome around AD 57.

No Soft Glamour Filters

Paul of course wasn't trying to describe Tenochtitlan. He wasn't a time traveler. Yet Paul precisely described Tenochtitlan during the sixteenth century. He described American slavery in the nineteenth century. He described Enver Pasha's Turkey, Joseph Stalin's Soviet Union, Adolf Hitler's Germany, Mao Zedong's China, and Pol Pot's Cambodia in the twentieth century. He described the death cult of Jonestown, the genocidal horrors of Darfur and Rwanda, and countless other abominations. Paul described the human condition and our undeniable tendency to turn on each other with malice. Say what you will about Paul, but he wore no rose-colored glasses when he looked into the human heart.

Paul's refusal to drop a soft glamour filter over humanity might seem outdated and pessimistic to us. But any honest look at the twentieth century makes it hard to write off Paul as a curmudgeon. As Jacques Maritain, originator of the UN's Universal Declaration of Human Rights, said after World War II, "We must have faith in man. But we cannot. . . . The present world of man has been for us a revelation of evil; it has shattered our confidence. . . . Our vision of man has been covered over by the unforgettable image of the bloody ghosts in extermination camps."[2]

> We are, each of us, far more corrupt and corruptible, capable of unleashing far more injustice, than we admit to ourselves.
>
> ▪ ▪ ▪

It would be easy (and self-serving) to single out the Nazis, some who dropped Zyklon B canisters into the gas chambers, as some aberrant subhuman species spawned from hellfire. Read up on Stanley Milgram's electrocution experiments, or simply show up at midnight for Black Friday deals at a local Walmart. You will learn the unflattering truth. SS officers are not the only corrupt ones. As Paul argues, "None is righteous, no, not one."[3] We are, each of us, far more corrupt and corruptible, capable of unleashing far more injustice, than we admit to ourselves.

Giving the Creator His Due

Let's dig deeper into Paul's teaching. Paul refuses to interpret any inch of reality apart from God. To cut God off from our understanding is to block out the sun and bump around in the dark. We see everything in its truest light when we view it in light of God's existence. That includes the way we see humanity's grim track record of injustice as well as our own underrated capacity for evil. Paul highlights God's invisible attributes: "namely, his eternal power and divine nature, have been clearly perceived, ever since the creation of the world, in the things that have been made."[4]

We pretend otherwise, but a transcendent power runs the universe, and deep down we know we are not him.[5] God is God and we are not. We aren't the Creator; we are creatures. But we suppress that most fundamental truth about the basic structure of existence. This blurs our vision of everything else. Like the guilt-wracked protagonist of Edgar Allan Poe's "The Tell-Tale Heart," we hide the old man under the planks. But his heart still beats. We plug our ears, we fabricate just-so stories in our own defense, we express #solidarity to feel good about ourselves, we entertain ourselves into a foggy-headed stupor—but his heart still beats.

Paul's unflattering description of us continues: "Although they knew God, they did not honor him as God or give thanks to him, but they became futile in their thinking, and their foolish hearts were darkened."[6]

Refusing to give the Creator the honor and gratitude he is due, we turn and bow to the cosmos. We endow created things with an ultimate value that they are not due. This is a double injustice. We fail to give both the Creator and the creation what they are properly due. In Paul's language, we "exchanged the truth about God for a lie and worshiped and served the creature rather than the Creator."[7]

That is what happened at Tenochtitlan. The Aztec rulers brutalized and murdered the vulnerable. The conquistadors coveted their neighbors' gold. They lied to the natives. They raped their wives and daughters. They took them for slaves. They broke a long list of commandments. In breaking those commandments, they broke the first commandment. They had gods before God. They worshiped creation rather than the Creator. The Aztecs bowed to the gods of sun and rain. The conquistadors exalted gold and power. That turn from Creator to creation worship was the first injustice of the Aztecs and conquistadors, the broken command that formed the essential premise and toxic fountainhead of all their other injustices.

This tragedy plays out in gruesome detail throughout the Old Testament. Slavery, murder, rape, child abuse, and theft happen when people worship idols instead of God. The first commandment, to have no gods before God, is where any authentically Christian vision of justice begins. Devalue the original by putting something else in his place and it's easier to treat the images like garbage.

That is what is so profound about Paul's take on injustice in Romans 1. He does not merely note that humanity is "full of envy, murder, strife, deceit, [and] maliciousness,"[8] then blame all that injustice on society and dream up a utopian political solution the way Karl Marx and Friedrich Engels did. Paul does not look at the bad fruit on the human tree and then suggest replanting it in the different soil of some new political ideology. Paul knows that the human tree is so hopelessly sick that whatever soil you plant it in, toxic fruit will form. No amount of political revolution, social engineering, or policy tweaking will stop envy, strife, deceit, and maliciousness from sprouting out of our sick hearts.

Why were all the utopias of the modern era doomed to fail? Because the evil did not originate in politics, society, or the economy. It is *expressed* there, but evil *originates* in human hearts that "exchanged the glory of the immortal God for images resembling mortal man and birds and animals and creeping things"[9] and the sun and water and gold and sex and power.

Consider white supremacy. The belief that white-skinned humans are superior to other humans has led to many nonwhites not receiving what they are due. We must work to make white supremacy a dead relic of the past. But the injustice of white supremacy has a transcendent dimension, something almost no one talks about that keeps us swatting at the bad fruits rather than chopping at the sick roots of racism. It makes race, not God, supreme. It worships and serves created things rather than the Creator. Racism, therefore, is not merely horizontally unjust, depriving other creatures what they are due; it is also vertically unjust, failing to give the Creator his due by making race an ultimate object of devotion. Why is racism so evil? If we leave God out of our answer to that question, we will fail to grasp the true diabolical depths of racism and find ourselves boxing ghosts of the real problem.

This, then, is how Paul adds deeper hues to our picture of injustice. *Look deep enough underneath any horizontal human-against-human injustice and you will always find a vertical human-against-God injustice, a refusal to give the Creator the worship only the Creator is due.* All injustice is a violation of the first commandment.

Calling Our Bluffs

A skeptic may object, "If you're saying that the injustices people commit against each other are really failures to give God his due, then why are so many culprits of injustice the very people who worship the God of the Bible?" Why indeed. The conquistadors were Roman Catholic, after all. If you could time-travel back five hundred years and ask them, they would likely tell you that they worship the Christian God. That's the beauty of Paul's view of injustice. It calls our bluffs. It reveals what we *actually* worship regardless of what we *say* we worship. Yes, the conquistadors *claimed* to worship the God of the Bible. But their unjust actions falsified their claims. Their "envy, strife, deceit, and maliciousness" exposed them for what they were—not Creator-worshipers but creation-worshipers groveling on their knees to the false gods of power and profit. If we treat others unjustly, then we too are on our knees to creation rather than the Creator.

There is a reason that the first of the Ten Commandments—to have no gods before God—is the *first* of the Ten Commandments. Acknowledging that God is God—not the universe, not physical sensations, not shiny objects, not government, not our own desires—is where real justice starts. If justice means giving others their due, then we must ask the question, "What is due to the ultimate Other?" That is the first question toward a deeply biblical justice. God, the divine Other, is due *everything*. We have him to thank for all that is true, good, and beautiful in the universe. We owe him our obedience, our next breath, our very selves. If we shy away from that truth then we should not be surprised to find that—just like Marxists, white supremacists, the Gestapo, and the KKK—we think we're doing justice when we're really just unleashing more havoc on earth. If our vision of social justice does not take the godhood of God seriously, then it is not really social justice.

EDDIE'S STORY

I loved every part of pastoring in South Korea—the shepherding, the teaching, the discipleship, and the evangelism. But in the fall of 2010, while I was walking through the busy streets of Seoul, God opened my eyes to a group of people I had completely missed. In the alleyways in Gangnam, one of Seoul's bustling consumer areas with a booming nightlife, I found thousands of young women and girls had been forced into sexual slavery. What was even more disturbing was that no one was doing anything to end this evil or care for these victims. As a pastor, I knew our church had to get involved. So we began a justice ministry and opened the first Christ-centered aftercare center for survivors of sex trafficking in Korea.

God further opened my eyes as I read in the gospel of Matthew how the hungry, the thirsty, the poor, and the prisoner matter profoundly to Jesus. Throughout Scripture I saw God's heart beating for the orphan, the widow, the fatherless, and the foreigner. What did these people have in common? They were the most vulnerable groups in their society. Scripture is crystal clear—the deeply vulnerable are deeply valuable to God.

Taking our cues from God's character and commands, our church moved into those areas of vulnerability, looking for ways to serve. We helped rescue a fifteen-year-old named Jinny, who had been violated by a close relative at the age of six. The abuse continued until she was ten. That's when she decided that the streets might be safer than her home. Within hours of her running away, an online trafficker lured Jinny into his home. From that day, she was abused ten to fifteen times a night for the next five years. By God's grace, she was able to run away and find our aftercare center. Jinny had felt worthless her whole life. But through the life, love, and words of her new caregivers, she experienced unconditional love for the first time.

"Why do you care about us?" That was the most common question we would get from those whom society treated as mere sex objects. It was also the easiest question to answer. "We love you because God loves you.

We love you because we love God. And God loves you infinitely more than we ever could!" We could credibly verbalize the gospel with them because they could see how the gospel had reshaped our lives.

As we, as a church, stepped out in obedience to the Bible's justice commands, God empowered us to change fifteen laws in Korea concerning human trafficking and adoption. He inspired us to begin Christ-centered ministries to care for the least of these. He allowed us to shine light into some of the darkest places on earth. We discovered justice as a way of loving God by imitating the passions of his heart. We found that a deep love for God has a way of changing our desires so that we want to love others. We wanted to love what he loves. God says point-blank, "I the LORD love justice" (Isa. 61:8). God's heart beats with a passion for the vulnerable in our communities. So should ours.

In some ways, justice seems trendy in our day. But for the believer, we must remember that justice is not a fad; it is the foundation of God's throne (Ps. 89:14). And the One who sits on that throne is the One we seek to honor, love, and follow all our days. Let's start by giving God his due so that we may "truly execute justice one with another" (Jer. 7:5).

–Eddie Byun

Eddie is an associate professor of Christian Ministries at Biola University's Talbot School of Theology and author of the award-winning book Justice Awakening: How You and Your Church Can Help End Human Trafficking *(InterVarsity, 2014).*

Questions for Personal or Small Group Study

1. How much of your justice-seeking energy is focused on giving God his due as your Creator and Redeemer? What are three ways our justice efforts would look different from today's popular visions of social justice if we made revering God the number one priority?
2. What is something you could do every day this week to demonstrate true reverence for God? What long-term habits could you form to orient your life around glorifying God first?
3. Why do you think God *commands* rather than *suggests* that we do justice? What do such commands have to do with God's character, with our chief end to glorify him, and with the mission of the church?

Chapter 2

The *Imago* Question

Does our vision of social justice acknowledge
the image of God in everyone, regardless
of size, shade, sex, or status?

Celebrated philosopher Charles Taylor pulls another puzzle piece from the carpet to help us fill in a bigger picture of justice. A defining mark of our secular age is what Taylor calls "the immanent frame."[1]

Justice in a Box

"The immanent frame" is Taylor's fifty-cent philosophy term to describe that we, Christians included, tend to operate in the universe as if it is a closed box. We assume that the best way to make sense of the universe—what's inside the box—is by *other stuff inside the box.* Charles Darwin and Richard Dawkins would have us make sense of all of life in terms of biology. Stephen Hawking and Neil deGrasse Tyson would reduce reality to physics. Sigmund Freud and Steven Pinker would point to psychology, Karl Marx and Friedrich Hayek to economics, Herbert Marcuse and Hugh Hefner to sex, Steve Jobs and Elon Musk to technology, Disney and TMZ to entertainment. Invoke God as an explanation of reality—Someone good who is *unconfined* by the box because he *made* the box—and, to most people, you might as well play in the fiery apocalypse on a handcrafted Swanson flute, yelling "Hail Zorp!" at strangers in the park.[2]

What if the joke is on us? What if many of today's attempts at justice have become so laughable precisely because we have laughed out of the room the Being who is most serious about true justice? Nothing inside the box grounds equality or dignity or value. If we're all just bodies in a box, then mine is not equal with Usain Bolt's, which can run the forty-yard dash in about four seconds, or Brad Pitt's, which can pull off skinny jeans without looking ridiculous. Only if there is Someone good, Someone beyond the box who made the box, Someone whose image all of us bear—regardless of our physical, economic, sexual, or political status—that things like equality, dignity, and value become more than bumper-sticker slogans. Limiting ourselves to "the immanent frame" is hardly a recipe for long-term justice or progress. That's why about 99.9 percent of MLK's "Letter from Birmingham Jail" appeals to equality, dignity, and values beyond the immanent frame.

By starting our exploration of justice with the question "What is due to God?" let me be clear: we are committing twenty-first-century heresy. We are starting from beyond the immanent frame. But any truly Christian approach to justice must be an outside-the-box perspective. We must be heretics in the culture's eyes, willing to risk all kinds of unsavory labels, if we are to "truly execute justice" as Scripture commands.

By starting with "What is due to God?" we have hit on the same insight that the great North African theologian Augustine discovered over a millennium ago. In a sermon on love, he attempted to sum up the entire Christian ethic with the famous line, "Love God and do what you want."[3] If I treasure God as God, that first affection should recalibrate all my other affections, my other wants. I won't *want* to lie to you, since you bear the noble image of the God I love most. I won't *want* to steal your stuff or your spouse, because you carry the unique image of the God I love most. I won't *want* to exploit you as a means to my own selfish ends, since you are made in the irreducibly valuable image of the God I love most. Love God, the ultimate Other, and you will give those who bear your Beloved's image the respect they are due.

Idolatry, then, is the first injustice and the carcinogenic source of every other injustice.

Had the Aztecs loved the actual God more than they loved the sun and water, they would not have wanted to treat people like chopped meat. Had the conquistadors loved the actual God more than they loved gold and power, they would not have wanted to treat the Aztecs like rats to be exterminated, sex toys to be exploited, or property to be owned. The tens of thousands of victims at Templo Mayor and the hundreds of thousands of victims of *encomienda* did not receive what was due them because other people's wants were disordered. They were not loved like the image-bearers of God that they were, because the Aztecs and conquistadors did not love the God whose image they bore.

Opening the Box

In a tightly reasoned article entitled "Does Naturalism Warrant a Moral Belief in Universal Benevolence and Human Rights?" Notre Dame sociologist Christian Smith helps us deepen Augustine's insight. Smith argues that naturalism—the belief that there are no supernatural realities, only nature and its processes—is often espoused by those who are zealously committed to universal human rights. But, Smith argues, we can't have it both ways. Take, for example, the rally cry of "Equality!" If naturalism is true, then human beings *are* their bodies. There is nothing more to us. Atheists like Jean-Paul Sartre, Arthur Leff, and Alex Rosenberg have bolstered Smith's point.[4] If we're nothing more than matter, then there seems to be no meaningful way to talk about justice.

If we are reducible to our bodies, then what is the foundation for human equality? Charles Darwin saw none and explicitly argued against human equality.[5] Our bodies are not equal. Michael Jordan's body could slam dunk a basketball from the free throw line. Mine cannot. Alex Honnold's body can free-climb the three-thousand-foot face of El Capitan. Mine cannot. Some of us were born with a higher genetic propensity to develop certain ailments. Others were born winning a genetic lottery, with low chances of getting certain diseases. If atheist Jacques Monod was right that "man is a machine," then some of us are Ford Pintos and some are Teslas. Some of our bodies are a boxy 1980s PC and others are the latest Mac. If we are to speak meaningfully about human equality, then there must be something more to us than our bodies— something beyond Taylor's immanent frame—that anchors our shared value.

There is a tendency today to reduce people not to bodies but to ideologies. We don't see a human being so much as we see social justice snowflakes to our left and neo-Nazi fascists to our right. Or we see and treat people on the basis of their skin color or gender or whom they want to sleep with. That is why giving God his due is so important to real justice. We were born into the box. We spend every day bumping around inside the box. If we imagine that the box is closed, then bumping around in the dark, we hear what people say, feel them bump into us and assess how much inconvenience or pain they cause us, grope around and feel the size of their wallets, and categorize everyone and hypothesize how to make life inside the box happier.

It is easy to see one another not theologically in light of God's existence but in terms of the categories culture supplies. Take the experience of Antonia Diliello ("Grandma Tony" as my wife and I call her or "Great-Grandma Tony" for my children). In the early 1930s in Oxnard, California, Grandma Tony attended Roosevelt School, which had segregated classrooms and playgrounds. Mexican students even had a ten-minute longer school day "to avoid interracial socializing."[6] One day, she recalls, she was caught speaking Spanish: "I had to get a rock, draw a circle in the dirt, and stand in the middle . . . until the bell rang, and I felt like a weird person because, you know, everybody would come by and look at me, like I was on display. . . . And I felt like the ugliest, the dirtiest little girl around, you know, really bad."[7]

Dirt circles aren't the only way we've categorized people; there is a lamentable history of yellow star patches and numbered tattoos on Jewish image-bearers, lashing scars and lynching nooses on black image-bearers, and, more recently, one-eyed happy faces in red spray paint (representing the Arabic letter "noon," for Nasara or Nazarenes) to mark Christian homes for destruction by the Islamic State in Iraq. When we reduce people to inside-the-box categories, we become oblivious to the beyond-the-box fact that every human being is a divine image-bearer. Justice requires that they be treated as such, regardless of size, shade, sex, or status.

> When we reduce people to inside-the-box categories, we become oblivious to the beyond-the-box fact that every human being is a divine image-bearer.

That is far easier said than done. We need supernatural help. We need the Holy Spirit's power to gift us with new sight, clearer vision to see others not as the prejudices of our subculture would have us see them or how social media propaganda would have us see them but as the God of the universe sees them. Lord, give us eyes to see.

A Simple Thought Experiment

This brings us full circle to our definition of justice. What is due to a "human being"—which I take as shorthand for an unfathomably precious image-bearer of God? It seems like not being defrauded, raped, brutalized, exploited, or murdered is a reasonable place to start. That's why truth-telling, sexual boundaries, and treating people the way you want to be treated are all justice issues. They are all essential to treating human beings like the unfathomably precious image-bearers of God we are.

As we seek a more just world, if we see those who disagree with us as Republicans or Democrats, progressives or conservatives, radical leftists or right-wing fundamentalists first and as image-bearers second, or not at all, then we aren't on the road to justice. We're on history's wide and bloody road to dehumanization.

Take a moment to think of specific people whose ideology you disagree with most. Pick your top three. It might be a public figure, a politician, a family member, a coworker, or a neighbor. Picture someone specific who you see as the living, breathing antithesis of everything you believe to be true and just. Picture that person, with all his or her smugness, in your mind's eye. Now think this true thought toward that person. "Image-bearer." Say it again. "Image-bearer." Once more for good measure. "Image-bearer." Next time you see that person, before your blood pressure starts to rise, repeat, "Image-bearer. Image-bearer. Image-bearer." Then treat that person as an image-bearer because that is who they were long before you found yourselves on opposite sides of a culture war. Then, when it starts to set in how incredibly difficult it is to treat people as image-bearers for more than five minutes, pray for yourself what Paul once prayed for the Thessalonians: "May the Lord make [me] increase and abound in love for one another and for all."[8]

WALT'S STORY

"Has anyone seen Kyle? He's about this tall," an acquaintance asked with his arm outstretched in a Nazi salute. I did not know what his mother called him, only his screen name. For security purposes, that was the norm. It felt like a group of trolls, a hodgepodge of people who had taken the red pill and met up in the Matrix. We were united in our love for one thing: European man.

Ethnically, we were predominantly Americans, but our family backgrounds were Anglo, Irish, Scottish, Russian, Czech, Danish . . . so long as you were not Jewish, you were all right. Ideologically, we were Fascists, National Socialists, monarchists, and Republicans. Socially, we were poor kids who grew up as skinheads, wealthy Mormons, lonely divorced women, and dedicated husbands. Religiously, we were predominantly godless, though some who identified as Christians and even Buddhists joined our ranks. What brought us together was the ideology of white supremacy.

Reflecting back on this point in my life is quite surreal. Had you asked me ten years ago if I detested *any* group of people, I would have wholeheartedly exclaimed, "No!" Yet I ended up in a racist hate group. How on earth did I get there?

I, and many of the predominantly young men with me, felt forced into a corner. From our public institutions and the culture writ large, we had all heard something to the effect of "Well, you all deserve what's coming to you" or "Well, you can't have an opinion about that" or "Well, you must be racist" or "Well, these other peoples might be worth protecting, but you are expendable." Our sense of self-worth was shattered by a never-ending stream of cultural voices declaring that by virtue of our skin tone, we were all members of the privileged group and, therefore, the enemies of social progress.

The constant stigma about being white leads young men right into the arms of radicals. Invert everything I said, and you get a radical leftist. "You wanna play the identity politics game? Fine, let's play. We'll win!" seems to be the message coming from loud voices on both sides of the political spectrum.

How did I escape this hopeless game? I can't think of a specific time or place in which I surrendered to God's grace. It was incremental. But if I were to talk to a younger version of myself, what could I possibly say that would make him think, "I am going to be okay. My life is worth living. Stop fearing the Light." I would say this: "Your value is not rooted in creation but in the Creator. Your value is not rooted in the coincidental happenstance surrounding your birth but in infinite love from he who is Love."

For anyone swept into identity politics, right or left, I realize simply saying "Jesus loves you" may not help you stop feeling bad about the world. Many Christians you know may seem completely against you. I get it. It hurts. But don't fall into the trap of defining your life mission by how other people may see you. Define your life on the basis of God, who knew you in the womb and loved you from Eternity's Gate. He has not forgotten you, nor could he. He knows and loves you enough to literally *die* for you. How can we see God crucified for every tongue, tribe, and nation and still think ourselves worthy because of our own melanin or merit?

Dear friends who may feel estranged and angry, come and achieve your long-sought revolution! Revolt against your own sin nature. Revolt against hate. Let God graciously turn your heart of stone into a heart of flesh. Look to Jesus and be saved!

—Walt Sobchak

Walt graduated from Biola University and is currently studying for lifelong ministry.

Questions for Personal or Small Group Study

1. Why is it sometimes so difficult to see people as divine image-bearers? Why does this make Paul's prayer for Christians to "increase and abound in love" so important for us to pray ourselves?

2. Are there any particular individuals you have a challenging time seeing and treating as image-bearers? For you personally, what might it look like to start treating them as divine image-bearers?

3. Are there any particular groups defined by inside-the-box categories—race, political persuasion, mental or physical disability, economic status, religion, etc.—whom you tend to look down on? What can you do this week to show love for anyone in those groups?

Chapter 3

The Idolatry Question

Does our vision of social justice make a false god
out of the self, the state, or social acceptance?

There aren't many Huitzilopochtli and Tlaloc worshipers left in the world. But the human heart, which John Calvin famously described as an idol-making factory, has not changed in the last five hundred years. If the first injustice of the Aztecs was worshiping the sun and rain gods, if the first injustice of the conquistadors was worshiping power and precious metals, then what are the idols of our age? And how might these false gods skew our vision of social justice?

During a ministry stint in Nepal years ago, I marveled that the Hindu religion boasts of over thirty-three million deities. But the West could give the East a run for its money. With all the West's rugged individualism, we might say there are as many gods in the West as there are Westerners.[1] Fallen human nature constantly cranks out new objects of worship.

We rarely recognize our idols for what they are. At different stages of my life, I would say, "I'm using my God-given mind to study theology," "I'm just looking for full-time employment doing what I love," "I simply want to buy a home for my family," "My wife and I want another child," or "I am writing another book." The truth is that I turned each of those good things into something ultimate. My sense of self was more wrapped up in these finite pursuits than in the infinite God of the universe. My heart is an idol factory, and if it weren't for Jesus taking my place on the cross, I would be on the eternal receiving end of divine justice for worshiping and serving created things rather than my Creator.

Idols of the Right

Idolatry happens when we make some good thing an ultimate thing, in which case it becomes a destructive thing. Given our tendency to make good things into ultimate things, it would be naive to think idolatry can't creep into our justice pursuits. Social Justice B is on the political left, and we will examine its favorite idols shortly. But the political right has its own idols. These include (but aren't limited to) stuff, solitude, sky, and the status quo.

By "stuff" I simply mean material prosperity for its own sake—hoarding wealth and celebrating reckless consumption without regard for the corrosive effects that too much stuff can have on our souls and our society.

By "solitude" I mean the kind of rugged individualism by which we think every man is an island unto himself instead of seeing ourselves and our actions as inevitably impacting those around us. It cares only about what Francis Schaeffer called those two "horrible values" of "personal peace and affluence," with blinders on to the oppressed.

By "sky" I refer to the versions of Christianity in which the whole point is to simply float off into the clouds after we die. The lordship of Jesus extends to every square inch of reality, as Abraham Kuyper noted. That includes poverty, race, sexuality, and politics. A super-spiritualized Christianity that has no implications for real pain in the here-and-now is hardly worthy of the word *Christian*.

By "status quo" I mean a tendency to accept the way things are with no recognition of how many are languishing and the urgent need to bring the lordship of Jesus to bear in such tragic spaces. Given Calvin's insight into our idol-factory hearts, we must be ever cautious never to bow before stuff, solitude, sky, or the status quo.

There is a fifth idol—skin tone—the point at which the right becomes the "alt-right." Racial idolatry motivated Dylann Roof to shoot up Emanuel Church in Charleston, a mob of tiki torch–carrying men to chant, "You will not replace us" through the streets of Charlottesville, and a white supremacist to open fire, killing twenty image-bearers in an El Paso mall mere days before I typed this. It shouldn't have to be said, but it *must* be said: claims to racial superiority have no place whatsoever in a Christian view of the world. We must work to make them a *permanent* thing of the past, never to be resurrected. It has been well said that the cross and the swastika cannot coexist without one burning up the other.[2] Given God's vision for salvation of every tongue, tribe, and nation, heaven would be a white supremacist's hell.[3]

Idols of the Left

If stuff, solitude, sky, and the status quo can be idols for the right, and skin tone for the alt-right, then what, we may ask, are the favorite idols of the left? To some, the question may seem strange. After all, doesn't the left simply care about the oppressed? If we don't think idols can lurk behind care for the oppressed, then we have yet to grasp Paul's view of just how sweeping and seductive idolatry really is.

A growing congregation of scholars are catching up with Paul's ancient insight. Feminist author and atheist professor Camille Paglia acknowledges that "human beings need religion, they need a religious perspective, a cosmic perspective. And getting rid of the orthodox religions because they were too conservative has simply led to [a] new religion."[4] Paglia identifies this new religion as "political correctness." She labels it a form of "fanaticism," citing her experience with second-wave feminists, whom she likens to "the Spanish Inquisition" seeking to "destroy" her for committing "heresy."

Culture commentator Andrew Sullivan notes that "critical race and gender theory and postmodernism, the bastard children of Herbert Marcuse and Michel Foucault—have become the premises of higher education, the orthodoxy of a new and mandatory religion."[5]

Elizabeth Corey recognizes similar undercurrents in the rise of the intersectionality movement, which she identifies as "a quasi-religious gnostic movement, which appeals to people for precisely the reasons that all religions do: It gives an account of our brokenness, an explanation of the reasons for pain, a saving story accompanied by strong ethical imperatives, and hope for the future. In short, it gives life meaning."[6]

Caring about the oppressed is a good thing. It is a deeply biblical thing. But when we make that good thing an ultimate thing, it becomes a destructive idol. The most pressing cultural and political issues of our day are, fundamentally, *worship* issues. They are contemporary expressions of our insuppressible religiosity. We would do well to wake up to this fact.

Back in 1981, Francis Schaeffer released *A Christian Manifesto*, a believer's riposte to *The Communist Manifesto* and *Humanist Manifesto*. Schaeffer opens with a great line: "The basic problem of the Christians in this country in the last eighty years or so, in regard to society and in regard to government, is that they have seen things in bits and pieces instead of totals."[7] Schaeffer cites the American church's hand wringing over sexual immorality, secular indoctrination in public education, the assault on family life, and the trampled rights of the unborn. "But," Schaeffer laments, "they have not seen this as a totality—each thing being a part, a symptom, of a much larger problem."[8]

Three years before, the Russian novelist Alexander Solzhenitsyn had delivered his seminal commencement speech at Harvard. Like Schaeffer, Solzhenitsyn argued that addressing society's problems at the surface of legal and political categories, rather than root moral and spiritual categories, "prevents one from seeing the size and meaning of events" and "makes space for the absolute triumph of absolute Evil in the world."[9]

Eighty years before that, Abraham Kuyper began his Stone Lectures at Princeton with the observation that there are "two life systems wrestling with one another, in mortal combat." The combatants were those seeking to "build a world of [their] own from the data of the natural man, and to construct man himself," striving to vanquish "with violent intensity" those "who reverently bow the knee to Christ." Kuyper saw this as *the* struggle in Europe" and "*the* struggle in America."[10]

The "bits and pieces" approach that Schaeffer criticized, the superficial "legalism" that Solzhenitsyn rejected, and the failure to reckon with the epic worldview showdown that Kuyper saw raging behind the headlines remain just as relevant in the early twenty-first century as they were in the late nineteenth and twentieth centuries. These three thought leaders beckon us to behold a bigger picture. We must reckon with the fact that every quest for a better world works outward from the premise of either Creator worship or creation worship. To ignore Paul's insight here is to limit ourselves to "bits and pieces," miss "the size and meaning of events," and render ourselves oblivious to "*the* struggle" in the West.

What, then, are the idols that may hide behind the banner of social justice? Again, those on the right have their own favorite idols and may even bow to some of the following idols. So don't take what follows as partisan bashing. But since this is a book about social justice—a moniker mostly chosen by those on the left—we must ask, "How might we start out with a noble concern for social justice and end up unwittingly on our knees to false gods?" Here are three good things we must be careful not to make ultimate things as we seek justice together.

The Idol of Self

Eighty-four percent of Americans believe "enjoying yourself is the highest goal of life." Eighty-six percent believe that to enjoy yourself you must "pursue the things you desire most." Ninety-one percent affirm the statement "To find yourself, look within yourself."[11] Anthropologist Paul Hiebert sees a new "dominant religion in the West" in which "self has become god and self-fulfillment our salvation."[12]

One of the many differences between God and us is his unique role in determining not only *that* humans would exist (we are contingent; he is not) but also *why* we exist. The built-in meaning of human nature, what we exist *for*, our telos, traces its origin to our transcendent Creator. Human nature is *not* like a bowl of alphabet soup—a senseless jumble of floating letters that can be arranged at our leisure. Human nature is more like a book—we are *authored* beings with meaning and purpose that we don't *invent* but we *discover*. Authoring the meaning of human nature is a God-sized task. Creator-worship gives us the humility to acknowledge our own fallibility because God is the standard of truth.

Read Social Justice B literature and you will find that the author of the human telos is not the Creator but the creature. This bait-and-switch is baked into its definition of justice. As RuPaul put it in an interview with *Time*, "Drag has always served a purpose. We mock identity. We're shape-shifters. We are God in drag. And that's our role to remind people of that."[13] The autonomous "I," the self-creating self, takes the sovereign mantle of identity-making that God held in historic Christianity.

The question is, "Who has the right, the trustworthiness, the goodness, and the authority to render the verdict about who we really are?" Social Justice B answers, "We do." Herein lies one of the deepest problems with idolizing the self as sovereign. The omnipotence-demanding task of constructing an entire person's nature is forced onto our all-too-shaky and finite shoulders. Tragically, we buckle under the impossible weight.

It is not a coincidence that the meteoric rise of the gospel of autonomous self-making since the 1960s corresponds with a crescendo of brokenness. "From 1960 to the turn of the twenty-first century, America doubled its divorce rate, tripled its teen suicide rate, quadrupled its violent crime rate, quintupled its prison population, sextupled out-of-wedlock births, and septupled the rate of cohabitation without marriage (which has been established as a significant predictor of divorce)."[14]

In sum, making an idol out of the self is just plain mean. We were never designed to bear the God-sized weight of creating and sustaining our own identities. It puts an unbearable weight on people's shoulders, especially children, when they are indoctrinated to follow their hearts, be true to themselves, and dream up their own identities. It deprives them of the unspeakable joy and meaning that go with being authored by Someone far more brilliant, strong, and loving than we are. Our churches must serve as trauma recovery centers for those crushed by the mainstream credo of self-creation.

The Idol of State

The problem with the idol of self is that only the Creator has what it takes to truly construct and sustain a creature's identity. Identity-making is a God-sized task. This leads to a second idol. To offset this crushing weight of autonomy, many turn to other finite creatures to validate their self-made selves. The collective "we" is invoked to do the existential heavy lifting that the autonomous "me" cannot muster. For deeply spiritual reasons, not merely political ones, people seek universal celebration of their constructed identities. As Chesterton observed, "Once we abolish God, the government becomes God."[15]

Consider the doctrine of justification, a core truth of a Christian worldview. Justification refers to the divine act by which God declares sinners like us "not guilty!" on the basis of Christ's redemptive death and resurrection. God is the judge, Satan is "the accuser," and Jesus is our defense attorney who appeals to his own completed death sentence so we can be declared not guilty.[16]

But what happens if we leave God out of the picture? Does our need for the not guilty sentence magically disappear? No. The need to feel justified is irrepressibly human.[17] Every Muslim on his knees toward Mecca, every Hindu plunging into the Ganges, and every atheist arguing online about the evils of religion is attempting the same feat. They are all trying to achieve status as *good people*. We all do that.

When we leave God out of the process of living free from guilt, we turn to the next biggest entity we can imagine. We turn to society. Government, media, law, education, entertainment, the local business owner—*everyone* must declare us, in unison, "not guilty!" We must silence anyone who fails to acknowledge and celebrate our guiltlessness. The Little Sisters of the Poor, the baker, the photographer, and the Christian university become equivalent to Satan and his minions in historic Christian theology.

The great triumph over evil, then, *must* be political. We must use the power of law to squash those who dare question our self-defined selves. Political activism becomes a spiritual quest to usher in a new heaven and new earth. This quest is every bit as eschatological and utopian as it was for the eighteenth-century French Revolutionaries and the twentieth-century Marxists. But, we must say with tears, this new revolution, like the old ones, renounces the Creator-creature distinction. Drastically overestimating our goodness and underestimating our propensity for evil, the quest will prove just as dystopian.[18]

Make no mistake: Social Justice B seeks a theocracy, a theocracy of creation worship that seeks to silence its heretics. Like our brothers and sisters living under a false theocracy in first-century Rome, we need the guts to say in our century that Jesus, not Caesar, is Lord.

The Idol of Social Acceptance

This leads us to a third idol. Let's face it. As Christians, we like to be liked. We crave culture's applause. We want to be marketable, we want to be mainstream, and we want to be moral, depending on whatever the mainstream defines as "moral" this week. The last thing we want is to be branded with the scarlet *B* for bigot or *I* for irrelevant. We often care more about offending fellow creatures than we care about offending the Creator, and we let that inverted emotion determine the way we think about everything from social policy to sexuality. We often care more about being on "the right side of history"—as the culture's trendsetters define "right"—than we care about being on the right side of Scripture. As David French points out, "You're begging the world for its love. It will not love you back."[19]

Our deities shape our identities.[20] If we make a God out of culture, then we will become like the culture. We never ponder injustice in a vacuum. Our idols will always shape our concept of what is just and unjust. But as Fulton Sheen cautioned, "Marry the spirit of the age and you will be a widow in the next one."[21]

I don't believe that most Christians who embrace Social Justice B set out to deny the godhood of God. Rather, they set out to do justice and combine it with an innocuous desire to be liked and relevant. They don't want their faith lumped in with those "God hates fags" sign-waving hyperfundamentalists. And yes, there is something to breaking such stereotypes. There is something to not being needlessly offensive, rude, or self-righteous. There is something to seeking to live peaceably with all, speaking kind words to settle raging nerves, making our love known to all, being gentle as doves, overcoming evil with good, and loving our enemies. Those are good things. Those are biblical things.

But Jesus said, "You will be hated by all for my name's sake."[22] James tells us that "friendship with the world is enmity with God" and "whoever wishes to be friends with the world makes himself an enemy of God."[23] This, then, is the telltale sign that we have crossed the line from real justice into Social Justice B: Does our vision of justice include anything the mainstream would reject? What if God's Word clearly said something that was so culturally unpopular, something considered so backward that you would be called unsavory names, lose your job, and be shunned by your neighbors? Be honest with yourself. Would you side with the masses or the Maker of heaven and earth?

Don't underestimate the seductive power of the idol of social acceptance. When Luther stood before the Diet of Worms, he faced tremendous social pressure to recant his writings and go along with the status quo. Had he budged, it would have saved his life, called off the pope's hired hit men, and instantly lifted an elephant's worth of weight off his shoulders. Before the assembled powers at Worms, Luther, whom the pope had nicknamed a "wild boar," was more of a chicken. In a quivering, hushed voice, he requested another day to think it through, which was reluctantly granted. That night Luther prayed, "O Lord! Help me! O faithful and unchangeable God! I lean not upon man. . . . Whatever is of man is tottering, whatever proceeds from him must fail."[24] The next day came the historic exchange. "I ask you, Martin—answer candidly and without horns—do you or do you not repudiate your books and the errors which they contain?"[25]

"Since then Your Majesty and your lordships desire a simple reply, I will answer without horns and without teeth. Unless I am convicted by Scripture and plain reason—I do not accept the authority of popes and councils, for they have contradicted each other—my conscience is captive to the Word of God. I cannot and I will not recant anything, for to go against conscience is neither right nor safe. Here I stand. I cannot do otherwise. God help me, Amen."[26]

Picture yourself as a young Luther, but you stand before the virtual Diet of Worms that is social media, or perhaps before a jury of your neighbors and friends. Like Luther on his first day at Worms, most of us stutter and quiver before judging eyes. Worse yet, we simply parrot what we think they want to hear. But we need our own "Here I stand" moments. We need our own realization of the "faithful and unchangeable God" and that "whatever is of man is tottering" and "must fail." We must decide in our hearts, once and for all, whom we answer to—creatures or the Creator.

And if we answer that question incorrectly, what we call "social justice" will certainly become something different from the Creator's justice.

> We must decide in our hearts who we answer to—creatures or the Creator.

Christians across the political spectrum should unite around the conviction that we should reject anything marketed as justice, by the right or left, that draws us to our knees before anything other than God. Like Jezebel turning ancient Israel to false gods, visions of social justice can lure us toward false gods. Despite our differences, we must never bow to the status quo, stuff, solitude, sky, skin tone, self, state, or social acceptance. As we seek justice together, let us resist our idol-factory hearts and have no gods before God.

BECKET'S STORY

On September 20, 2009, I walked into a church in Hollywood for the first time. I was a gay man and a professing atheist. Two hours later, I walked out a born-again Christian who no longer identified as gay. The "idol of self" had been smashed into a million pieces, and a new self took its place, a self "created after the likeness of God in true righteousness and holiness" (Eph. 4:24).

I spent fifteen years working in Hollywood as a set designer in the fashion industry for magazines such as *Harper's Bazaar* and *Vogue* and ad campaigns for Gap and Nike. I attended the Oscars, Emmys, and Golden Globes. I spent summers swimming in Drew Barrymore's pool and having dinner parties at movie stars' houses and spent a magical night at Prince's house in Benedict Canyon, where he performed for three hours in his backyard! I was happy in this milieu of fascinatingly creative people.

I knew from an early age that I was attracted to the same sex. But growing up in Dallas in the 1980s, being gay wasn't an option. Through my late teens and early twenties, I found other young gay men who helped me finally feel comfortable in my own skin. This was who I was, and nothing was going to change that. As the glamorous years in Los Angeles went by, I had my share of boyfriends, attended annual pride parades, and marched in rallies for gay marriage. Then the law of diminishing returns began to set in. After more than a decade of decadence, I wondered, "Is that all there is?"

In March 2009, I was at Paris Fashion Week and ended up at Stella McCartney's after-party, sipping champagne with the who's who of the fashion world. I suddenly felt an overwhelming sense of emptiness. I knew that the life I was living couldn't sustain me anymore. I needed answers, but becoming a Christian was out of the question. How could I join a club that thought *who I was* was wrong?

Six months later I was at an LA coffee shop with my best friend. We noticed a nearby group of millennials with Bibles on the table. We were stunned. Bibles in public in Los Angeles? I asked what their church believed about homosexuality, and they answered frankly, saying that that they believed it is a sin. I appreciated their honesty. Five years earlier I would have snap-judged them as bigots still living in the Dark Ages. Instead,

I was able to really hear their perspective and thought, "Maybe I'm wrong. Maybe this is a sin. What if I've built my life on a false foundation?" They invited me to church.

I found myself in an evangelical church in Hollywood the following Sunday. Every word from the pastor's mouth rang true. *This is the gospel?* It turned everything I had understood about religion on its head. It truly was good news! The Holy Spirit overwhelmed me. God revealed himself to me. I began bawling uncontrollably. I knew God was real, Jesus was his Son, heaven was real, the Bible was true—all in an instant. I also knew homosexual behavior was a sin. The Holy Spirit made it as clear as day. I knew being gay was no longer who I was. It was part of my past. But I didn't care. I had just met the King of the Universe—Jesus—and his love is all-consuming. Ten years later, I am still single and celibate and have never been happier. I am more than willing to deny myself, take up my cross, and follow Jesus. He's worth it.

What happens when we make personal sexual desires supreme markers of our identity? What happens when we want government to punish those who reject today's sexual orthodoxy? What happens when we sacrifice the truths of God's Word on the altar of cultural trends? We tell the lie that Jesus is not worth it. We bow to idols. We do not give the Creator his due, and that is not justice.

—Becket Cook

Becket is a graduate of Biola University's Talbot School of Theology and author of A Change of Affection: A Gay Man's Incredible Story of Redemption *(HarperCollins, 2019).*

Questions for Personal or Small Group Study

1. Of the idols explored in this chapter—status quo, stuff, solitude, sky, skin tone, self, state, social acceptance, or sex—which are you most likely to bow down before?
2. Are there any other idols in your life or in the broader culture that can distort our vision of true justice?
3. What are some metrics or barometers we could use to discern when we have crossed the line and turned our political convictions or affiliations into idols?

So You're Saying . . .

Given the power of the Newman effect in our day (see pp. 8–9), here are five points some may have heard me advancing in part 1, "Jehovah or Jezebel? Three Questions About Social Justice and Worship":

1. "So you're saying the pursuit of justice is optional for Christians."
2. "So you're saying that people who don't worship the God of the Bible have no true insight into justice and contribute nothing to making the world a better place."
3. "So you're saying that Christians should be known more for what we are against than what we are for."
4. "So you're saying the only way to agree with the political left about anything is if you are worshiping some false god."
5. "So you're saying right-wing politics are not plagued with idolatry too."

No. I am not saying any of that. I don't believe any of that. If you are hearing any of that, then either the Newman effect is at work or I have simply done a poor job communicating, for which I pray you forgive me.

A Prayer to Worship Jehovah over Jezebel

God,

As we seek to obey your commands to do justice in the world, help us keep the first commandment to have no gods before you. When we do not exalt you, when glorifying and enjoying you is not our highest aim every day, when our inescapable, built-in impulse to worship veers from you—our Creator—to creation, then our justice becomes injustice. We do not give you your due. We do not give your image-bearers what they are due. Forgive us for our idolatry. We have bowed to the false gods of stuff, solitude, sky, the status quo, the self, the state, social acceptance, and sex. Help us worship you in Spirit and in truth, that we might become true agents of justice in the world. Amen.

PART 2

UNITY OR UPROAR?

■ ■ ■

Three Questions about Social Justice and Community

Now in Christ Jesus you who once were far off have been
brought near by the blood of Christ. For he himself is
our peace, who has made us both one and has broken
down in his flesh the dividing wall of hostility.

–Ephesians 2:13-14

ime magazine polled Americans on the one hundred worst ideas of the twentieth century. Fast food, aerosol cheese, thong underwear for men, plus-size spandex, breast implants, and a purple dinosaur named Barney all made the list. Of 232,919 votes cast, the number one answer was telemarketing.[1]

What if, however, we defined "worst" not in terms of the annoying, ridiculous, gross, or silly but in terms of actual human suffering and evil unleashed? One bad idea, related to lives lost, dominated the twentieth century. It proved to be a pathological and fatal idea for over a hundred million people.

It inspired the lynching trees of America, the smokestacks of Auschwitz, the gulags of Siberia, the killing fields of Khmer Rouge, and the butchery of those in Rwanda, Darfur, Congo, and more. Given its bloody track record, you would think this idea would be universally rejected; but it is staging a massive comeback in the twenty-first century, rebranding itself as "justice." What is this bad idea?

Tribalism is the idea that we should divide people into group identities, then assign undesirable or evil traits to that group in such a way that we don't see the unique image-bearers of God before us. As Shelby Steele points out, collective identities tend to reduce individual human beings to ciphers or nonindividuated members of a particular group or class. As an ex-Social Justice B devotee put it, "I did not engage with individuals as individuals, but as porcelain, always thinking first and foremost of the group identities we inhabited."[2] Such group identities take many forms:

> We are Aryan, we are good; they are Jewish, they are bad.
> We are Brahman class, we are good; they are Untouchables, they are bad.
> We are Hutu, we are good; they are Tutsi, they are bad.
> We are white, we are good; they are black, they are bad.
> We are the Islamic State, we are good; they are infidels, they are bad.

The list could go on, and so could the body counts.

A Good Need Twisted

If tribalism has proved to be such a devastating idea, then why is it so enduring? After the bloodshed it unleashed in the twentieth century, why are group identities trending so sharply in the twenty-first century?

Harvard researcher Robert Putnam found that "if you belong to no groups but decide to join one, you cut your risk of dying the next year in half."[3] One famous study found that group-connected people with unhealthy habits like smoking, poor diet, and heavy drinking consistently outlive disconnected people with otherwise healthy lifestyle habits.[4] Pull a leaf off a tree and it dies. Pull a red-hot ember from a fireplace and it turns to ash. Pull a human out of a meaningful group and he or she starts to fall apart. Every "me" needs a "we."

Biblically speaking, the need to live as more than an isolated me is far from trivial. The Bible begins with a series of benedictions, or good words, that God speaks over his creation. Heavens and earth—good. Oceans, clouds, fruit, and animals—good. Then we reach the first malediction, or bad word, God speaks over his creation. "It is not good," says God, "that the man should be alone."[5] Our Creator, who is community as Father, Son, and Holy Spirit, designed us for meaningful community.[6]

The God-given need for community has not gone away since the fall in Genesis 3. It has been twisted, like everything else, since that catastrophic day in the garden. Take a good need for community—a desire to belong to a group bigger than our lonesome selves—then add our fallenness to the mix, and what do you get? You get a gang, a mob, a cult, an abusive church, a hate group, or a totalitarian political party—one self-righteous tribe seeking to vanquish all others. This is the dilemma of our century, and indeed every century: *How do we meet our irrepressible God-given need to belong in groups without those groups becoming self-righteous and resorting to full-blown tribal warfare?* The Bible has an answer to that question. So does Social Justice B. The answers are very different. So we ask three questions about social justice and community:

> Does our vision of social justice take any group-identity more seriously than our identities "in Adam" and "in Christ"?
>
> Does it buy into divisive propaganda?
>
> Does it replace love, peace, and patience with suspicion, division, and rage?

Chapter 4

The Collective Question

Does our vision of social justice take any
group-identity more seriously than our
identities "in Adam" and "in Christ"?

Christian Picciolini was sixteen years old when he joined the Chicago Area
Skinheads. He rose quickly through the ranks to become a leader of the
neo-Nazi hate group. "I felt abandoned and that led me to this community."[1]
After the birth of his first child, by God's grace, Picciolini was set free from the
sin of white supremacy and went on to colead a new group called Life After
Hate. "I think ultimately people become extremists not necessarily because of
ideology," Picciolini observes. "They're searching for three very fundamental
human needs: identity, community and a sense of purpose."[2]

If we swing from far right to far left, we meet Conor Barnes. At eighteen
years old, Barnes was "depressed, anxious, and ready to save the world." He
moved in with what he calls his "radical community." To hear Barnes describe
this community is like hearing someone jump from the screen during the
movie *Fight Club* to tell you what it's like living on Paper Street with Tyler
Durden as he launches Project Mayhem to topple the evils of the capitalist
West. In Barnes's words, his group was "a community that shares both an
ideology of complete dissatisfaction with existing society due to its oppressive
nature and a desire to radically alter or destroy that society." Thankfully, after
finding himself "exhausted and misanthropic," Barnes found freedom. His
advice to anyone still swept up in far-left groups is simple: "Flee the cult!"[3]

Christian Picciolini and Conor Barnes are mirror images. Both were swept
up in groups that used categories like race, economic status, and oppression to
see themselves as angels and others as demons, although one man's angels were

the other man's demons. Christian found community fighting against immigrants and people of color, while Conor found a community that "lived and breathed concepts and tools like call-outs, intersectionality, cultural appropriation, trigger warnings, safe spaces, privilege theory, and rape culture." Both now work to set others free from such self-righteous communities. Yet Christian and Conor were propelled by the same human drive—the need to belong.

Strange Comradery

The Bible has a beautiful and unifying answer to the longing for belonging. Social Justice B tries to answer the same need.

We've all felt hurt, lonely, and aimless. We all seek a proxy card to the top floor offices, a passport into a better country, a password into the hippest speakeasy—someplace to feel important, to feel included, to ease our pain. Social Justice B seeks to meet these needs by dividing humans into two groups, the oppressed and the oppressors. Your skin tone, your gender, or your economic or social status may grant you a warm welcome into the virtuous group, which will take you seriously, pat you on the back, and hand you a drink.

This promise of becoming an insider has a powerful draw for people God designed for community. That draw is particularly magnetic for those who bear the heartache of having been ostracized by their families, churches, or societies. In short, Social Justice B scratches a real itch. It touches our God-given need to belong. It offers "church" to many who have never had or who have been burned by the actual church.

One way Social Justice B draws members is by marketing itself as radically inclusive. It is not. How can it be? If markers that not everyone shares are the passwords for entry, then inevitably some will be insiders and others outsiders based on the level of oppression attached to certain skin tones, genders, sexual desires, or economic or social statuses. If such unshared features determine the virtue and credibility of human beings, then we will always count some people among the "saints" and exclude others as "sinners" (unless the "sinners" perform enough penance to prove themselves worthy of inclusion).

The Bible's answer to the need for belonging is far more inclusive. Biblically, there is such a thing as being damned by belonging to a people group—namely, the group called *people*. This damnation has nothing to do with our gender, our income, our national origin, or the melanin in our skin cells. It has to do, on the deepest level, with being a human being. According to Paul, every person on planet earth—rich or poor, male or female, black or white, religious or secular, right or left—stands united in this scandalous group identity. "All have sinned and fall short of the glory of God," say the Scriptures.[4] We are, each and all of us, born under the curse of Genesis 3. Adam's sin has affected all of us from our days in diapers. None of us had to be taught how to be selfish, how to bend the truth in our favor, how to worship things that are not God, how to be ungrateful for what we have and jealous of what others have, how to push others down in an attempt to bump ourselves up, or how to make up absurd self-justifications when we know deep down we're wrong. All of that comes quite naturally to us, *all* of us in the dysfunctional human family.[5]

This is the truth that millions of Christians around the world acknowledge every Sunday when rich, poor, male, female, black, brown, and white say out loud together: "We confess that we have sinned against you in thought, word, and deed, by what we have done, and by what we have left undone. We have not loved you with our whole heart; we have not loved our neighbors as ourselves."[6]

Many think such a doctrine of sin leads only to shame. Social Justice B proponents explicitly reject this doctrine. They tend to prefer Jean-Jacques Rousseau's far more flattering dogma: "There is no original perversity in the human heart.... Man is naturally good.... It is by our institutions alone that men become wicked."[7]

What if, in a strange way, a biblical understanding of sin leads to exactly the kind of authentic community we all long for? If we believe, with Rousseau, that human institutions are the primary source of evil, then we can divide the human race into good and bad groups on the basis of whether those institutions help or hurt them. If we believe, with Paul, that evil is our shared human heritage—that our hearts share the same corruption, that those at the top and the bottom are united in having idol-factory hearts—then something powerful and ego-deflating happens. It becomes impossible to go through life with a self-serving mindset that envisions halos over your own head and horns on everyone else's.

> Gut-wrenching malevolence cannot be reduced to a color, a gender, an economic problem. It is a *human* problem.

What if we soaked into our bones the unflattering truth of our tragic group identity in Adam's fall? We would see that gut-wrenching malevolence can't be reduced to a color, a gender, an economic problem. It is a *human* problem. Since I'm human, it's *my* problem. And if you are a descendent of Adam—which is to say if you're not a toad or a squirrel but a member of the human race—then it is *your* problem. It is all of our problem.

Howard Zinn's *A People's History of the United States* rewrites history from the perspective of the oppressed, as Zinn imagines their perspective. A biblically informed reading of history would tell us to care for the oppressed and to take their stories seriously as God's downtrodden image-bearers, but it would also do something Zinn never dreamed of. It would inspire us to see history not purely through the perspective of the oppressed but also through the lenses of the oppressors. Why? Because the same human nature in the Aztec slayer, the Atlantic slave trader, and the Auschwitz executioner resides in us too. If we don't seriously reckon with that uncomfortable truth, then we can all too easily become the next round of self-righteous oppressors.

Had a sixteen-year-old Christian Picciolini believed that *all* fall short, he could have seen through the neo-Nazi propaganda that equates white skin with goodness. Had an eighteen-year-old Conor Barnes reckoned seriously with the universal depravity of the human heart, he could have seen through the self-exempting leftist narrative that lays all human suffering at the feet of cops and capitalists. The doctrine of human depravity swings like a wrecking ball, leveling any ideology that says, "*My* gender group, *my* ethnic group, *my* economic group makes me good, and *their* group is evil."

Our hearts are just as susceptible to evil as the hearts of those atop the bloody steps of Templo Mayor, those grinning under America's lynching trees, or those dropping Zyklon B canisters into German gas chambers. Those who committed such atrocities were not extraterrestrials or some animal species. They were humans, like us, with the same corruptible hearts. We are *all* in desperate need of grace, forgiveness, and atonement.[8]

Try to find such humble self-awareness in Social Justice B literature. Instead, you will find humanity divided into subgroups of damnable oppressors and the blameless oppressed. You will find the same identity game played in far-right literature. That is not a recipe for inclusivity but for self-righteousness and never-ending tribal warfare.

How Paul Inspired Unity

It is important to understand the context of Paul's statement: "All have sinned and fall short of the glory of God." Trying to gain superiority over others using a group identity wasn't something the American slave traders invented. Yes, they took such tribalism to new diabolical depths, but the world Paul traveled had plenty of folks using their ethnicity to feel superior. He, along with other first-century evangelists, faced the impossible task of church. *Church*, from the Greek *ekklesia*, simply means "gathering." How do you gather people from long and bitterly divided social tribes under the same roof to worship the same God, break bread together as equals, and unclench fists to embrace one another as brothers and sisters? It's not easy. Such gathering, such church, was a Herculean task, or rather a Holy Spirit–sized task. But it happened. And in many places around the globe today, it still happens every week.

Here is what Paul and the first-century evangelists did *not* do. They did not play a game of grievances. First-century Jews could easily have said, "Look at all the oppression the non-Jews have unleashed on us! We've been oppressed by Egyptians, Babylonians, Assyrians, Persians, Greeks, and now Romans. They banished us from Rome nearly two hundred years ago and tried again thirty years ago. Romans have invaded and now occupy Jerusalem, our most sacred city. Their economic system of mass taxation has left most of our fellow Jews languishing in poverty. The whole system is rigged against us by the Roman supremacists, enforcing their cultural hegemony on us at every turn. And we're supposed to break bread with them and call them brothers? No way! They must prove their spiritual merit and solidarity with us by becoming 'Judaized' and divesting themselves of their Roman-ness."

Paul would have none of this. Paul does not say to the non-Jews, "Look at all the horrors your ancestors unleashed on the Jews." He does not say, "Jewish believers, wake up to the fact that the gentiles have long oppressed you and that they are presently benefitting from all that injustice." Paul did not treat people like what Thomas Sowell calls "intertemporal abstractions" of their ethnic identity groups, then pit one group against another in tribal warfare. That would be like rigging explosives to the foundations of the temple that is God's church. And it would demolish the gospel itself, giving people a way of feeling justified and free of blame on the basis of ethnic identity in an oppressed group rather than on the finished work of Jesus. Paul cared far too much about the church and the gospel to split believers into such oppressor/oppressed binaries.

Here is what Paul *did* do. He spoke three unifying truths into communities where historic grievances could have easily torn the body of Christ limb from limb. First, *Paul told the truth that sin is not exclusively the oppressor's problem, but a human problem.* Some Jews thought that, by virtue of their Jewishness, they were superior to non-Jews. Paul counters, "What then? Are we Jews any better off? No, not at all. For we have already charged that all, both Jews and Greeks, are under sin."[9] Then Paul cites Psalm 14:

> None is righteous, no, not one;
> > no one understands;
> > no one seeks for God.
> All have turned aside; together they have become worthless;
> > no one does good,
> > not even one.[10]

No ethnic or religious group identity can absolve anyone from evil. "For there is no distinction"—meaning no difference between one people group and another—"for all have sinned and fall short of the glory of God."[11] By telling the truth that all people sin, Paul dealt his first blow against tribalism.

Second, *Paul told the truth that being "in Christ Jesus" is a new identity that transcends other group identities.* "In Christ Jesus you are all sons of God, through faith. For as many of you as were baptized into Christ have put on Christ. There is neither Jew nor Greek, there is neither slave nor free, there is no male and female, for you are all one in Christ Jesus."[12]

Jews shouldn't resent Greeks or vice versa, though it would have been easy to build a historic case for such resentment. Slaves shouldn't resent the free or vice versa, though it would have been easy to build a historic case for such resentment. Women shouldn't resent men, or vice versa, though it would have been easy to build a historic case for such resentment. All us-versus-them thinking, all group divisions, all grievances are wonderfully transcended by a shining new group identity—"you are all one in Christ." In Christ, ethnic enemies become family, oppressed and oppressors become brothers and sisters, and privileged and underprivileged become equally loved siblings under the same all-loving Father.

> In Christ, ethnic enemies become family, oppressed and oppressors become brothers and sisters, and privileged and underprivileged become equally loved siblings under the same all-loving Father.

Third, *Paul told the truth that God and God alone grants us our "not guilty" verdict on the basis of the justifying death of Jesus.*

But now in Christ Jesus you who once were far off have been brought near by the blood of Christ. For he himself is our peace, who has made us both one and has broken down in his flesh the dividing wall of hostility.[13]

[God is the] just and the justifier of the one who has faith in Jesus.[14]

There is therefore now no condemnation for those who are in Christ Jesus.[15]

Who shall bring any charge against God's elect? It is God who justifies. Who is to condemn? Christ Jesus is the one who died—more than that, who was raised—who is at the right hand of God, who indeed is interceding for us.[16]

Paul or Cone?

Contrast Paul's approach with that of James Cone. Cone, the father of black liberation theology, has become a celebrated voice among many Christians, particularly those adopting more of a Social Justice B perspective on race. Here is his vision in his own words. It is worth quoting at length if we want to understand the vision behind what has been dubbed "racial reconciliation" in much of today's church.

> When whites undergo the true experience of conversion wherein they die to whiteness and are reborn anew in order to struggle *against* white oppression and *for* the liberation of the oppressed, there is a place for them in the black struggle of freedom. Here reconciliation becomes God's gift of blackness through the oppressed of the land. But it must be made absolutely clear that it is the black community that decides both the *authenticity* of white conversion and also the part these converts will play in the black struggle for freedom. The converts can have nothing to say about the validity of their conversion experience or what is best for the community or their place in it, *except* as permitted by the oppressed community itself. . . . White converts, if there are any to be found, must be *made* to realize that they are like babies who have barely learned to walk and talk. . . . They must be told when to speak and what to say, otherwise they will be excluded from our struggle. . . . Unless whites can get every single black person to agree that reconciliation is realized, there is no place whatsoever for white rhetoric about the reconciling love of blacks and whites. . . . Just because we work with them and sometimes worship alongside them should be no reason to claim that they are truly Christians and thus part of our struggle."[17]

Cone inverts all three truths that Paul uses to bring the church together. First, rather than sin being a universal human affliction, Cone equates sin with oppression, and oppression, for Cone, is a white man's game.[18] Second, for Paul, being "in Christ Jesus" transcends all other group identities. Reading Cone, we get the clear sense that black identity and white identity outweigh our "in Christ Jesus" identity. Such ethnic identifiers are paramount for Cone and ought to form hierarchies of power in the church—determining who can and who cannot speak. And why should whites be allowed to speak if, as Cone argues, "whites are incapable of making any valid judgments about human existence"?[19] Third, it is not God who is the Just and the Justifier, not God who decides the authenticity of conversion; it is the totality of the black community that decides such weighty matters.

When people are to be treated like babies on the basis of their skin color, we must ask ourselves honestly, "Whose vision of reconciliation holds more hope for bringing deeper unity to the multiethnic body of Christ, Paul's or Cone's"?

Be Found *in Him*

In Philippians 3, Paul lists his spiritual credentials. He was circumcised on the eighth day, of the people of Israel, of the tribe of Benjamin, a Hebrew of Hebrews, a law-abiding Pharisee, a zealous defender of his Jewish tribe against all ideological threats foreign and domestic. In essence Paul is saying, "So you guys want to play either the tribalists' game of proving your goodness by group identity or the individualists' game of proving your goodness by your own accomplishments? Fine, let's play. I played that game a long time, and I've got all of you beat."

Then comes a breakthrough so joyous and freeing for Paul that he spent his life, literally, to proclaim, "Whatever gain I had, I counted as loss for the sake of Christ. Indeed, I count everything as loss because of the surpassing worth of knowing Christ Jesus my Lord. For his sake I have suffered the loss of all things and count them as rubbish, in order that I may gain Christ and be found in him, not having a righteousness of my own that comes from the law, but that which comes through faith in Christ, the righteousness from God that depends on faith."[20]

Paul considers his credentials and group status nothing, rubbish, dung, compared with being found in Christ. When we come to that same realization of the treasure that is *in Christ-ness*, it becomes difficult if not impossible to use our color or credentials to create race-based hierarchies—black, white, brown, or other—in the church. This is why white supremacists in American history were so woefully heretical. They made "in whiteness" more important than "in Christ–ness."

One of the most inspiring facts about the early church was how, for all its imperfections, it managed to take hands off throats and raise them together in worship. "Here there is not Greek and Jew, circumcised and uncircumcised, barbarian, Scythian, slave, free; but Christ is all, and in all."[21] If we can't see "the surpassing worth of knowing Christ Jesus"[22] as infinitely more important than everything else—including our ethnic differences, our political passions, and our historic grievances—that he "is all, and in all,"[23] then there is little hope of unity in the twenty-first-century church.

This raises a vital question: Couldn't this make for a whole new form of self-righteous tribalism, those "in Christ" versus those who aren't? That's the beauty of being in Christ. *Our qualification for entry has nothing whatsoever to do with our being better than anyone else in any way.* There is zero room for self-righteousness. Unlike every religious system in history in which our performance is the determining factor of our status, being "in Christ" means that Jesus's performance alone is the determining factor. Any other claim to be "better than" is sheer self-deception. Any and all righteous status we have is solely in Jesus, not our color, not ethnicity, not gender, not the amount of oppression we or our ancestors have or haven't experienced, not our good works, our ticking the right squares on the ballot, or our height on a hierarchy of privilege or pain; it is nothing but Jesus. The cross of Christ forms the spear through the heart of both far-right and far-left ideologies. Only when very different people with very different credentials and very different circumstances come to see their main identity as Jesus followers, we have the foundation on which real community—a community that doesn't devolve into tribal warfare—is built.

EDWIN'S STORY

When I was "woke," I did not realize how much resentment I harbored. Only after rejecting the ideas of the woke movement and the Social Justice B doctrines it preaches was I able to see my own sinful biases. By that time I had unwittingly hurt many people and severed friendships. I used my social media platforms to vent my self-righteous indignation toward white America. I believed the lie that everyone who is white is privileged and everyone who isn't white is oppressed.

I imbibed such racist ideas from theologians like James Cone. In applying Cone's teachings, I struggled to see fellow church members as equally forgiven, loved, and embraced by God. Why? Because of the color of their skin. After weekly sermons, people would gather, and I prepared for verbal combat against anyone who did not see all the oppression I saw. I couldn't enjoy the saints for who they were as individuals. Everything was about racism all the time. If a white person did not see things my way, I convinced myself that their racial bias left them hopelessly blind to social injustice.

Then the Lord opened my eyes and set me free in an unexpected place, a rural, predominantly white church that I visited with my family. We began singing one of my favorite songs, "Behold Our God." Scanning the room, my eyes fell on an older lady whose face was filled with joy as she worshiped our God. Then it hit me: "That older white lady is my sister in the

Lord!" Bible passages about the redemptive work of Christ rushed through my mind. Then came the voice of God in verses commanding Christians to love one another. I left the church humbled by the reality of my own weakness and utter dependence on Christ. I had been so blinded by an ideology that divided people by skin color that I missed the blessing of seeing the sufficiency of Christ's atonement. Though I considered myself woke, my bitterness toward white people had closed my eyes to God's marvelous saving power in the gospel.

If you're not heavily involved in Social Justice B or the woke movement, don't feel like you are missing out. You are not. Rather than trying to wrap your brain around all the slanted sociological terms and ideologically edited historical narratives, I encourage you to look to Christ in Scripture. Rather than being versed in the ever-changing cannon of woke literature, aim to be rooted in theological truths, such as the doctrines of justification and sanctification. Look at the unity within the godhead, and seek to live out that kind of unity in the context of your local church, as Jesus prayed in John 17.

For those who consider themselves woke, please hear the loving caution of a former outspoken voice from your ranks: examine your hearts. What effect is reading oppression into virtually all of life having on your soul? What do you see first when you encounter a fellow Christian, their "in Christ" identity as your brother or sister or whether their appearance places them in the oppressed or oppressor group? Does your wokeness give you a sense of moral superiority or make you utterly dependent on the righteousness of Christ that becomes ours through the gospel? Do you prejudge people by their melanin (or lack thereof), or do you love your brothers and sisters in the Lord with an open heart? I know from experience how a noble desire for justice can replace love in our hearts with resentment and hate. I know because it happened to me. But by God's grace, and God's grace alone, I have been set free. I pray that you too can exchange the suspicion and rage of wokeness for the love and joy of the gospel of Christ, who "himself is our peace, who has made us both one and has broken down in his flesh the dividing wall of hostility" (Eph. 2:14).

–Edwin Ramirez

Edwin hosts the podcast The Proverbial Life *and blogs regularly at www.theproverbiallife.com.*

Questions for Personal or Small Group Study

1. Try to identify five major differences between what the church is supposed to be according to the New Testament versus according to the tribalism of our culture.
2. In your own words, how does the biblical doctrine of universal human depravity prevent us from falling into tribalism or identity politics, left or right?
3. What can we as Christians do practically to live out our shared "in Christ" identity with those from different tongues, tribes, and nations?

Chapter 5

The Splintering Question

Does our vision of social justice
embrace divisive propaganda?

W hat would it take to totally invert the second great commandment—to love our neighbors as ourselves—and rally neighbors to turn on one another with bloodthirsty rage? The answer is, in a word, propaganda.

An old Nazi pamphlet says that the Jew "only looks human, with a human face, but his spirit is lower than that of an animal.... [He represents] unparalleled evil, a monster, subhuman."[1] The Tutsis in Rwanda were called *Inyenzi*, or "cockroaches." KKK literature reduced blacks in the US to "gorillas." The two million victims of Khmer Rouge were deemed "microbes" who must be "swept aside" and "smashed." White supremacists of the 2017 Unite the Right rally in Charlottesville spoke of the "parasitic class of anti-White vermin." Propaganda is the uranium that powers tribalism and the social meltdown it incurs.

If you ever find your day going too well or your stomach *too* calm, then go read through propaganda—whether that of the SS, the KKK, or the RTLM[2]— that inspires one group of people to think of some other group as subhuman. I have spent hundreds of hours doing precisely that while researching for this book. Frankly, it is profoundly depressing and profoundly eye opening.

We find three common marks. One, propaganda offers a highly edited history that paints the most damning picture it can of a given people group. Two, it encourages us to treat individual neighbors as exemplars of their damnable group. Three, it gives us a way to blame all of life's troubles on that damnable group and its members. This has been precisely the logic used to oppress black people throughout history. Read the propaganda behind the twentieth-century genocides and you will find the same three marks.

The optimist in me would like to think that after a hundred million casualties in the last century, we would see through such propaganda. I would like to think we have moved past telling the most damning revisionist histories of people groups, making individuals into exemplars of those damnable groups, and blaming our current problems on those groups. Sadly, we have not moved past it.

Damning Revisionist Histories

Just like other propaganda throughout history, Social Justice B edits history in the most damning way possible against particular people groups. Facts that undermine the Social Justice B version of history are simply not mentioned or can be mentioned only if you want to incur public wrath.

Take the history of slavery. Social Justice B tells us that slavery is the legacy of a particular people group—white, European, imperialistic, and usually Christian males. If that's the story we want to tell, then we must blot many important historical facts from our collective memory. Thomas Sowell documents some of these in "The Real History of Slavery":

- "Slavs were so widely used as slaves in both Europe and the Islamic world that the very word 'slave' derived from the word for Slav—not only in English, but also in other European languages, as well as in Arabic."[3]
- "China in centuries past has been described as 'one of the largest and most comprehensive markets for the exchange of human beings in the world.' Slavery was also common in India, where it is estimated that there were more slaves than in the entire Western Hemisphere.... Slavery was also an established institution in the Western Hemisphere before Columbus' ships ever appeared on the horizon."[4]
- "While slavery was common to all civilizations ... only one civilization developed moral revulsion against it, very late in its history—Western civilization.... Themselves the leading slave traders of the eighteenth century, Europeans nevertheless became, in the nineteenth century, the destroyers of slavery around the world."[5]
- "The British stamped out slavery, not only throughout the British Empire ... but also by its pressures and actions against other nations" including Brazil, Sudan, Zanzibar, the Ottoman Empire, and Western Africa, often at the great loss of British lives and money.[6]
- "Americans stamped out slavery [not only in America itself, but also] in the Philippines, the Dutch stamped it out in Indonesia,

the Russians in Central Asia, the French in their West African and Caribbean colonies."[7]

- The Westerners who stamped out slavery did so "over the bitter opposition of Africans, Arabs, Asians, and others. . . . On the issue of slavery, it was essentially Western civilization against the world."[8]
- "Moreover, within Western civilization, the principal impetus for the abolition of slavery came first from very conservative religious activists—people who would today be considered 'the religious right.' Clearly this story is not 'politically correct' in today's terms. Hence it is ignored, as if it never happened."[9]

Such facts don't sit well with today's fashionable, group identity–based version of history. When we buy into the Social Justice B narrative that one particular group is best thought of as oppressors, we have to take scissors to our history books. We must not talk about how many members of the group—white, Western, usually Christian men—labored to stamp out slavery in the UK or how many died on Civil War battlefields to help topple the system of Southern slavery. We must suppress the historic fact that white Western males formed the tip of the spear plunged into the heart of slave systems not only in the West but also in the African, Arab, Indian, Asian, and South American worlds.

Am I arguing that American race-based slavery was somehow excusable? Not in a million years. It was an appalling evil. Am I arguing that white men are somehow supreme? Of course not. White men are fallen, depraved, twisted, capable of tremendous harm, *like everyone else in Adam's tribe called humanity.* There is no shortage of historical proof that white male members of Adam's tribe have committed heinous evils against other members of Adam's tribe, a fact conveniently edited out of far-right propaganda. I am not excusing such evils for one second. I am critiquing the way Social Justice B simplifies history to push a narrative that fosters us-versus-them tribal warfare.

So I say again: *slavery, racism, and sexism are inexcusable, and anyone who has participated in such sins should repent and run as fast as possible to the cross of Jesus.* Yet we must say with equal clarity that telling lopsided stories to paint damnable pictures of entire people groups—whether that group happens to be black, brown, white, male, female, or whatever—is also a sin we must take to the cross. In biblical terms, it is a form of bearing false witness, a form of slander, a form of not loving our neighbors. And it devalues the God whose image our neighbors bear.

Individuals as Group Exemplars

Damning revisionist history is the first mark of propaganda and, increasingly, a mark of Social Justice B. This leads us to a second mark. Once history has been edited in the most condemning way possible for certain groups, propaganda ensures that individual members of that group can be judged on the basis of that group identity, regardless of how they live their lives. To grasp the point, take a moment to read through two abbreviated newspaper articles from opposite sides of the world.

. . . here in the land of legislatively legitimated toxic masculinity, is it really so illogical to hate men? But we're not supposed to hate them because . . . #NotAllMen . . . but when they have gone low for all of human history, maybe it's time for us to go all Thelma and Louise and Foxy Brown on their collective butts. . . .	Every Hutu should know that every Tutsi is dishonest in business. His only priority is the supremacy of his ethnic group. . . . The experience of the October war has taught us a lesson. . . . The Hutus must be firm and vigilant against their common Tutsi enemy. . . .
[Men should] pledge to vote for feminist women only. Don't run for office. Don't be in charge of anything. Step away from the power. We got this. . . .	All strategic positions, political, administrative, economic, military and security should be entrusted only to Hutu. The education sector (schools pupils, students, teachers) must be majority Hutu. . . .
Growing movements challenge a masculinity built on domination and violence and to engage boys and men in feminism are both gratifying and necessary. Please continue. . . .	Hutu ideology must be taught at every level to every Hutu. Every Hutu must spread this ideology widely. . . .
And please know that your crocodile tears won't be wiped away by us anymore. You have done us wrong. #BecausePatriarchy.	The Hutu should stop having mercy on the Tutsi. . . .
It is long past time to play hard for Team Feminism. And win.	The Hutu must be firm and vigilant against their common enemy: the Tutsi.

Simply swap out the word *women* for *Hutu* and the word *men* for *Tutsi* and you are essentially reading the same article.

The parallels are chilling. Both articles come from media outlets with wide audiences in their respective countries—the *Washington Post* in the US and *Wake Up* in Rwanda. Both articles cite historical grievances to villainize an entire group of people. Both call readers to see every individual in that group as the enemy. Both express group solidarity among an oppressed people group and boldness to fight the oppressor group, remove them from society's positions of power, and refrain from showing them mercy.

One article is from 1990 and called "The Hutu Ten Commandments." The man behind it, Hassan Ngeze, was eventually arrested and sentenced by the International Criminal Tribunal for Rwanda for his role in inciting hatred against Tutsis. The other is from 2018 and entitled "Why Can't We Hate Men?"[10] and its author Suzanna Danuta Walters is a celebrated professor of sociology at Northeastern University, Boston, and director of the Women's, Gender, and Sexuality Studies Program. Ngeze's "Hutu Ten Commandments" is recognized for the tribalizing, hate-inspiring propaganda that it is.

Thankfully, Walters wasn't calling for genocide as Ngeze did. Yet her version of tribal thinking in "Why Can't We Hate Men?" is not harmless. That a call to hate an entire people group could be issued in a major national newspaper is, frankly, appalling. The twentieth century should have taught us with gruesome clarity the consequences of ascribing blame and inciting hate against entire people groups. Yet Walters's article is hardly a fluke. Read law professor Ekow Yankah's "Can My Children Be Friends with White People?"[11] from the *New York Times* or Michael Harriot's "White People are Cowards."[12] Calls to hate entire people groups have been platformed by major media outlets and become orthodoxy in departments of Women's, Gender, and Race Studies. I have personally witnessed the heart-wrenching effects of this ideology. It turns bright-eyed, articulate, caring students into chronically triggered, ever-suspicious, resentment-fueled soldiers, well trained to make snap judgments against others on the basis of their appearance.

If we think this is not happening, then we simply aren't paying attention. As Christians commanded to care about justice for *all* divine image-bearers, we *must* pay attention.

A serious charge could be leveled at me here. "Aren't you a big hypocrite? Aren't you doing the same thing as those you're critiquing, lumping Dr. Walters, individuals in the media, and tons of people in higher education into one big evil group—whether you brand them 'lefties,' 'snowflakes,' 'Social Justice B advocates,' or whatever? Don't you see the same dangers of tribalizing in what you are saying?"

To the first charge, yes, I am a big hypocrite. I fail to live up to God's standards of justice, goodness, and consistency every day. Thank God my identity does not rest on my ability to measure up, because I have no such ability. To the second, no, I am not doing the same thing as those I'm critiquing. I am critiquing their *ideas*, not their gender or skin tone, and we should never call for hatred or unfriending or use a morally charged word like *cowards* to generalize any particular people group. Allow me to write a brief article entitled "Why Can't We Hate All Social Justice B Advocates?" Here goes:

"Why Can't We Hate All Social Justice B Advocates?"
Because the Bible commands us to love our neighbors. The End.

Walters, Yankah, Harriot, and anyone else espousing Social Justice B are our neighbors. We can think Suzanna Danuta Walters is wrong, that her ideas are dangerous and even hateful, and still love the divine image-bearer Suzanna Danuta Walters. The same goes for all those who advocate for Social Justice B. Hating people is simply not an option for the Christian.

Blaming Life's Troubles on a Damnable Group

Now we come to the third mark of propaganda—scapegoating. Once we have rewritten history to demonize a given people group and trained our eyes to see horns on the heads of individuals in that group, the final step is to blame life's troubles on them. How do the KKK, the Aryan Nations, and other neo-Nazi groups find recruits to hate black, brown, and Jewish people? It's simple. Just blame all white folks' problems on minorities. Life isn't going well? You're struggling to pay the bills? Things seem hopeless? Your culture isn't thriving? You feel depressed, anxious, and angry? It's all the foreigners' fault—the invaders, the infiltrators, the leaches, the parasites! When Christian Picciolini, whom we met in the last chapter, was in the Chicago Area Skinheads, this was the kind of toxic, racist air he breathed.

This group blame game is also played on the left. Barnes recalls,

I was a depressed and anxious teenager, in search of answers. Radicalism explained that these were not manageable issues with biological and life-style factors, they were the result of living in capitalist alienation. . . . The force that causes depression is the same that causes war, domestic abuse, and racism. By accepting this framework, I surrendered to an external locus of control. Personal agency in such a model is laughable. And then, when I became an even less happy and less strong person over the years as an anarchist, I had an explanation on hand.[13]

Picciolini and Barnes were both taken in by ideologies that offered them easy scapegoats for every problem in their lives. "It's the minorities' fault!"

thought Picciolini before he saw the light. "It's the white cisgender capitalist pigs' fault!" thought Barnes before he fled the cult. In my home country, at the moment, we find ourselves in a situation, full of irony, in which the far-right and far-left sides of the political spectrum are playing exactly the same game they think the other side is so deplorable for playing.

The truth is that because Genesis 3 happened, because we are fallen creatures inhabiting a fallen cosmos, life is hard. The problem of evil is not just the Christian theologians' problem. It is *everyone's* problem. The unexpected brutality, the unrelenting pain, the seeming absurdity and senselessness of so much suffering are realities we all try to come to terms with somehow. For theologians, the task of accounting for evil in the universe goes by the fifty-cent term *theodicy*. Everyone needs a theodicy, an explanation for the twistedness of the world. My first book—*Love, Freedom, and Evil*—focused on the free will defense, the most influential explanation of evil throughout Christian history. I spent nearly fifteen years wrestling through the free will defense to the problem of evil. I came to the conclusion that this answer to the problem makes the problem of evil worse, for reasons I unpack in that book.[14]

Since then I have come to see that there is an even more dangerous answer to the problem, an answer that adds to the net suffering in the world. It is the attempt to explain the world's suffering by finding a collective scapegoat. In this sense, Nazism was a theodicy. It attempted to explain the existence of evil by saying, "It's all the Jews' fault!" That theodicy added to the evil in the universe by exterminating six-plus million precious Jews from the planet. Marxism was a theodicy. It attempted to explain evil by saying "It's all the capitalists' fault!" That theodicy cost the world over a hundred million lives in less than a century. The caste system, Jim Crow segregation, and jihadism are all theodicies—pointing to the poor, the black, or the infidel as convenient scapegoats for the travails of life in a fallen world.

We must see Social Justice B for what it is. It too is a theodicy. It attempts to explain the world's evil and suffering by making group identities the primary categories through which we interpret all pain in the universe. No matter how much it waves the banners of "justice," "equality," and "liberation," do we really think such a grand experiment in collectivist group blaming will end well?

If the body count of the last century has taught us anything, it is that ideas have consequences, and bad ideas have bad consequences. Telling damnable stories about entire people groups, seeing individuals as exemplars of their groups, and blaming the hardness of life on them are really bad ideas. They should be given no foothold in the church of Jesus Christ.

SURESH'S STORY

I was born into a destitute Dalit family in the Gorkha district of Nepal in 1979. A Dalit is known as "Achhut" (Untouchable), a term invented to humiliate the downtrodden. Though the Nepal government has recently declared caste-based discrimination a crime, the Dalit community still strives for dignity.

When I was growing up, children from the higher caste were told not to befriend Dalits like me. If they happened to play with us, they had to be sprinkled with gold-touched water to purify them from our Dalit defilement. I had to bow down to Hindu gods and goddesses from outside the temples where non-Dalits worshiped freely. In restaurants, I had to wash my own plates because no one would dare wash a Dalit's dishes. Even dogs are allowed to enter the houses of the upper caste, but not Dalits. We are treated as subhuman.

In the summer of 1999, I had a breakthrough at the Monkey Temple in Kathmandu. I met a Biola University theology student on a mission trip. We walked the temple steps for hours, talking about the differences between grace-based Christianity and karma- and caste-based Hinduism. At last, a truly humanizing way to see my identity! That night, I accepted Jesus as my Savior. I found a dignity in the eyes of my Creator who didn't see me as "untouchable" but reached down to love me, embrace me as his son, and offer me "every spiritual blessing in the heavenly places" (Eph. 1:3). Jesus welcomes us regardless of our social status or religious performance!

I wish I could say my last twenty years as a Christian have ended my experience of caste-based discrimination. My dream of being treated with dignity as an image-bearer of God is still a far cry in Nepali society. I live in a small flat in Kathmandu with my wife and children where we would be swiftly evicted if our landlords discovered that we are Dalit. We train our children to hide their caste membership.

What is truly scandalous is that Nepali churches are no different. Many churches ask attendees to identify their caste. When they find out we are Dalits, attitudes change dramatically. We hear propaganda, even within the church, that "people of lower castes have lower intellectual ability." It makes no difference that I recently earned my master's degree in theology and plan to embark on PhD studies to better serve the church. It only matters that you are "untouchable," which disqualifies you from church leadership. As a result, Dalits are compelled to either hide their identities or start their own churches.

Instead of mirroring Jesus, who loves every tongue, tribe, and nation, the church has simply gone with the flow of Nepal's caste-based discrimination. Many Nepali Christians were formerly Hindus but still have Hindu hearts toward their brothers and sisters in Christ. Ephesians 2:14 teaches that Jesus has made the Jews and gentiles one, having broken down the dividing wall of hostility through the cross. Why, then, would we keep intact the dividing wall between non-Dalit and Dalit?

It is time for the church not only in Nepal but around the world to show what true social justice looks like. How do we do that? We must live out the biblical truth that everyone bears God's image and should be treated as such. We must preach the gospel of Jesus's death and resurrection that gives dignity and worth not only to Dalits in my country but to the downtrodden around the world. We must follow God's command to "show no partiality as you hold the faith in our Lord Jesus Christ" (James 2:1). And finally, we must pray. Pray for the church in Nepal. Pray for the church around the world. Pray that we would truly do justice, because Jesus has turned the walls of hostility into rubble.

–Suresh Budhaprithi

Suresh earned his Masters of Divinity at the Kathmandu Institute of Theology and is continuing his training for lifelong ministry. To help him and his family overcome injustice, visit his page at gofundme.com/f/gofundmecombless-the-budhaprithis.

Questions for Personal or Small Group Study

1. Why it is so easy for us as humans to blame our life troubles on other people groups?
2. Think of specific people groups who have been made scapegoats in our society today. How can you be countercultural by loving people in those groups this week?
3. One powerful remedy to propaganda is spending time with people who disagree with us, deliberately escaping our echo chambers. What are the current echo chambers you may be occupying, and how can you venture beyond them this week?

Chapter 6

The Fruit Question

Does our vision of social justice replace love, peace,
and patience with suspicion, division, and rage?

Real community—something we all long for and were created for—does not come easy. Think of how easily our hearts harbor grudges and assume the worst of others to feel better about ourselves and our clans. That is what our hearts do in their fallen default mode. That is one reason Paul talks so much about *schismata*—the sin of divisiveness[1]—and why he talks about "the fruit of the Spirit." For quick-to-quarrel, easy-to-offend, clique-forming people to have any hope of experiencing real community, of gathering, of doing *church* together, then we need love, joy, peace, patience, kindness, faithfulness, goodness, gentleness, and self-control to deal with other far-from-perfect people. These "fruits" must be Spirit-produced. Without the Spirit's fruit, we fall into tribal default mode. That is why any approach to social justice that encourages suspicion and rage instead of the fruit of the Spirit has no place in Jesus's church.

A Flood of Healing Warmth

To see what I mean by the need for supernatural fruit produced by the Spirit, consider the case of Corrie ten Boom as she confronted the Nazi SS officer responsible for the death of her sister at the Ravensbruck concentration camp. It is one of the most moving stories to emerge from the darkest days of the twentieth century and worth quoting at length:

> Betsie and I had been arrested for concealing Jews in our home during the Nazi occupation of Holland; this man had been a guard at Ravensbruck

concentration camp where we were sent. Now he was in front of me, hand thrust out: "A fine message, *fraulein*! How good it is to know that, as you say, all our sins are at the bottom of the sea!"

And I, who had spoken so glibly on forgiveness, fumbled in my pocketbook rather than take that hand.... "You mentioned Ravensbruck in your talk," he was saying. "I was a guard in there." ... "But since that time," he went on, "I have become a Christian. I know that God has forgiven me for the cruel things I did there, but I would like to hear it from your lips as well. Fraulein"—again the hand came out—"will you forgive me?"

And I stood there—I whose sins had every day to be forgiven—and could not. Betsie had died in that place—could he erase her slow terrible death simply for the asking?

It could not have been many seconds that he stood there, hand held out, but to me it seemed hours as I wrestled with the most difficult thing I ever had to do. For I had to do it—I knew that ... "If you do not forgive men their trespasses," Jesus says, "neither will your Father in heaven forgive your trespasses." I knew it not only as a commandment of God, but as a daily experience. Those who were able to forgive their former enemies were able also to return to the outside world and rebuild their lives, no matter what the scars. Those who nursed their bitterness remained invalids. It was as simple and as horrible as that.

And still I stood there with the coldness clutching my heart. But forgiveness is not an emotion—I knew that too. Forgiveness is an act of the will, and the will can function regardless of the temperature of the heart. "Jesus, help me!" I prayed silently. "I can lift my hand. I can do that much. You supply the feeling."

And woodenly, mechanically, I thrust my hand into the one stretched out to me. And as I did, an incredible thing took place. The current started in my shoulder, raced down my arm, sprang into our joined hands. And then this healing warmth seemed to flood my whole being, bringing tears to my eyes.

For a long moment we grasped each other's hands, the former guard and the former prisoner. I had never known God's love so intensely as I did then.[2]

I don't know about you, but I am astounded by ten Boom's utter lack of self-righteousness. She had the humility to ask Jesus for help. She saw herself as a sinner, rather than doing the easy thing of projecting all injustice outside herself, even though she had experienced devastating injustice from outside herself. She did not villainize all Germans. She did not think rehearsing historical grievances would make her some kind of noble heroine against oppression. She recognized that her seething was something to progress beyond, not defend. She questioned her (understandable) emotions to withhold her hand from the Nazi complicit in her sister's murder. As a result, she experienced the flood of healing warmth in her whole being.

When Jesus commanded his listeners to love their enemies and pray for those who persecute them, he was talking to real people with real enemies and real oppressors. The kingdoms of the world play the self-defeating game of tribalizing, retaliation, and escalation, running up body counts in the name of "justice." The kingdom Jesus invites us into does not play by those rules. Corrie ten Boom showed her citizenship in Jesus's kingdom rather than the world's kingdoms when she extended forgiveness to the Nazi.

> The kingdoms of the world play the self-defeating game of tribalizing, retaliation, and escalation, running up body counts in the name of "justice."

This same kingdom shone through the darkness of Dylann Roof's racist shooting spree that left nine precious black image-bearers dead at Emanuel Church in Charleston in 2015. Roof tried to start a "race war." But rather than supplying the reciprocated rage to fuel such a war, those who lost loved ones to Roof's racial hatred responded with forgiveness:

> You took something really precious from me. I will never talk to her ever again. I will never be able to hold her again, but I forgive you and have mercy on your soul.[3]
>
> —*daughter of shooting victim Ethel Lance*

> I've realized that forgiving is so much tougher than holding a grudge. It takes a lot more courage to forgive than it does to say, "I'm going to be upset about whatever forever." . . . After seeing how people could forgive, I truly hope that people will see that it wasn't just us saying words. I know, for a fact, that it was something greater than us, using us to bring our city together.[4]
>
> —*son of shooting victim Sharonda Hughes-Singleton*

> I would just like him to know that . . . I forgive him and my family forgives him. But we would like him to take this opportunity to repent. Repent. Confess. Give your life to the one who matters most: Christ. So that he can change him and change your ways, so no matter what happens to you, you'll be okay.[5]
>
> —*relative of shooting victim Myra Thompson*

I acknowledge that I am very angry. But one thing that DePayne always enjoined in our family . . . is she taught me that we are the family that love built. We have no room for hating, so we have to forgive.[6]

—*sister of shooting victim DePayne Middleton Doctor*

Wow! These big-souled believers reflected their Savior far more powerfully than I ever have (or ever could). Read my friend John M. Perkins's *One Blood*, *Let Justice Roll Down*, or *Dream with Me* to be further awestruck by the power of love over hate. These stalwart saints each demonstrated the love and forgiveness of our Savior, who prayed "Father, forgive them" over the very oppressors hammering nails into his wrists, and died to redeem us when we were his enemies. Such grace must be supernatural. It comes from a kingdom not of this world. It requires the power of the Holy Spirit, and couldn't we all use more of that?

Hooks's "Killing Rage"

From a Social Justice B perspective, things look different. Contrast Corrie ten Boom and the saints of Charleston's stories with a bit of required reading in many humanities and sociology departments around the West, an essay called "Killing Rage." Its author, Gloria Watkins, is better known by her nom de plume "bell hooks." She is former Yale faculty, distinguished professor of English at City College of New York, hailed as "the most prominent exponent of black feminism" by the *New York Review of Books*, and a celebrated voice of many Social Justice B advocates. She coined the term *white supremacist capitalist patriarchy*, a concept that has soared to the status of orthodoxy in activist communities, academia, and much of the church.

Disclaimer: It would be easy to read what follows as a personal attack against bell hooks and those who process the world as she does. It is not an attack against her. Hooks is a divine image-bearer of inestimable value. It is a love-motivated plea to process the injustices of the world in a way that is less toxic for her and for our souls.

In "A Killing Rage," she begins with the line, "I am writing this essay sitting beside an anonymous white male that I long to murder." The impetus for this murderous rage was a seating mix-up on a commercial flight. Hooks takes her first-class seat beside a friend she simply identifies as "K." The plane intercom requests that K make her way to the front of the cabin to have her ticket inspected, revealing that her first-class upgrade wasn't properly processed and she must relocate to coach. An "anonymous white male" with the first-class ticket replaces K. He apologizes for the inconvenience. Here is what bell hooks has to say:

> I stare him down with rage, tell him I do not want to hear his liberal apologies, his repeated insistence that "it was not his fault." I am shouting at him that it is not a question of blame, that the mistake was understandable, but that the way K was treated was completely unacceptable, that it reflected both racism and sexism.... I let him know he had an opportunity to not be complicit with the racism and sexism that is so all pervasive in this society.... I felt a "killing rage." I wanted to stab him softly, to shoot him with the gun I wished I had in my purse. And as I watched his pain, I would say to him tenderly "racism hurts." ... As though I were the black nightmare that haunted his dreams, he seemed to be waiting for me to strike, to be the fulfillment of his racist imagination. I leaned toward him with my legal pad and made sure he saw the title written in bold print: "Killing Rage."[7]

Some may think I have cherry-picked an extreme example to paint Social Justice B in a bad light. Granted, it is an extreme example. And, of course, we should not picture Social Justice B proponents sitting around fantasizing about murdering anonymous white men. Murderous rage aside, bell hooks's personal account of oppression on an airplane is highly instructive if we want to understand the basic categories of Social Justice B thinking and why it is so divisive. Note three aspects of hooks's account.

First, at no point in her narrative does hooks question whether racism and sexism are the best explanations for her and K's experience. Racism and sexism aren't conclusions that necessarily *follow* from her experience but premises that necessarily *frame* her experience. Socially uncomfortable, unfortunate encounters happen on airlines every day. Airlines often botch their bookings, leaving passengers in a lurch. Airline employees, like the rest of us, have bad days and, like the rest of us, fail to treat people with courtesy at times. (Having flight attendants in my family, I can tell you they often get the brunt of people's bad days.)

Could K's experience have been something people of all colors and both genders experience daily? Could there have been an honest seating mix-up? Is it possible that the "anonymous white man" in this scenario was simply seeking the seat he paid for? No, he was *clearly* an accomplice in a grand plot of white male subjugation of black women. She was clearly the "black nightmare" of his "racist imagination." This mishap was *clearly* evidence of the rampant racism and sexism, yet another instantiation of centuries of what hooks would call white supremacist capitalist patriarchy.

Or was it? Hooks would never know, since her mentality makes it impossible to even entertain any less rage-inducing explanations for what happened on that tense flight. This unwillingness to consider less infuriating explanations or entertain the benefit of the doubt on others' behalf has become a mark of Social Justice B.

Second, throughout the essay, individuals become exemplars of entire groups and those groups' cumulative injustices. Notice that hooks identifies the object of her rage as an *anonymous* white man. She didn't know his name. She didn't need to know his name. All she needed to tap into her self-described "militant rage" was to look at his color and gender. That was enough to channel all her rage for the full historic sum of injustices black women have suffered. His skin and sex identified him as part of the oppressor group and therefore as an oppressor himself. She might have been sitting next to a civil rights attorney, a firefighter in underprivileged neighborhoods, or a paper pusher who had never had a racist thought in his life. Perhaps his ancestors were abolitionists or died in blue coats fighting Southern slavery. Hooks would never know. In her style of group-identity-think, she might as well have been sitting next to the Imperial Wizard of the Ku Klux Klan. If K had been replaced by another black female, would hooks have inked the words *killing rage* in bold so her new neighbor could see? Of course not. It was the skin and gender that made the difference for hooks. This has become a growing tendency of Social Justice B supporters, a tendency to turn the particular people sitting beside us into poster boys for all the wrongs committed by those who happen to share their pigmentation or Y chromosomes.

Third is the obvious rage from which hooks's essay takes its title. There is little room in hooks's account for anything resembling grace, kindness, forgiveness, or peacemaking. Let's assume that the anonymous white man and the airline staff involved in the relocation of K were truly racist and sexist. The Bible commands, not suggests, that we love our enemies.[8] The Holy Spirit, through Paul, commands us to "let all bitterness and wrath and anger and clamor and slander be put away from you, along with all malice. Be kind to one another, tenderhearted, forgiving one another, as God in Christ forgave you."[9] He also says,

> Repay no one evil for evil, but give thought to do what is honorable in the sight of all. If possible, so far as it depends on you, live peaceably with all. Beloved, never avenge yourselves, but leave it to the wrath of God, for it is written, "Vengeance is mine, I will repay, says the Lord." To the contrary, "if your enemy is hungry, feed him; if he is thirsty, give him something to

drink; for by so doing you will heap burning coals on his head." Do not be overcome by evil, but overcome evil with good.[10]

This leads to a fourth and final point we can draw from hooks's "Killing Rage." Nowhere in the essay does she turn from criticizing the assumed motives of those around her to question her own heart. There is no sense that fantasizing about stabbing or shooting an anonymous white man might expose a problem—dare I say, *sin*—in her own heart. If the all-pervasive problem is white patriarchal oppression, then what incentive would hooks have to search her heart or confess any evil there?

Instead of humility and repentance, hooks speaks in high terms of "black rage . . . as a potentially healthy, potentially healing response to oppression and exploitation. . . . [Rage is] a necessary aspect of resistance struggle. . . .Rage can act as a catalyst inspiring courageous action. . . .It is humanizing to be able to resist it [racial hatred] with militant rage."[11]

The Bible commands, not suggests, that we love our enemies.

▪ ▪ ▪

What if someone were to question her killing rage? It would only prove their white supremacy. Says hooks, "To perpetuate and maintain white supremacy, white folks have colonized black Americans, and a part of that colonizing process has been teaching us to repress our rage, to never make them the targets of any anger we feel about racism. Most black people internalize this message well."[12]

If white people question hooks's rage, they are oppressors; if black people question her rage, they are victims of colonization who have internalized white racism. Such ready-made explanations effectively shield hooks from ever having to look in the mirror. Envisioning ourselves as noble revolutionaries against a white supremacist patriarchy is far easier than taking a long, hard look in the mirror.

To see hooks consumed with such "militant rage" is a tragedy that moves me to tears. I long and pray for hooks and those caught up in her ideology to experience the breakthrough from rage to a flood of joy, peace, and healing as Corrie ten Boom and those traumatized in Charleston did.

The problem is that bell hooks's "Killing Rage" is standard fare in universities around the West. I have seen the rage, resentment, and quickness-to-be-offended it inspires in students. It injures their souls and breaks my heart. They are rarely, if ever, offered a more humbling and humanizing alternative to hooks's rage. I would be shocked to find Corrie ten Boom's personal account of forgiving an SS officer in the syllabus of any humanities or social science department of our day. But ten Boom's humility, love, grace, forgiveness, self-criticism, and willingness to seek supernatural help are exactly what such students need to escape the vertigo of rage that would, before long, have them self-righteously seething on airplanes or social media news feeds.

Militant Rage or the Fruit of the Spirit

The way Corrie ten Boom and the saints at Charleston confronted injustice is what Paul calls "the fruit of the Spirit" in Galatians 5. "The fruit of the Spirit," says Paul, "is love, joy, peace, patience, kindness, goodness, faithfulness, gentleness, self-control."[13]

Here are some clues that we may have been taken in by an anti-Spirit ideology: Instead of being love-filled, we're easily offended, ever suspicious, and preoccupied with our own feelings. Instead of being filled with joy, we're filled with rage and resentment, unable to forgive. Instead of striving for peace, we're quarrelsome—dividing people into oppressed or oppressor groups instead of appreciating the image-bearer before us. Instead of having patience, we're quickly triggered and slow to honestly weigh our opponents' perspectives. Instead of being kind, we're quick to trash others, assuming the worst of their motives. Instead of showing gentleness, we use condemning rhetoric and redefined words to intimidate others into our perspective. Instead of showing self-control, we blame our issues exclusively on others and their systems, not warring daily against the evil in our own hearts.[14]

May we surrender our quick-to-tribalize hearts to the Holy Spirit so that our justice seeking brings more unity than uproar.

MICHELLE'S STORY

When I was growing up in Minnesota, one of the things that made me acutely aware of being a racial minority was the seemingly endless "So where are you from?" questions. I quickly learned that people didn't want an answer like "Minnesota," or "Hibbing," which was the town where I lived. They were satisfied only once I said something about my parents being born in Korea. The question was so difficult, even if the person was well-intentioned, because of the implied message that surely I wasn't "from" someplace in the United States. Even though my siblings and I were born in America, meaning this was the only country we knew, we were assumed to be foreigners, unlike my white classmates. Life was a constant reminder that we didn't belong, which is especially hard when you're a kid trying to figure out your place in the world.

It's easy to be angry at those who seem to want to remind you that you don't fit in. But I've learned that's not the only way I can respond. As a graduate student, I observed an incident that changed my perspective. My friend, who enjoys meeting new people and learning about new cultures, approached a shop owner who was clearly not white and asked, "So where are you from?" I was horrified. But to my astonishment, the man was delighted. He shared story after story about Egypt, the country he loved, and even thanked her for being interested in where he was from! When you meet someone, you can't immediately tell just from looking at them whether they will be offended or delighted if you ask where they are from. This taught me the importance of grace in our interactions.

Of course, truly terrible interactions happen and need to be seen for what they are. But sometimes a well-meaning person sincerely wants to make things better but is afraid of being called racist for accidentally offending someone. And if someone is to be called racist for making a mistake, then they'll likely conclude it's better to not take the risk. So we end up not talking at all or being on the defensive when we do. As Christians, we are called into deep relationships with one another, but it's hard to do that if we feel like we have to walk on eggshells.

Grace takes our human limitations into account. Do people ever say something to me I don't like? Certainly. I have also said many things others don't like, and they gave me grace. None of us has a monopoly on giving or receiving offensive comments. That's why giving grace has become so important for me personally. Focusing on how I've been offended may make me feel good for a moment, but it also leads me down the path of bitterness that can overtake my soul and trap me in resentment. It's hard to see how staying stuck in that mindset can lead to anything but strife and more hard feelings.

The Bible calls us to the kind of love that is not easily offended (1 Cor. 13:5). Grace doesn't mean I think terrible words or actions are okay, but it does compel me to remember that I am relating with someone who is imperfect, just as I am imperfect. The gospel is based on the truth that we all fall short of God's ideal (Rom. 3:23). If we're going to have truly productive conversations about race and other controversial social justice topics, we have to be willing to give people space to make honest mistakes. As a follower of Jesus, I am called to build up others in the body instead of shaming them (1 Cor. 14:26). As flawed human beings, we shouldn't expect instant perfection but realize we are all constantly growing in grace and truth (John 1:17). And we all deeply need the Holy Spirit's help to do that (Gal. 5:16-25)!

–Michelle Lee-Barnewall

Michelle is an associate professor of New Testament at Biola University's Talbot School of Theology and blogs regularly at https://www.biola.edu/blogs /good-book-blog.

Questions for Personal or Small Group Study

1. We all from time to time may experience something like the rage bell hooks expresses in her essay "Killing Rage." In those moments, what specific Christian truths can we preach to ourselves to replace rage with the kind of grace and love we see in Corrie ten Boom?
2. How do you think preaching the gospel to ourselves every day— reminding ourselves of the amazing grace God extended to us when we were hostile to him—could impact our approach to social justice? How might excluding the good news of God's forgiveness from our daily thought lives and emotions pollute our passion for social justice?
3. In our social media age of daily online warfare and polarization, what are some specific ways to embody the fruits of the Spirit online with those who disagree with us?

So You're Saying . . .

Given the power of the Newman effect in our day (see pp. 8–9), here are five points some may have heard me advancing in part 2, "Unity or Uproar? Three Questions About Social Justice and Community":

1. "So you're saying our 'in Christ' identity as Christians means we should ignore harsh realities people face on account of their skin tone, sex, or economic status."

2. "So you're saying, like the white Christians who opposed Martin Luther King Jr., that we shouldn't speak out against injustice because that risks being divisive."
3. "So you're saying that minorities should surrender their own cultural and ethnic identities to white majority culture in the church in the name of unity."
4. "So you're saying that the long history of oppression against black and brown people should be swept under the rug in the name of unity."
5. "So you're saying that victims of oppression have no right to be angry about injustice."[15]

No. I am not saying any of that. I don't believe any of that. If you are hearing any of that, then either the Newman Effect is at work or I have simply done a poor job communicating, for which I pray you forgive me.

A Prayer to Seek Unity over Uproar

God,

You designed us for community, but in our fallen state, we take the good relational drives you gave us and we twist them into tribalism. Help us humbly recognize our shared fallenness in a way that smashes all claims to ethnic, gender, or economic superiority. Help us to see our "in Christ" identity as infinitely precious so that people from every tongue, tribe, and nation can transcend our grievances and embrace one another as brothers and sisters with whom we will enjoy eternity. Help us see through and stand against vicious propaganda that pretends to be justice but rewrites history, treats individuals as group exemplars, and blames all life's problems on different people groups. Replace suspicion and rage inside us with the life-giving fruit of the Spirit. Fill us with the supernatural love, joy, peace, patience, kindness, goodness, faithfulness, gentleness, and self-control we need in order to have real unity in your church. Amen.

PART 3

SINNERS OR SYSTEMS?

Three Questions about Social Justice and Salvation

For I delivered to you as of first importance what I also received:
that Christ died for our sins in accordance with the Scriptures,
that he was buried, that he was raised on the third day.
—1 Corinthians 15:3-4

Twenty years ago I sat across the table from a Hindu monk, whom we'll call Sid, at a monastery in Los Angeles. I was preparing for a mission trip to Nepal to share the gospel in a predominantly Hindu culture, so I wanted more than just book knowledge of Hindus. Sid described the torment he once felt over the inequality in the world. Why were some born into mansions with silver spoons and others born in mud huts with malaria? The question had kept him up at night. How could such unfairness be explained?

Eastern philosophy, particularly the doctrines of karma and reincarnation, seemed to do the trick for Sid. Little Richie Rich was reborn in Bel Air because he had earned a surplus of good karma in his last life cycle. Sad little Sunji was reborn in the Kathmandu slums because of his poor prebirth karmic performance.

Sid was tapping into a cosmic question—a good question—that animates today's Social Justice B movement. Why is there so much inequality in the universe? I was born in Orange County, California, with toys on the shelf, an air-conditioned house, and a backyard spa. One of my best friends, Suresh, whom I met at the Monkey Temple in Kathmandu back in 1999, was born in abject poverty in a town called Gorkha with a tin roof over his head, a family goat, and the stigma of being a Dalit from birth—a member of Hindu culture's untouchable class. Could we have traded places at birth? Could he have been born into the global 1 percent, while I was born an untouchable? Yes. Did either of us have a say in being born to rags or riches? No. That seems unfair.

Sid's way of coping with the unfairness was to embrace a doctrine of individual responsibility so radical it could make Ben Shapiro and Jordan Peterson blush. Some sad untouchable was born in a slum because he *merited* slum life from his personal choices in a former life. I was born in suburban Southern California because, apparently, I did a stellar job scoring karma points in my last life.

In the West, many struggle to make sense of the same unfairness that drove Sid to the Hindu monastery. Except in the West, the current trend in academia, entertainment, and media is to go the exact opposite way that Sid did. It is not the self and the self's personal choices that explain inequalities; rather, it is *systems*. That poor man is poor because of capitalism, a system, we are told, that makes the rich richer by making the poor poorer. That person of color is stuck in dire straits because of all the systems of white supremacy stacked against him—the racist criminal justice, racist housing, and racist education systems. That woman struggles to get ahead because of the patriarchy—the vast network of institutions founded and run by the kind of men who would love to see Margaret Atwood's *The Handmaid's Tale* become more than fiction.

Is there such a thing as systemic injustice? Of course. What else do you call slavery in antebellum (pre–Civil War) America or Jim Crow laws in postbellum America? What else do you call apartheid? What else do you call the caste system? What else do you call human trafficking?

The Bible warns us to not be allied with those who "frame injustice by statute,"[1]—that is, those who inject disobedience to God's law into human legal codes. Evil humans make evil laws. We build our sins into our systems. Heinrich Himmler, Hermann Goering, and Adolf Hitler's sin of anti-Semitism wasn't just individually expressed; it was systematized into ghettos and gas chambers. The sin of antiblack racism wasn't just expressed by individuals; it was framed by statute through the American slave trade, the Supreme Court's infamous Dred Scott ruling, Jim Crow laws, the Alabama statute that required black people to surrender their bus seats to white people (a law Rosa Parks courageously broke), redlining, and more. The caste system of India, which branded most citizens "untouchable," was an injustice baked into the very systems by which Hindu society functioned. Apartheid in South Africa, China's one-child policy, the list of systemic injustices could go on ad nauseam.

The Bible had it right thousands of years ago. We indeed "frame injustice by statute."

But this biblical insight that sin can be supersized and systematized is usually not what Social Justice B means by "systemic injustice." There are important differences. If we don't ponder these differences, the church will find itself bowing down to a trendy ideology rather than to Jesus as Lord. In this chapter we will ask three questions about social justice and salvation that will make those fundamental differences clear and, Lord willing, keep the church from losing the gospel as we seek to love the oppressed.

Does our vision of social justice prefer damning stories to undamning facts?

Does it promote racial strife?

Does it distort the best news in history?

Chapter 7

The Disparity Question

Does our vision of social justice prefer
damning stories to undamning facts?

Putting the words *systemic* and *injustice* together is a lot like putting the words *social* and *justice* together—there are biblical and unbiblical meanings we can pour into those word combinations.

The Bible nowhere uses the word *systemic*. But we would have to take scissors and do some serious Jeffersonian slicing and dicing to the inspired text to believe sin cannot be expressed systemically. The Jews' captivity in Egypt wasn't just Pharaoh and some slave-whipping Egyptian underlings treating God's people as subhumans. It was also a system. King Darius, who decreed that a person praying to anyone but him would become lion lunch, and King Nebuchadnezzar, who decreed that anyone refusing to bow to his golden idol would become fuel for the furnace, set up unjust systems. From steep interest rates to ritual child sacrifice, the Bible has much to say about confronting the kind of injustice that is bigger than this or that individual sin. The Bible's commands aren't merely for personal piety, but guide us to display God's justice more radiantly in the systems of earth as it is in heaven.

Two Kinds of "Systemic Injustice"

If we infuse the terms *systemic* and *injustice* with biblical meaning, then systemic injustice is *any system that either requires or encourages those within the system to break the moral laws God revealed for his creatures' flourishing*. Darius and Nebuchadnezzar set up systems that required citizens to self-destructively break the first commandment to have no gods before God. The imperial cult of the New Testament era did the same thing when the Romans legislated the lordship of Caesar over Christ. Nations that worshiped Molech, the god of fire, had laws that permitted child sacrifice, much like abortion laws in today's world, which formed unjust systems. These laws encourage the breaking of the sixth commandment: "You shall not murder."

Systemic injustice is any system that requires or encourages us to defy the Creator by breaking his good commands. That is the implicit biblical definition that empowered Frederick Douglass and Sojourner Truth to subvert the systems of American slavery, Sophie Scholl and Dietrich Bonhoeffer to resist the systems of Nazism, and Alexander Solzhenitsyn and Vaclav Havel to undermine the systems of Soviet Communism.

But that is *not* the way Social Justice B defines "systemic injustice." If we can't tell the difference between these definitions and their implications, then we may think we are doing justice for the oppressed, when we are really doing the bidding of political ideologues.

If we go with the Social Justice B definition, then these are real-world scenarios that count as systemic injustice:

- In California's Silicon Valley, women make up a mere 15.67 percent of tech jobs (e.g., programmers and engineers) at tech giants Apple, Google, Twitter, Facebook, LinkedIn, and Yahoo.[1]
- On the New Jersey Turnpike, black drivers received nearly twice as many speeding tickets as white drivers.[2]
- Mortgage lenders rejected twice as many blacks as whites for home loans, 44.6 percent compared with 22.3 percent according to data from a 2000 US Commission on Civil Rights Report.[3]

Examples like this abound. From a Social Justice B perspective, the way you spot systemic injustice is by looking for unequal outcomes. An unequal outcome becomes damning evidence that sexism, racism, or some other evil "ism" is at the foundation of a system. The system, therefore, must be reduced to rubble for everyone to have a fair shot at the good life. Social Justice B thinking follows a straightforward equation:

Disparity = Discrimination

The Bible is clear that discrimination exists and that Christians must resist it.[4] Sinful discrimination indeed causes some disparities. But the Bible never goes to the extreme that we find in the thinking of Ibram X. Kendi.

In his award-winning bestseller *Stamped from the Beginning*, Kendi argues that "racial disparities must be the result of racial discrimination."[5] Notice the language: "must be." In the *New York Times*, Kendi states his doctrine bluntly: "When I see racial disparities, I see racism."[6] Automatically equating disparity with discrimination is not just something that happens in six-hundred-page bestsellers or in many sociology and humanities departments around the US. It has gone mainstream as the way most conversations about social justice are framed in the twenty-first century. That includes conversations in the church.

> The Bible is clear that discrimination exists and that, as Christians, we must resist it.
>
> ▨ ▨ ▨

On a Social Justice B view, working for a socially just world follows three steps:

Step 1. Spot an unequal outcome.
Step 2. Interpret that unequal outcome as damning evidence of a racist or sexist system.
Step 3. Overthrow that system.

When we import this view into Christianity, there is often a fourth step.

Step 4. Identify overthrowing that system as "a gospel issue" and indict fellow believers for white supremacy or patriarchal oppression if they do not join us in the fight.

Undamning Facts

In Social Justice B's definition of systemic injustice, step 2 sends many Christians with great intentions down a path that leads to a space where their faith can no longer breathe. On this road, we learn to assume the worst. We accept the most damning conclusions about others, often at the expense of both facts and biblical charity.

Take one particular unequal outcome that made the headlines around the turn of the millennium. On the New Jersey Turnpike, more black drivers than white drivers were pulled over and written up for speeding tickets. Step 1—unequal outcome identified. Then came step 2. Take that finding as evidence that the system of New Jersey traffic law enforcement is racist. Many were content to go from there to step 3 and launch a social justice crusade against the state troopers. In today's American Christian context, many would happily go to step 4 to proclaim that the Christian community's failure to address this systemic injustice of racism on the New Jersey Turnpike serves as evidence of a "truncated gospel" or "white supremacy" in the church.

Then came the Public Services Research Institute's *Speed Violation Survey of the New Jersey Turnpike: Final Report.* Researchers used high-speed cameras and a radar gun on 38,747 turnpike drivers to get to the bottom of the issue. The study found that "in the southern segment of the turnpike, where the speed limit is 65 m.p.h., 2.7 percent of black drivers were speeders, compared with 1.4 percent of white drivers. Among drivers going faster than 90 m.p.h., the disparity was even greater. . . . The study concluded that blacks make up 16 percent of the drivers on the turnpike and 25 percent of the speeders in the 65 m.p.h. zones, where complaints of profiling have been most common."[7]

The researchers pointed out, "Demographic research has shown that the black population is younger than the white population, and younger drivers are more likely to speed."[8] This is not a breakthrough; it is common knowledge— older people drive slower. (This does not mean there is no such thing as racial profiling, only that in this particular case, factors other than race better accounted for the disparity.)

Or take the fact that bank lenders across the US rejected twice as many blacks as whites for home loans, 44.6 percent compared with 22.3 percent. Taken alone, that fact seems damning. But the same US Commission on Civil Rights report found that white Americans are turned down nearly twice as often as Asian Americans and Native Hawaiians for those same mortgages (22.3 percent versus 12.4 percent)?[9] Does this prove systemic racial discrimination against whites? Of course not. How about the fact that "black-owned banks turned down black applicants for home mortgages at a *higher* rate than did white-owned banks"?[10] Is that systemic racism?[11] No.

Granted, such facts aren't very useful for whirling people into a tizzy for justice. They are undamning explanations, and ones that happen to be backed by empirical evidence. Undamning and perhaps even boring explanations go a long way to making sense of many inequalities. The following list includes just a few:

1. *Location, Location, Location.* People who live on coasts and people who live on mountains, people who live on fertile soil and people who live on sand, and people near or far from cultural hubs of innovation experience different outcomes. *In a world, unlike ours, with zero racism or sexism or any other evil ism, there would still be inequalities based on something as boring and undamning as geography.*[12]

2. *Candles.* The number of flames that flicker on our birthday cakes each year has a big impact on unequal outcomes. "In the United States, for example, the median age of Japanese Americans is 51 and the median age of Mexican Americans is 27. How likely is it that these two groups—or others—would have the same proportions of their populations represented in occupations, institutions or activities requiring long years of education and/or long years of job experience?"[13] *In a world, unlike ours, with zero racism or sexism or any other evil ism, there would still be inequalities based on something as boring and undamning as age.*

3. *Calendars.* There is a remarkable inequality between hockey pros born between January and March and those born in December. In his book *Outliers,* Malcolm Gladwell tries to explain the overrepresentation of January–March born players in the NHL. The cutoff for Canadian youth hockey programs is January 1. When coaches start marking kids for promotion to the more elite hockey programs—programs with more practice, more games, better coaching, and a more likely path to the NHL—a kid born in January of year X is not just *older* than his teammate born in December of year X; he is *better.* Says Gladwell, "When you are 8 years old, 10 or 11 months of maturity means a lot."[14] (Is the NHL guilty of "Decemberism," discrimination against those with birthdays later in the year?) The same phenomenon shows up in even more extreme ways, Gladwell argues, in European soccer and American baseball. *In a world, unlike ours, with zero racism or sexism or any other evil ism, there would still be inequalities based on something as boring and undamning as birthdays.*

Twenty-two of the twenty-nine astronauts in the original Apollo space program were firstborns. People living in the US experience 90 percent of the world's tornadoes. Asians are underrepresented in the NBA, NFL, NHL, and MLB. Woman are overrepresented in health care, in attaining university degrees, and in setting consumer trends that determine the actions of the world's biggest corporations. Men make up an overwhelming majority of soldiers who perish on battlefields and have a virtual monopoly of the bricklaying, plumbing, and carpentry industries. Jewish people, "being less than 1 percent of the world's population . . . received 22 percent of Nobel Prizes in chemistry, 32 percent in medicine and 32 percent in physics."[15] Middle and old-aged white men make up the majority of those who enjoy shows like *Frasier,* music by Creed, and golf.

The point is *not* that there is no such thing as racism or sexism or other vicious isms wreaking havoc on earth. Sinful isms inflict hurt on some people groups that other people groups never have to cope with. The point is that shouting, "Systemic injustice!" at every unequal outcome is too easy. *In a world, unlike ours, with zero racism or sexism or any other evil ism, there would still be vast inequalities based on things as boring and undamning as geography, age, birthdays, birth order, shopping habits, desire to lay bricks, and so much more.*[16]

When we automatically assume damning explanations for unequal outcomes, we not only lock ourselves in a prison of never-ending rage but also dull our senses to the point that we will be useless for the sacred task of recognizing and resisting the real racism, real sexism, and other real vicious isms around us.

The Magic Equality Wand

Another factor in understanding unequal outcomes is the simple fact that different people make different life choices. Different life choices yield different life outcomes. That doesn't mean choice is the *only* determining factor behind different outcomes, of course. But personal choice is *a* factor. If we ignore that truth, our vision of social justice will become harder and harder to reconcile with a biblical worldview in which

> A slack hand causes poverty,
> > but the hand of the diligent makes rich.[17]

> In all toil there is profit,
> > but mere talk tends only to poverty.[18]

> The sluggard does not plow in the autumn;
> > he will seek at harvest and have nothing.[19]

> If anyone is not willing to work, let him not eat.[20]

> By wisdom a house is built,
> > and by understanding it is established;
> by knowledge the rooms are filled
> > with all precious and pleasant riches.[21]

> I passed by the field of a sluggard,
> > by the vineyard of a man lacking sense,

and behold, it was all overgrown with thorns;
> the ground was covered with nettles,
> and its stone wall was broken down.
Then I saw and considered it;
> I looked and received instruction.
A little sleep, a little slumber,
> a little folding of the hands to rest,
and poverty will come upon you like a robber
> and want like an armed man.[22]

"Between 2007 and 2011, the percentage of Asian and Jewish students at Ivy League universities was 16 percent and 23 percent respectively, compared to their representation of 5.6 percent and 1.4 percent in the U.S. population. In other words, they're overrepresented by factors of 3 and 16."[23] Does this prove that the Ivy League is riddled with Asian and Jewish supremacy? Of course not.

Or consider that conservative Protestants have far less wealth than Catholics and mainline Protestants, with Episcopalians and Jewish Americans earning far above the rest. The median net worth of conservative Protestants came to $26,000 compared with a median net worth of $150,890 for proponents of Judaism.[24] Are such inequalities evidence of systemic anti–conservative Protestantism? Should we protest America's widespread discrimination against conservative Protestants? No. The numbers support the commonsense fact that different life choices yield different life outcomes.

Imagine we could wave a magic equality wand that erased inequality around the world. This wand is so magical that it can even wipe away all discrimination from the planet. We all wake up in a discrimination-free world with a million dollars in our bank accounts, big homes, the best name brands in our closets, and an equally wide-open horizon of options and opportunities. No oppressive systems stand in anyone's way. How long could we who care about justice enjoy a vacation from protesting inequality? It would be more like a bathroom break than a vacation.

Since people have different priorities and make different life choices, inequalities would manifest within five minutes and grow larger by the day. Consider how different characters in the NBC sitcom *Parks and Recreation* might react to such a sudden influx of cash. Donna expands her real estate business. Ben sinks his million into building Ice Town. Ron buys gold and buries it in the woods. Tommy throws a lavish red-carpet party, complete with six open bars, a Bengal tiger, and a shrimp wall. Chris invests in a vegan market chain. Andy blows his money on Skittles, while Jean-Ralphio is livin' large with a high-end scarf collection and a RoLexus. Soon the social scientists go to work studying inequalities. Massive disparities between individuals and groups come to light. Activists take to their Gryzzl devices to protest the injustice of it all.

Two points follow from our magic equality wand thought experiment. First, we are being far too simplistic if we take discrimination as a one-size-fits all explanation of inequality. Notice that in this fictional world, there is zero discrimination. Yet there are huge disparities. What both worlds share is that different people have different priorities and make different choices. Should we expect those different people, priorities, and choices to yield equal (or even equal-ish) outcomes, even in a discrimination-free world? There is a sickening amount of discrimination-based inequality in our fallen world. But there are also inequalities that have nothing to do with discrimination. If we buy into the Social Justice B formula that disparity equals discrimination, then we will likely find ourselves in many situations swinging swords against perceived injustices when we are only beating the air. The tragedy is that we will be too blurry eyed and exhausted to recognize and stand against the real injustices around us.

Second, notice that different outcomes result from different people with different priorities making different choices. Here is an ironclad law of the universe: *Different people with different priorities making different choices will experience different outcomes.* Should we expect the Donnas and Rons of the world to fare equally with the Jean-Ralphios of the world? No. But here is the crucial point: The more fully committed we become to a vision of justice in which unequal outcomes are automatically assumed to be the result of injustice, the more our quest for justice will lead, indeed it *must* lead, to the use of power to enforce sameness. Only people who are forced to be, believe, and behave alike could have any hope of reaching the sacred goal of equal or equal-ish outcomes. In the name of "justice" we would have to turn different choices into brainwashed obedience. Different priorities would be swallowed up by some grand collectivist ideology. Different people would be remolded into an unquestioning legion of goose-stepping clones. Then and only then would we have the sameness that can forever save the world from the curse of unequal outcomes. As the Party slogan goes in George Orwell's *1984*, "War is peace. Freedom is slavery. Ignorance is strength."

Some will think I'm resorting to scare tactics. How, after all, could a noble goal like ending inequality bring on the apocalypse? If by ending inequality we mean "ending inequality that comes from discrimination or any other sin," then I am right there with you. But if we don't bother to distinguish between inequalities that come from sin and those that don't, then we are well on our way not to a fictional dystopia but to repeating the bloodiest mistakes of modern history. "Equality" was a waving banner of France's Reign of Terror, Russia's Gulags, and Mao's Great Leap Forward. "Equality" was also the banner over true leaps forward, such as Wilberforce's abolition, Dr. King's civil rights, and Desmond Tutu's antiapartheid movements. Working to free the world of some inequalities is just, good, and biblical. Working to free the world of other inequalities will turn us into monsters who think of ourselves as angels.

Social Justice B advocates find free markets repulsive because they lead to different outcomes for different people. Because different people with different priorities making different decisions experience different outcomes, any system that maximizes people's freedoms to be their different selves will end up with different outcomes. If we believe that different outcomes are *a priori* evidence of injustice, then *freedom itself is unjust*. Moreover, any systems that seek to maximize freedom, such as free markets, must be abolished as "systemic injustice." Different outcomes are the price of freedom. The converse is also true. Tyranny is the price of equal outcomes.

Let us return to our magic equality wand to grasp the point. Social scientists find that within a year Donna's real estate business, Chris's investment in the organic food chain, and Gryzzl's tech research have paid off big. There is massive wealth inequality between them and the Andys, Tommys, and Jean-Ralphios of the world. Again, in this fictional world there is zero discrimination to cause unequal outcomes. By the standards of Social Justice B, these massive disparities are unjust and must be undone. How could we do that? Some people who believe they have big enough hearts to care about injustice and big enough heads to fix it band together to do what the old magic equality wand did. They level the playing field again. Since they don't have magical power like the wand, they must resort to political power to wipe out the "injustice." These heroic justice seekers grab the opposite ends of the wealth gap and use their Herculean power to pull the haves and the have-nots together. Soon history repeats itself. Different people with different priorities making different choices leads to another round of different outcomes. The great equalizers must step in yet again, make more laws, redistribute more wealth, enforce more "social justice" until the quest for "equality" turns us into Communist Russia, North Korea, or Venezuela 2.0.

The Harry Potter in All of Us

We have challenged the dogma that disparities equal discrimination. Social Justice B leaves little to no room for factors like location, age, or life choices to help explain unequal outcomes. Whether such undamning explanations of inequalities are happily welcomed or written off says a lot about the state of our hearts. C. S. Lewis makes the point:

> Suppose one reads a story of filthy atrocities in the paper. Then suppose that something turns up suggesting that the story might not be quite true, or not quite so bad as it was made out. Is one's first feeling, "Thank God, even they aren't quite so bad as that," or is it a feeling of disappointment, and even a determination to cling to the first story for the sheer pleasure of thinking your enemies are as bad as possible? If it is the second then it is, I am afraid, the first step in a process which, if followed to the end, will make us into devils.[25]

Over the last five years in many Christian churches, the number of people who take the posture of charity that says, "Thank God, even they aren't quite so bad as that" has declined. As with chameleons taking on the colors of the culture, our default mode is becoming not righteous indignation but *self*-righteous indignation, assuming we are on the side of the angels and drawing damning conclusions about anyone who disagrees. When we start down that road, we become devils, and, as Lewis warns, "we shall insist on seeing everything . . . as bad, and not be able to stop doing it: we shall be fixed forever in a universe of pure hatred."[26]

Why do we often prefer damning explanations over undamning ones? Thomas Sowell points out that the most damning explanations of inequalities offer many "a moral melodrama, starring themselves as crusaders against the forces of evil."[27]

Let's expand on Sowell's point theologically. God designed us to find meaning as characters in a grand adventure, to participate in the epic triumph of good over evil. This God-given drive is one reason why our species, unlike any other on the planet, tells stories. The ancient world had Thor of Nordic mythology, Ulysses of Greek mythology, Arjuna of Hindu mythology, and more. Today we have Luke Skywalker, Frodo Baggins, and Harry Potter. Such stories resonate profoundly with us because they awaken our divinely infused desire to be swept into a morally rich drama far bigger than us. Deep down we all want to be Aragorn or Arwen, Luke or Leia, Harry or Hermione. God designed us to "stand against the schemes of the devil," to "wrestle . . . against the rulers, against the authorities, against the cosmic powers over this present darkness."[28]

If unequal speeding tickets turn out to be as mundane as median age differences between blacks and whites, then how can we fly down the New Jersey Turnpike to destroy the Death Star of discrimination?

If unequal loans turn out to be a dull matter of basic economics—lenders taking credit scores seriously to better ensure that their money will be repaid—then how could we march like Gondor against the Black Gate of big banking?

If we factor in women who freely leave full-time work to pursue family life and find that the gender pay gap either disappears or reverses, then how can we take up our wands and band together to destroy the snake of sexism?

What would happen if we lost the dragons, the Orcs, and the Voldemorts of systemic injustice as defined by Social Justice B? Would the Harry or Hermione inside us be condemned to a life sentence of meaninglessness, filling out endless TPS reports? No. Instead, we just might find our daily lives *more* adventurous, *more* meaningful, *more* just—slaying the real dragons of sin in our own hearts, charging the real Orcs of injustice in our culture, and destroying real Horcruxes in spiritual warfare against Satan. There is real racism, sexism, and other forms of discrimination in the world. It is damnable and should be vanquished. If we aren't willing to put in the effort to thoughtfully separate damning disparities from the undamning, then we don't take discrimination and its victims seriously enough.

SAMUEL'S STORY

The parable of talents in Matthew 25 is one of my favorite parables. Jesus's story opens with a wealthy man entrusting his property to three of his servants before leaving on a journey. The wealthy man gave "talents," which were large sums of money in the ancient world. He entrusted five to the first, two to the second, and one talent to the third servant, according to their individual abilities. The first and second servants immediately worked hard to make a profit for their master. By the time their master returned, they had each doubled the money he had entrusted to them. The second servant didn't receive as much money as the first. Although he also returned a 100-percent profit, he did not equal the first servant's total profit. Despite this disparity between the first and second servant, Jesus made it clear that the master was equally pleased with them because both were faithful with what they had been given. He said, "Well done, good and faithful servant[s]. You have been faithful over a little; I will set you over much. Enter into the joy of your master" (Matt. 25:23).

But remember, there were three servants, not two. The third received one talent but failed to steward his master's money. He didn't even store the money in a bank to earn interest. Instead, he hid it in the ground and accused his master of exploiting others to increase his wealth. He blamed his lack of profit on his master's character, not his own. So the master punished him and rewarded the other servants.

The master represents God, the first and second servants represent faithful Christians, and the third represents unfaithful, false converts. This parable has implications for how Christians should think about disparities, including racial disparities. If you learned that the first and second servants where white and that the third was black, would it change your perception of the parable? What if you learned that the first servant was white and that the second and third were black? Would you think the master was racist? Keep in mind that under this scenario, the master's character and motives, as Jesus described, would be unchanged. The servants' character and abilities would remain unchanged too. The only new information under this scenario would be the servants' skin colors.

If we accept the doctrine that racial disparities are evidence of racial discrimination, then we are forced to conclude that the master was racist. Many of us embrace this kind of unhelpful thinking when we suggest racial disparities are best understood as evidence of ongoing systemic racism. But racial disparities are not—on their own—evidence of racial discrimination. Laws or policies that discriminate against people because of their skin color would indeed be evidence of ongoing systemic racism. Slavery and Jim Crow segregation were tragic cases of this. But, thankfully, such laws have been abolished in the United States.

As a black man, I understand the temptation to ascribe racial disparities to racial discrimination, especially since racism did create vast disparities between black and white Americans through history. But things have changed and, while blaming today's disparities on ongoing *systemic* racism may win us the applause of the mainstream, it is no longer true or helpful. The Bible teaches me that I shouldn't compare my blessings with those of my (white) neighbors. It teaches me that accusing white people of racism without evidence is slander. It teaches me that if I am grateful and faithful over the little blessings God gives me, God will bless me further. It teaches me that different trees bear different fruits. Disparities are often evidence of differences, not discrimination. God entrusts people with different blessings or privileges—because he values faithfulness, not parity. We should do the same. We're not instructed to pursue parity. We're instructed to pursue faithfulness and biblical justice.

−Samuel Sey

Samuel works at the Canadian Centre for Bio-Ethical Reform and writes extensively about racism from a biblical worldview perspective at www.slowtowrite.com.

Questions for Personal or Small Group Study

1. There is real systemic injustice in our fallen world. What are three reasons it is so important, as we seek to love the oppressed, to distinguish between inequalities that are unjust and sinful and those that have other explanations?

2. In many spheres of our culture—in much of our media, entertainment, and higher education—you aren't allowed to question whether discrimination is the best explanation of most disparities without facing serious consequences. Why is it important for the church to be different—a place where we can graciously ask hard questions—as we pursue justice together?

3. C. S. Lewis warns us about clinging to damning explanations and taking pleasure in thinking our enemies are as bad as possible. In today's political climate, that has, sadly, become the norm. Are you guilty of an assume-the-worst mindset? If so, take it to the cross of Jesus and ask the Holy Spirit to generate love, peace, and patience in your heart.

Chapter 8

The Color Question

Does our vision of social justice
promote racial strife?

Black lives matter. It's true. From a Christian worldview perspective, we can plumb even deeper than a three-word catchphrase or hashtag. Black lives don't merely matter; every black life was fearfully and wonderfully made by God himself. Every black life bears the divine image. Black lives are worth enough for the Creator to take on flesh and endure torture, execution, and infinite wrath. Do our words and actions reflect those truths?

There are far too many blood-boiling examples of people—including some who claim to follow Christ—living as if such biblical insights are not true. We must do better to speak and live out the boundless value of black lives. To really do that, instead of just easy virtue-signaling, we must go beyond the narratives of our day, whether they come from the political right or left.

Listen hard to conversations about racism—conversations that often turn into shouting matches—and you will hear one issue come up again and again—racism in American policing. In particular, the tragedy of black men killed by officers who usually get off the hook is Exhibit A for just how deeply racism is embedded in our systems of law enforcement. It is why the Black Lives Matter organization was founded, why people riot, and why athletes kneel for the National Anthem. "It feels like open season on black men in America, and I'm outraged."[1] Those were the words of Georgia Democrat Hank Johnson on the House floor in 2015, giving voice to the angst of millions of Americans.

Shots Fired

In January 2015, a police officer remarked to his partner about the "little f*cker" of the sort who "go steal cars, they go break into sh*t." Minutes later, the officers fired twenty-four rounds at a young man in a stolen Ford Explorer. He suffered a fatal AR-15 rifle shot to the back of the head. An internal review board found the officers innocent of breaking departmental policy.

A year later, a young man on his knees pleaded, "Please don't shoot me!" Following orders to crawl toward police officers, the young man reached for his waistband and was instantly shot dead. No gun was found on him, only an air rifle in his hotel room. The jury acquitted the officers.

Six months later, an unarmed teenager reached for his waistband after repeated warnings from officers. He reached and was shot four times. The police chief ruled the shooting justified, and the county district attorney refused to file charges against the officers.

Have you heard of Trayvon Martin, Tamir Rice, or Alton Sterling? It's likely. The tragic stories of these three black image-bearers of God are chillingly similar to the three fatalities above. Have you heard of Loren Simpson, Daniel Shaver, and Dylan Noble? Probably not. But these were three white men who each met their fatal demise to police gunfire as described before. They were three of the 2,352 white men fatally shot by police officers from January 2015 to July 2020.[2]

In *Time* magazine, Columbia University professor John McWhorter observes, "We operate according to a meme under which cops casually kill black men under circumstances in which white men are apparently let off with a hand slap. . . . That meme is quite understandable given the existence of racism in America."[3]

McWhorter identifies as "neither Republican nor conservative" and rejects "right-wing dismissals of Black Lives Matter." After weighing the evidence, he concludes, "That meme is vastly oversimplified. . . . There is a Daniel Shaver for John Crawford, a Michael Parker for Walter Scott, a James Scott for Laquan McDonald. . . . Our conversation must be based on facts."[4]

What are the facts? Here are some details according to the *Washington Post* database on people shot and killed by the police in America:

Between 2016 and 2019, 3,939 image-bearers of God were fatally shot by image-bearing police officers, averaging just under 1,000 deaths per year.

Of those deaths, roughly half of those victims were white and a quarter
were black.

Of those deaths, about 4 percent involved the shooting of an unarmed
victim, averaging twenty-five unarmed whites and eighteen unarmed
blacks per year.

Of those unarmed victims, an average of sixteen whites and eight blacks
per year were not fleeing the scene.

Of those twenty-four unarmed victims per year who were not fleeing the
scene, nearly all of them involve victims physically attacking police
officers, usually under the influence of drugs or alcohol.[5]

"Yes," we might think, "'the likelihood of being gunned down by the police
is relatively low, and, yes, nearly twice as many whites as blacks are shot by cops
each year. But whites are a whopping 62 percent of the American population,
and blacks are around 13 percent. The fact that 13 percent of the population
accounts for nearly a quarter of police shooting victims proves that there is
widespread racial injustice in our police system!"

This conclusion, however, leaves out a factor that should matter to us if
we care more about pinpointing real racism than clinging to popular political narratives. That factor is simply this: if police are doing their jobs, then
we should expect to find greater force where there are higher rates of violent
crime. A cop who discharges his weapon equally whether he finds himself in
office buildings fighting fraud or in back alleys encountering armed criminals
would not be a good cop. Whether criminals use computers, cell phones, and
secret bank accounts or whether they use guns, knives, and fists will make a
difference—and *should* make a difference in how often officers reach for their
holsters. This is not saying that one type of crime is worse than another. It is
simply saying that violent crime is more likely to be met with violent force than
nonviolent crime.

Where, then, do we find more violent crime? Peter Kirsanow, a prominent
black attorney and member of the US Commission on Civil Rights, carefully
documents disparities between blacks and whites when it comes to experiencing violent crime in the United States.[6] This body of research, of course,
does *not* mean there are few violent white criminals. It does *not* mean most
black people are violent criminals. The overwhelming majority are *not* violent
criminals, and we must say so emphatically, lest we slap a pathological stigma
on an entire group of image-bearers, as has been done so egregiously in the past.
All it means is that in America, regardless of the rationales we might offer,
there are drastic disparities when it comes to violent crime. Such disparities

should never be used to villainize or dehumanize an entire people group who should be treated with all the dignity and respect that goes with bearing the divine image. High rates of violent crime in black communities should matter, however, if we want to separate fact from fiction in understanding the scope of racism today so we can fight real evil and not a boogeyman.

Harvard's Roland Fryer carried out a thorough investigation of police shootings in ten major cities across the United States. Fryer, who happens to be black, concluded that there is no evidence of racial bias in police shootings.[7] In Houston, for example, he found that blacks were 24 percent less likely than whites to be shot by officers even though the suspects were armed or violent. A Washington State University study found that police officers were *less* likely to shoot black suspects than white suspects in realistic simulations of both armed and unarmed scenarios.[8]

Why do such facts matter? Because black lives matter. Each and every black life should matter to Christians because it is the beautiful, irreplaceable, creative handiwork of God. The more politicians and activists with great intentions push the false narrative of widespread racist police shootings, the more police forces around the nation will withdraw from neighborhoods ravaged by violent crime. Yes, the politicians and activists may feel the warm, inner glow of doing their part to fight racism. But ideas have consequences, and false ideas have bad and even fatal consequences for real people. With less of a law enforcement presence, more people meet their tragic demise at the hands of armed criminals—fathers, mothers, sons, and daughters are murdered and no justice is served. This is not a political opinion; it is an empirical fact.[9] Yes, parroting the narrative of widespread, race-motivated, and deadly police shootings may win us the approval of a woke intelligentsia, kneeling athletes, and our progressive neighbors. But it will not help us love our suffering black neighbors who bear the precious glow of God's image. To take an important action step, I highly recommend looking into the vital ministries, training, and opportunities offered by the John and Vera Mae Perkins Foundation at www.jvmpf.org or the Center for Biblical Unity at www.centerforbiblicalunity.com.

> Each and every Black life should matter to Christians because it is the beautiful, irreplaceable, creative handiwork of God.

The Other Saint Thomas

We have not yet scratched the surface of the massively complex questions of systemic injustice. Racial profiling, mass incarceration, home ownership, education, health care, employment, and even church life are all complex issues. I am *not* saying there is no racism, sexism, and other evil isms expressed in such systems. There is. The dismal callback rates on identical resumes with black-sounding names compared with white-sounding names is one tragic case in point.[10] We also find evidence of enduring discrimination in American housing and criminal justice systems.[11] If we play by the all-or-nothing rules of today's political tribalism, many of us will hastily sweep such evidence under the rug, believing that discrimination is a thing of the past and that anyone who says otherwise is a brainwashed leftist. As Christians, we must do better. Remember, the God who commands us to seek justice is the same God who commands us to "test everything." If our political allegiances encourage us to swiftly write off all claims of discrimination rather than to test them, then we will fail to bring the lordship of Christ to bear in many of the world's most aching places.

The National Association for the Advancement of Colored People provides some of the following statistics:

> African Americans, according to 2014 data, make up 2.3 million of the 6.8 million Americans in correctional systems, which is 34 percent, despite being only 13.4 percent of the population.
> African Americans are five times more likely to be incarcerated than white Americans.
> African Americans, despite rates of drug usage similar to those of white Americans, are six times more likely to be incarcerated on drug charges.

According to US Census data, white households earn 65 percent more income than black households.[12] Such inequalities are as sad as they are shocking.

What are we looking at when we look at such numbers? On a Social Justice B interpretation, we are looking at the ongoing effects of American slavery, racist policies like Jim Crow, and racist practices like redlining.[13] We are looking at proof of white privilege in America, proof that racism does not go away but mutates into new forms. We are looking at proof that white supremacy is not just a few hate mongers with swastika tattoos chanting, "Blood and soil!" in the backwoods; it is a nationwide system designed to elevate whites and push everyone else down. Yes, it is true that we can't expect the effects of 345 years of legalized racial oppression in the US to have vanished in the last half century since the Civil Rights Act. Yet that is not the whole story. The popular narrative may blind us to certain facts and bar us from asking important questions. I offer three brief examples.

First, according to 2018 data from the US Census Bereau, whites rank sixteenth on the scale of "Median Household Income by Selected Ancestry Groups."[14] *How can we reconcile the Social Justice B narrative that America remains systemically white supremacist to its core when Indians, Taiwanese, Lebanese, Turkish, Chinese, Iranian, Japanese, Pakistani, Filipino, Indonesian, Syrian, Korean, Ghanian, Nigerian, and Guyanese earn more income on average than whites in the United States?*

Second, homes with a married mother and father correspond with higher levels of academic and career success for their children, as well as lower rates of criminality and mental disorder. The rate of black children born out of wedlock has jumped from 24 percent in 1965 to nearly 70 percent in 2016.[15] This tragedy has occurred *well after slavery and segregation were dismantled*, after the abolitionist and civil rights movements claimed their greatest victories. Lest we think this family breakdown is a uniquely black problem, the rate for white children born out of wedlock over the same fifty years has skyrocketed from 4 percent to 28 percent.[16] These steep spikes are devastating for black and white Americans alike. Nevertheless, a black child today is 2.5 times more likely than a white child to be born out of wedlock.[17] *Are we to believe that this heartbreaking reality has nothing to do with many of the sad disparities we see today?*

Third, Ian Rowe, CEO for a network of black charter schools in New York City, cites a recent study of thriving black men in America. The study found that the growing class of successful black men "followed the success sequence. They finished their education, got a full-time job, they got married, and then they had children, *in that order.* . . . If a kid grows up in a low income family and follows those steps, only 6 percent will end up in poverty."[18] The Brookings Institution likewise found that 98 percent of Americans who finish high school, get a job, any job, and wait until marriage to have children will not end up poor.[19] That is a hopeful message. In fact, a 2016 study found that the black poverty rate was 22 percent compared with an 11 percent white poverty rate, while the poverty rate for *married* black couples was lower than the white poverty rate (7.5 percent).[20]

The Social Justice B story, by contrast, tells us that American systems are so thoroughly racist that dark skin makes it virtually impossible to escape poverty. That is a profoundly uninspiring story. Why strive for excellence if society is going to smash your dreams because of your skin tone? Rowe makes this point: "If you're a kid and you keep hearing over and over and over that because of your race these are the outcomes that you're going to have in your life, it's really hard to feel a sense of personal agency."[21] *Is it possible that the Social Justice B story can have an unintended dream-crushing effect on the very communities it seeks to uplift?*

For many of my white friends whom I've had this conversation with, asking such questions would mute "the black voice." "Aren't you taking the side of the oppressors over the oppressed?" "Aren't you regurgitating arguments used by racists in the past?" "Aren't you failing to listen well to our black brothers and sisters?"

I learned the previously mentioned facts and questions precisely by listening to my black brothers and sisters. According to Pew Research, less than one-in-three black people without college degrees believe their race has made it harder for them to succeed (29 percent), while 60 percent believe "race has not been a factor in their success or failures."[22] According to a recent study by the nonpartisan research organization PRRI, a greater share of black and Hispanic Americans than white Americans (59 percent and 55 percent versus 52 percent of whites) agree that "children from different social classes have adequate opportunities to be successful."[23]

Indeed, it is possible that what is often considered "the black voice" is actually the white liberal voice. Consider a recent example. The Smithsonian's National Museum of African American History and Culture opened an online portal entitled "Talking About Race" to help inspire "productive conversation about race." Providing starting points for the conversation, the Smithsonian offers readers a crash course in three basic terms—*whiteness, white privilege,* and *white fragility.*[24] What may escape the reader who simply seeks out a more empathetic understanding of black perspectives is that all three of these concepts were crafted and popularized by liberal white women—*whiteness* from Judith Katz,[25] *white privilege* from Peggy McIntosh,[26] and *white fragility* from Robin DiAngelo.[27] Likewise, most conversations about race, including those within the church, begin by stipulating that *racism* does not mean discriminating against people on the basis of their race, but "prejudice plus power," a redefinition invented by a white sociologist named Patricia Bidol-Padva.[28] (I explore this redefinition of racism in Appendix B, "Black and White".) Concepts like whiteness, white privilege, white fragility, and the new definition of racism have cornered the market in education, diversity training, and the lion's share of recent Christian literature on race. But we must be careful not to confuse preaching such concepts with standing up for minority voices. They are often not the same thing. Citing a litany of recent sociological studies, Musa al-Gharbi points out that

relatively well-off, highly educated, liberal *whites* tend to be among the most zealous in identifying and prosecuting new forms of racism. . . . Whites tend to be more "woke" on racial issues than the average black or Hispanic; they tend to perceive much more racism against minorities than most minorities themselves. . . . Indeed, evidence is growing that many fashionable formulations of "racism" (and antiracist activism) may be directly pernicious for people of color.[29]

Of course, truth is never determined by what a majority believes, or the sun would have revolved around the earth for most of human history. But the research does show that arguing that America is systemically rigged against blacks is not the same thing as standing up for "the black voice." It may win us approval in our social, academic, or online circles, but it is, in fact, to stand against the majority of black voices on many questions of racial justice.

One of those voices, Jason Riley of the Manhattan Institute, raises an important point:

Many people have convinced themselves that evidence of ongoing racial bias proves beyond any doubt that racism in America today remains the major barrier to black progress. Whether other factors play a bigger role is a question seldom asked, let alone investigated with any rigor. In fact, to even ask such a question is enough to earn the wrath of those who believe racism is an all-purpose explanation for bad black outcomes in America today.[30]

Riley is right. The Social Justice B narrative is usually recited as if other perspectives either don't exist or are motivated by nothing but ignorance or animus. Challenges to Social Justice B are automatically chalked up to either shallow research or shameless discrimination, which may be as false as it is self-serving.

Take, for example, the curious case of Dr. Thomas Sowell, or "the other Saint Thomas," as I call him. From growing up on the streets of Harlem to graduating from Harvard, Columbia, and the University of Chicago, then teaching at Cornell, UCLA, Rutgers, Amherst, and now Stanford, where he serves as senior fellow for the Hoover Institution, Sowell is no lightweight. With over fifty books to his name and a Mount Everest of scholarly articles and essays, Sowell has done more serious research on justice, inequality, and racism than 99.99 percent of humans in history. Yet he sees the Social Justice B perspective on such issues as deeply flawed, even dangerous to those hanging on the lowest rungs of society.

I have asked friends and colleagues who maintain a Social Justice B perspective, "What's your take on Tom Sowell?" All but one have never read any of his books, but they have strong opinions of his work. Responses range from "He's racist and an Oreo for being black on the outside and white on the inside" to "Why would I waste my time with someone so ignorant about how widespread systemic injustice is?" Having read dozens of books on systemic injustice, I have yet to find one that interacts meaningfully with any of his fifty-plus books on the topic. The same could be said for such intellectual heavyweights as Walter Williams, Shelby Steele, Glenn Loury, John McWhorter, Coleman Hughes, and many other experts on race and inequality who dare question the Social Justice B narrative. When Social Justice B advocates call for more "voices of color" to be centered in our schools, our diversity seminars, and our political platforms, it is clear that they don't want voices of color like Sowell's or the many brilliant black thinkers like him who question the worldview of wokeness.

We find this same one-sidedness in much of today's church world. Our conversations about "racial reconciliation" often start with unquestioned Social Justice B premises. We assume that disparity is evidence of discrimination. We hear that society is a white supremacy and misogynist to its core, and it's too risky to raise questions. We are told that the church must join the Social Justice B fight against those systems, or else it suffers from a "truncated gospel." We choose the path of least resistance. But the path of least resistance is often not the same as the path to true justice.

We should heed Proverbs 18: "An intelligent heart acquires knowledge, and the ear of the wise seeks knowledge. . . . The one who states his case first seems right, until the other comes and examines him."[31] Scripture does not allow us to separate justice from the quest for understanding and knowledge. Here, then, is my friendly suggestion. Before assuming you are "woke" on issues of systemic injustice, I suggest reading at least one or two books about racism that challenge the dogmas of Social Justice B. See the notes at the back of this book for some of the best.[32] If that's too tall an order, then invest an hour in watching videos or reading articles by marginalized black voices who question the woke narrative.[33] Watch John McWhorter's "How Anti-Racism Hurts Black People," or watch "Barriers to Black Progress," a conversation among black scholars on YouTube. Then dive into resources from the Social Justice B perspective and make up your own mind. Again, check the notes for some of the best.[34] There is truth to be found in both sides. The best way to avoid being taken in by dangerous, one-sided ideologies is to expose ourselves to different perspectives with humble minds that say, "We don't know it all. What insight can we find here to bring our pursuit of justice into deeper alignment with truth and reality?"

"Whiteness Is Wicked"

If we take the time to hear both sides, we find that much of the communication breakdown has to do with the definitions or rather the *redefinitions* of words. Redefining words such as *tolerance, marriage, authenticity, bigotry* and *discrimination* is where Social Justice B draws much of its power to sway public opinion. (Appendix B examines these redefinitions, especially the new meaning Social Justice B pours into the word *racism.*)

When important words are redefined without any rational or biblical case offered, we have a recipe for endless confusion and strife. This is an especially pressing problem for the church when it comes to living out the kind of oneness that Jesus prayed for us to showcase to our racially tribalized world.[35]

In March 2019, Ekemini Uwan addressed the Sparrow Conference for Women in Dallas, Texas. The ad for the conference read, "The world needs peacemakers, because conflict is everywhere—in relationships, on social media, at work—so follow God's call and join an amazing community of peacemaking women at the 2019 Sparrow Conference!" At this conference to inspire peacemakers, Uwan, who brands herself "an anti-racist public theologian," had this to say:

> When we talk about white identity, then we have to talk about what whiteness is. Well, the reality is that whiteness is rooted in plunder, in theft, in slavery, in enslavement of Africans, genocide of Native Americans.... It's a power structure, that is what whiteness is.... Because we have to understand something—whiteness is wicked. It is wicked. It's rooted in violence, it's rooted in theft, it's rooted in plunder, it's rooted in power, in privilege.[36]

To grasp Uwan's perspective, a perspective she developed from critical theorists,[37] it is important to note that *whiteness* does not always mean having white skin. She calls on "people of color to divest from whiteness too."[38] Whiteness is not a skin tone so much as it is a plundering, thieving, enslaving, genocidal way of being in the world.

Surely, if we use *whiteness* to mean the devastating idea crafted by sinners that paler skin justifies treating darker skinned people like anything less than divine image-bearers, then, yes, that is an evil idea, and Uwan is right to expose its horror. Such "whiteness" is rotten to its slavery justifying, antibiblical, God-insulting core. Yet as the language of whiteness pops up in more Christian conversations about race, its meaning is all too easily muddled. So I offer three important questions we should ask together about whiteness.

1. *Does claiming that "whiteness is wicked" drop a glamor filter over nonwhite cultures?* Immerse yourself in "whiteness" studies and you will walk away with a sense that if we could only "decentralize," "destroy the idol" of, and "divest ourselves" from whiteness, then a multicultural heaven-on-earth is on the horizon. This brings out the Gauguin in all of us.

European painter Paul Gauguin followed Rousseau's philosophy that "man is naturally good. . . . It is by our institutions alone that men become wicked."[39] As with today's Social Justice B movement, Gauguin came to the conclusion that institutions of Western European civilization had become hopelessly oppressive. He left his family and fame in France for Tahiti to escape "everything that is artificial and conventional."[40] On the black sand beaches of the South Pacific, Gauguin believed he would discover Rousseau's "noble savage," "an idealized concept of uncivilized man, who symbolizes the innate goodness of one not exposed to the corrupting influences of civilization."[41] Instead of paradise, he found an island full of people enslaved to alcoholism, ravaged by sexually transmitted diseases, torn asunder by broken families, and oppressed by corrupt politicians. Gauguin realized to his great disillusionment that evil is not an exclusively white, Western problem; it is a *human* problem.

We see this human problem more clearly if we reckon with some untrendy facts:

- At least a million Europeans were enslaved by North African pirates alone from 1500 to 1800.[42]
- The Europeans who were enslaved in North Africa were despised and abused because they were Christians in a Muslim region of the world where they were called "Christian dogs."[43]
- "Europeans enslaved other Europeans, Asians enslaved other Asians, Africans enslaved other Africans, and the indigenous people of the Western Hemisphere enslaved other indigenous peoples of the Western Hemisphere."[44]
- "It was the Africans who enslaved their fellow Africans, selling some of these slaves to Europeans or to Arabs and keeping others for themselves. Even at the peak of the Atlantic slave trade, Africans retained more slaves for themselves than they sent to the Western Hemisphere."[45]
- "There were also slave plantations in East Africa and on the Island of Zanzibar, and some African and Asian slave owners used their slaves as human sacrifices in religious ceremonies, as did Mayans in the Western Hemisphere."[46]
- "Arabs were the leading slave raiders in East Africa, ranging over an area larger than all of Europe. The total numbers of slaves exported from

East Africa during the nineteenth century has been estimated to be at least two million."[47]

- "China in centuries past has been described as 'one of the largest and most comprehensive markets for the exchange of human beings in the world.'"[48]
- "Slavery was also common in India, where it has been estimated that there were more slaves than in the entire Western Hemisphere."[49]
- "Slavery was also an established institution in the Western Hemisphere before Columbus' ships ever appeared on the horizon."[50]
- "Brazil . . . imported several times as many slaves as the United States and perhaps consumed more slaves than any other nation in history."[51]
- "Even in colonial America, white indentured servants were a major part of the population and they were auctioned off just like black slaves."[52]
- The tragic fact is that slavery, while illegal in every nation on the planet, is practiced in every nation by and against people of every skin tone, to the tune of over forty million victims of modern day slavery.[53]
- According to the 2018 *Global Slavery Index*, the ten countries with the highest prevalence of modern day slavery are North Korea, Eritrea, Burundi, the Central African Republic, Afghanistan, Mauritania, South Sudan, Pakistan, Cambodia, and Iran.[54]
- The top ten countries with governments most actively fighting against modern day slavery are the Netherlands, the United States, the United Kingdom, Sweden, Belgium, Croatia, Spain, Norway, Portugal, and Montenegro.[55]

If we buy into the Social Justice B story of the world, then it is easy to view nonwhite majority cultures through primrose glasses. This blinds us to the universality of human wickedness and the need for repentance in *all* cultures.

Consider Idi Amin. While others dubbed him the "Butcher of Uganda," he gave himself the official title "His Excellency, President for Life, Field Marshal Al Hadji Doctor Idi Amin Dada, VC, DSO, MC, Lord of All Beasts of the Earth and Fishes of the Seas and Conqueror of the British Empire in Africa in General and Uganda in Particular." (Try fitting that on a business card!) Was Idi Amin guilty of "whiteness" when he unleashed his murderous project of self-glorification? Was Attila the Hun as he slaughtered and pillaged his way across the Roman Empire? Were Pol Pot, Mao Zedong, Enver Pasha, Ho Chi Minh, the Taliban, ISIS, Boko Haram, and the Aztecs? Genghis Khan spread his Mongol Empire through Eurasia through massive slaughter and subjugation of civilian populations, eventually claiming nearly one-sixth of the total land on earth. Was he guilty of whiteness? What about the killing fields of Khmer Rouge, or the Hutus and Tutsis in Rwanda, the cartel wars of South America, or the intertribal slaughterfests in precolonial America? Was Pablo Escobar guilty of whiteness as he murdered and exploited his way through Columbia to expand his cocaine empire? Of course none of these plundering, thieving, enslaving, genocidal power-seekers involved in such injustices were white.

In a biblical worldview, wickedness is never associated with a single skin color. Rather, "all have sinned and fall short of the glory of God."[56] We can empirically test a biblical worldview against Social Justice B to see which one checks out with reality. If Social Justice B is true, then we should expect to find oppression as a uniquely or overwhelmingly white western phenomenon. On a biblical view of the world in which every human being of every stripe and color and creed is fallen, we should expect to find oppression all over the globe and all throughout history. Sowell points us in the right direction: "From a narrow perspective, the lesson that some draw from the history of slavery, automatically conceived of as the enslavement of blacks by whites, is that white people were or are uniquely evil. Against the broader background of world history, however, a very different lesson might be that no people of any color can be trusted with unbridled power over any other people, for such power has been grossly abused by whatever race, class, or political authority has held that power."[57]

Sowell concludes, "The story of how human beings treat other human beings when they have unbridled power over them is seldom a pretty story or even a decent story, regardless of the color of the people involved."[58] Why, then, shouldn't we use "breaking the Ten Commandments" instead of the term *whiteness*? If "breaking the Ten Commandments" is too long and cumbersome, then how about the old-fashioned word *sin*?

2. *Does claiming that "whiteness is wicked" cherry-pick the most damning aspects of people-with-less-melanin's legacy?* To many, Britain is a prime historic case in point of imperialistic, greedy, oppressive white power. Britain was once the world's largest slave trader.[59] Combine all the havoc and hurt inflicted by the Brits with the horrors of American slavery and it is easy to conclude that history is a long sordid tale of pale Westerners running roughshod over the more melanized planet. But is there more to the story? Sowell thinks so. "What was historically unusual [in the West] was the emergence in the late eighteenth century of a strong moral sense that slavery was so wrong that Christians could not in good conscience enslave anyone or countenance the continuation of this institution among themselves or others."[60]

As noted earlier, Brits and Americans spent enormous resources and lives to end slavery not only in their own countries but around the world "over the bitter opposition of Africans, Arabs, Asians, and others."[61] Why are such courageous acts of historic justice on behalf of the oppressed not included in our definition of whiteness? Why does Social Justice B thinking allow only things like plunder, theft, slavery, and genocide to count as the identifying marks of whiteness? Why are people living today saddled with the collective historic shame of their identity groups but not the moral triumphs of those groups?

Yes, tragically, people who claimed the name of Christ were often perpetrators or spinelessly complicit in the evils of racism, a historic fact we must work to ensure has no place in our planet's future. Yet if we've been taken in by the loudest narrative of our day, then we are missing out on a lot of beautiful true stories. Though slavery had been practiced without question throughout history, it was Christians—both black and white brothers and sisters—who stood up for justice in the face of a long, horrific, and global history of treating people like property instead of people. Whether in Britain, America, Africa, Asia, the Caribbean, the Middle East, the pre-Columbus Western Hemisphere, or anywhere else on earth—it was Christians who first lit the sparks and fanned the flames that grew by God's grace into the blaze that incinerated legalized slavery around the globe.

3. Is the definition of whiteness as wickedness unnecessarily inflammatory?
This leads us to a third problem with redefining a color to mean oppression. Neil Shenvi makes the point: "If I insist on defining 'moron' to mean 'French hockey player,' I shouldn't be surprised if a roomful of French hockey players is offended by my definition! We should choose words that convey our meaning as clearly as possible and—as Christians—as charitably as possible."[62]

When Uwan declared that "whiteness is wicked" at the 2019 Sparrow Conference for Women, some women reportedly stormed out of the auditorium. The women who stormed out were criticized for their "white fragility," a term coined by critical theorist Robin DiAngelo in her book by that title, which Uwan recommended at the end of her talk. Could it be that white women were offended because using a word that in common parlance refers to one of their physical features, then using that word to saddle strangers at a peacemaking conference with the full weight of historic guilt from those in a color-based identity group is, well, offensive? Playing such group identity blame games has, sadly, become a mark of Social Justice B. God assesses blame differently. Scripture says, "Everyone shall die for his own iniquity."[63]

For we must all appear before the judgment seat of Christ, so that each one may receive what is due for what he has done in the body, whether good or evil.[64]

Fathers shall not be put to death because of their children, nor shall children be put to death because of their fathers. Each one shall be put to death for his own sin.[65]

The soul who sins shall die. The son shall not suffer for the iniquity of the father, nor the father suffer for the iniquity of the son. The righteousness of the righteous shall be upon himself, and the wickedness of the wicked shall be upon himself.[66]

Again, unity was crucial to the early church becoming a multiethnic family, brothers and sisters united by the same loving Father. They could have played the collective ethnic identity blame game. "That isn't just Rufus over there. He is Rufus *the Roman*, and let us not forget how his people banished us from Rome two centuries ago and how they tried again thirty years ago."

"Oh yeah?" comes the reply, "Rufus the Roman had ancestors who were brutally murdered during the Maccabean revolt led by *your* people!"

"Yeah, well, your people invaded and now occupy Jerusalem, our most sacred city! They tax the sandals off our feet and impose their Roman supremacy on us at every turn."

How would Christians ever show the tribalized world what real unity looks like if they got swept up in such a never-ending game of grievances—treating one another as exemplars of their ethnic groups rather than their shared identity in Christ?

Do you see the problem? Social Justice B singles out a physical feature that God gave some people and not others. It then uses that feature not as a physical descriptor but as a mark of evil. If we think playing a semantic game of associating evil with a physical feature (which some have and others don't) will not be used by fallen people to unleash hate and violence against people who have that physical feature, then we have made three lethal mistakes. First, we have underestimated human fallenness, the ease with which we can tribalize and turn on each other. Second, we have not learned the hard lessons of history. When has equating a physical feature that some have and others don't ever resulted in anything but catastrophe? Third, we have made it much more difficult for the church to "maintain the unity of the Spirit in the bond of peace."[67] Instead of adopting the redefined words crafted by Social Justice B theorists—with their inflammatory force—let us heed Scripture: "These are the things that you shall do: Speak the truth to one another; render in your gates judgments that are true and make for peace."[68]

In closing, some have a real concern that the kind of arguments I have offered may empower racists to be more racist. So let me be clear: If you have taken anything I have said as a justification for believing that white people are superior to black people or any other demographic, then you are wrong. You have contradicted the gospel. When it comes to salvation, it is not white or black or brown or any other color that matters, except red. It is the blood of Jesus and the blood of Jesus alone that sinners from every skin tone find justification in the eyes of God, and true equality in his kingdom, both here and for eternity.

MONIQUE'S STORY

At dinner, my pops uttered those five dreaded words: "Let's make America great again." I was shocked! America's history is slavery, lynching, and Jim Crow. I am adopted. My family is white. I am African American. When has America ever been great for me?

I spent my formative years in South Los Angeles. "Never trust white people!" was a running theme of my upbringing, and I carried those skin-deep judgments with me everywhere. As a sociology major, I found a label for the framework I had learned growing up. My professors espoused critical race theory (or CRT), which validated my biases. My belief that only people who looked like me would be able to understand my experience was sealed when my class read *Why Are All the Black Kids Sitting Together in the Cafeteria?* by Beverly Tatum. This book confirmed my tribalism. I spent the next two decades preaching CRT.

My family and I disagreed on issues of systemic racism. Why couldn't they see America as it really is? My sociology professor was right—white Christians hide behind Jesus to disregard everyone not like them. That night I prayed, "God, open my family's eyes to their privilege and how people of color live under nonstop oppression in America."

The answer to my prayer came as a deep shock to my system. "Monique, you need to repent of your views on social justice." The Holy Spirit spoke this clearly to my heart shortly after I prayed for my family to "receive" the social justice gospel. I pouted and protested. I was convinced the Lord would never say something like that. But he did. I have begun the painful process of untangling my faith from CRT. It's like prying candy out of a toddler's hands. I've put up a good fight, but God is gentle, faithful, and kind. He walks by my side on a liberating journey out of CRT.

The first step in that journey was taking a serious look at the roots of my faith. I discovered the deep conflict between a Christian worldview and CRT. With CRT's constant focus on evil systems, I had become oblivious to the evil in my own heart. I couldn't see aspects of my own privilege. I had become blind to my own prejudices. CRT encouraged my tribal favoritism that kept me from taking white voices seriously in conversations about justice. I wasn't just a victim of America's racist systems; I also perpetuated the racism I claimed to hate.

According to historic Christianity, salvation is the good news of Jesus's life, death, and resurrection so sinners of all colors can be saved by a free act of divine grace. CRT had pulled me away from that good news into a social justice gospel in which the finished work of Jesus wasn't enough. Activism to end "oppression" as redefined by CRT became a gospel essential. Scripture consistently defines us as brothers and sisters. CRT splits us into intersectional tribes. In God's eyes, humanity's fundamental problem is that we are all sinners in need of grace. According to CRT, humanity's fundamental problems are whiteness and oppression. The beliefs of CRT weren't "part of the gospel;" they formed a different gospel altogether.

The book of James is clear: we should not show favoritism or speak evil over each other. But with my black Christian friends, speaking of whites in derogatory ways was perfectly acceptable. I spoke words over whites that Christ would never speak over me. CRT made it nearly impossible to see white people as beloved image-bearers whom Christ died to redeem. This hampered my ability to treat people with the love and compassion that Christ has for me.

My family and I are still learning. They are becoming more aware of certain injustices they didn't see before. I am learning that God has a much better way to bring justice and unity than I do. And there's grace for all of us.

−Monique Duson

Monique studies at Biola University's Talbot School of Theology and serves as Founder of the Center for Biblical Unity, which offers resources, training, and videos on racial justice from a biblical perspective at www.centerforbiblicalunity.com.

Questions for Personal or Small Group Study

1. It is true that segments of the church through American history have championed or been complicit in vile forms of racism, including slavery, lynching, and segregation. Clarify three to five biblical doctrines that refute such white racial supremacy.
2. How does a biblical worldview enable us as Christians to say "black lives matter" in a manner more profound and expansive than the doctrines of today's secular movements that bear the Black Lives Matter label?
3. Why are claims such as "whiteness is wicked" and other charges that emerge from critical race theory unhelpful if the church seeks to be an every tongue, tribe, and nation witness of the unifying power of the gospel to the watching world?

Chapter 9

The Gospel Question

Does our vision of social justice distort
the best news in history?

How could you become the most miserable version of yourself? How could
you become the most unlikeable version of yourself? How could you
become the most anxious version of yourself?

First and Second Things

These may seem like random questions, but they have everything to do with
social justice. The answers are straightforward. To become the most unhappy version of yourself, spend all your time trying to make your three best friends—me,
myself, and I—happy. To become the most unlikeable version of yourself, spend
all your time trying to get everyone to like you. To become the most anxious
version of yourself, spend all your time trying not to be anxious. To become
irrelevant, the church need only spend all its energy trying to be relevant.

These four answers surface a deep principle that explains much of life in the
universe. In an essay called "First and Second Things," C. S. Lewis points us to
the principle behind these ironies: "Every preference of a small good to a great,
or partial good to a total good, involves the loss of the small or partial good for
which the sacrifice is made. . . . You can't get second things by putting them
first. You get second things only by putting first things first."[1]

Think about it. The woman who puts her own happiness first ends up
chronically dissatisfied with her life. The man who makes his first thing getting
everyone to like him becomes obnoxious. The poor soul whose first priority is
staving off another anxiety attack will feel constantly on edge.

Why? Because being well-liked, happy, and anxiety-free are not first things. They are second things. They are byproducts, not goals. Mistake a second thing for a first thing and you'll lose not only the real first thing; you'll lose the second thing too. If our sad woman put loving God and loving people ahead of her own happiness, she would end up far more satisfied with her life. If our obnoxious man genuinely cared about the people around him more than his own likeability, he would end up better liked. If people redirected energy from trying not feeling anxious into exercising at the gym, getting into God's creation, and caring deeply about other people, then their anxiety spikes would be less frequent.

What does all this have to do with the gospel and social justice? If we make social justice our first thing, we will lose not only the real first thing—the gospel—we will lose social justice too.

The Bible's First Thing

We don't have to speculate about what Scripture makes the first thing. In 1 Corinthians 15, Paul states one of the earliest creeds of the first-century church: "Now I would remind you, brothers, of the gospel I preached to you. . . . For I delivered to you as *of first importance* what I also received: that Christ died for our sins in accordance with the Scriptures, that he was buried, that he was raised on the third day in accordance with the Scriptures."[2]

The gospel is *en protois*, a Greek turn of phrase that could be translated "of first importance," "most important," or "of chief significance." In Lewis's categories, the gospel is "the first thing." What exactly is this gospel? According to the ancient creed, it is the good news of what God has done through the sin-atoning death and bodily resurrection of Jesus, the ascended King. That is Scripture's first thing; it should be ours too.

Does putting the gospel first mean justice becomes optional for us? Surely not. Let us be clear. God does not *suggest*, he *commands* that we "do justice and righteousness, and deliver from the hand of the oppressor him who has been robbed."[3] Jesus launched his public ministry with the stated mission to "proclaim good news to the poor . . . liberty to the captives and recovering of sight to the blind, to set at liberty those who are oppressed"[4] (This is a commonly cited proof text for Social Justice B proponents. I examine it in appendix G, "Good News to the Poor"). "Seek justice"[5] is a clarion call of Scripture. Justice is not the first thing. The gospel is. But that does not make justice optional to the Christian life.

The Bible also commands that we tell the truth, that we give generously, that we love our neighbor, and so on. None of these commands are optional. Yet none of these commands *is* the gospel. We should not confuse any of these commands with the first thing. If we do, then we will not only lose the gospel but also find ourselves adhering to these commands in a way that obliterates their essence. Without the gospel first, we become graceless in our truth telling, cheerless in our giving, and our neighborly love turns into self-righteous showmanship. Likewise, when the gospel is not our first thing, social justice becomes something else entirely.

> When the gospel is not our first thing, social justice becomes something else entirely.
>
> ▪ ▪ ▪

What Is a "Gospel Issue"?

"But," comes the reply, "you create a false dilemma between the gospel and justice, making two things out of one, to downplay the church's essential role in fighting injustice. I agree—seeking justice is not optional for believers. Social justice is, therefore, a gospel issue."[6] That is an important objection. If my claim that the gospel is the first thing can be taken seriously, then the objection can't be ignored. The gospel can't be the *first* thing, while justice is a *second* thing, if they are, in fact, the *same* thing.

Nevertheless, there is a reason that the gospel and the call to justice can't be the same thing. *Gospel* means "good news." News, good or bad, always takes the *indicative* form. It announces, or *indicates*, something that has happened. For the first time in history, obesity is a bigger problem than starvation. The Cubbies won the World Series. Scientists have made a new breakthrough in cancer treatment. That is all news. They are all indicative statements, statements that indicate what is now true of the world.

Imagine I tell my four-year-old daughter, "Eat your broccoli." That is not news (especially not good news from her perspective). Such a command is not an indicative statement. It is an *imperative* statement, something you *must* do, not something that *has been done*. Good news must take indicative form. "Your broccoli has already been eaten!" or "Mommy bought ice cream for dessert!" That would be good news.

The difference between an indicative and an imperative is no small matter for grammar nerds.[7] The good news upon which eternity depends hangs in the balance. When Paul wrote to the church in Galatia, he was deeply concerned that the good news was being twisted into bad news—an antigospel. Why? Because instead of the good news that we are saved by God's grace alone through faith alone in King Jesus alone for God's glory alone, the Galatians had turned circumcision and a Jewish diet into "gospel issues." A gospel with additional requirements is not good news. For those who know themselves well, if the gospel is not about Christ's finished saving work alone but about any commandment we must keep, then the good news turns out to be very bad news. If my salvation were 99 percent God's doing and 1 percent my own doing, I would find a way, in my fallenness and stupidity, to mess up that 1 percent and be damned.

So what happens when we make social justice not a mark of consistent Christian living but a requirement of the gospel itself? Consider the tens of millions of victims of modern-day slavery. The good news now entails the imperative "Work toward the liberation of human trafficking victims." On this scheme, you are saved by God's grace through Christ *plus* your efforts to end modern slavery. Herein lies the existential conundrum: How could we ever know if we had done enough to end this vile and dehumanizing practice to be saved? There is a qualitative difference between fighting the injustice of slavery to *become* saved versus fighting the injustice of slavery *because* you are saved. If we confuse the gospel—the indicative announcement of the salvation accomplished on our behalf through the death and resurrection of Jesus—with the imperative to help human trafficking victims, then the good news is no longer good news. We find ourselves right back in the hopeless plight of works-based righteousness.

In first-century Galatia, the Judaizers added the imperatives "Get circumcised" and "Eat kosher" to the gospel, incurring Paul's condemnation, "If anyone is preaching to you a gospel contrary to the one you received, let him be accursed."[8] This problem is compounded exponentially in our day. If doing justice is either identical to or part of the gospel, then we do not merely add circumcision and a handful of dietary restrictions to the gospel. We add a theoretically infinite set of imperatives. Counteract sex slavery in Thailand. Fight cocoa bean farm trafficking on the Ivory Coast. Abolish the carpet looms of India. The list of twenty-first century injustices stretches on and on.[9] I am not arguing that Christians should be apathetic about such injustices. On the contrary, we should care passionately about the dehumanization of God's precious image-bearers and work toward a more just world. I am arguing that making the imperative to work against such injustices either identical to or part of the gospel is to lose the gospel. Given Lewis's first thing principle, to lose the gospel is to lose justice for the oppressed too.

A Game You Can't Win

To take Paul's point deeper, consider a brilliant episode of NBC's hit show *The Good Place* (a synonym for heaven). A superhuman being named Michael, played by Ted Danson, is befuddled by the fact that, for centuries, no one on earth has accumulated enough good points to avoid eternal anguish in "the bad place." Keep in mind, the theology of the show, at least up to the third season, has no category of salvation by grace. You can make it to "the good place" only by accumulating enough good works. The plot unfolds in an all-law, no-gospel universe. Why has no one been worthy of the good place for centuries? Upon finding that simply buying a tomato counts as negative 12.368 points, Michael finally solves the problem: "It's impossible for anyone to be good enough for the Good Place.... These days just buying a tomato at a grocery store means that you are unwittingly supporting toxic pesticides, exploiting labor, contributing to global warming."[10] As condemned character Tahani, played by Jameela Jamil, laments that it "feels like a game you can't win."[11]

In a culture gripped by a Social Justice B mindset, we find ourselves in the same unwinnable game. Social Justice B professor Richard Day speaks of our "infinite responsibility" by which "we can never allow ourselves to think that we are 'done,' that we have identified all of the sites, structures, and processes of oppression 'out there' or 'in here,' inside our own individual and group identities."[12] Do you see how this becomes a game no one can win? As Social Justice B educators Ozlem Sensoy and Robin DiAngelo put it, we should "work from the knowledge that the societal default is oppression; there are no spaces free from it. Thus, the question becomes, 'How is it manifesting here?' rather than 'Is it manifesting here?'"[13] If everything is unjust all the time—since Social Justice B interprets all inequality as injustice—we end up in the chronically frazzled state of mind well described by an ex-radical: "Infinite responsibility means infinite guilt, a kind of Christianity without salvation: to see power in every interaction is to see sin in every interaction. All that the activist can offer to absolve herself is Sisyphean effort until burnout. Eady's summarization is simpler: 'Everything is problematic.'"[14]

When an ideology has no limiting principles, such that "everything is problematic," then we end up in a state of defeat and hopelessness, having a bottomless sense of never doing enough, of having more sin than we could possibly atone for.

If you know much about Martin Luther from the sixteenth century, then that state of "infinite guilt" will sound familiar. Seeing "sin in every interaction," exerting "Sisyphean effort until burnout," reaching the conclusion that "everything is problematic" are spot-on descriptions of young Luther not in a twenty-first century social activist's collective but in an early sixteenth-century monastery. In the last five hundred years, Western culture has become far less concerned about our moral standing before a holy God. But that paradigm shift from Creator to creation has done nothing to curb humanity's need for justification. Luther wasn't a freak of nature for his need to be good, clean, holy, and justified. These needs are irrepressibly human. "We all seek catharsis somehow" (catharsis from the Greek *kathairein* meaning "to be clean").[15] Just ask the Hindu in the Ganges, the Catholic in the confessional booth, the Muslim on his face toward Mecca, or the Jew at the Western Wall.

Or simply picture the social justice activist on the social media wall. How might posting our daily outrage online become a misguided quest for justification? Elizabeth Nolan Brown cites psychological research that the kind of moral outrage we typically classify as altruistic "is often a function of self-interest, wielded to assuage feelings of personal culpability for societal harms or reinforce (to the self and others) one's own status as a Very Good Person."[16] This constant imputation of guilt to others—*they* are the bigots, *they* are the phobics, *they* are the fascists—offers a subjective sense of something that may feel close to and yet is infinitely far from what Christ offers us in the gospel. (Note well, this false means of declaring ourselves "not guilty" is not just a problem for Social Justice B. We may find it among Christians on the right too. Rather than our justification coming from Christ, and Christ alone, we seek our own "not guilty" verdict by transferring all guilt to the left. With the alt-right, which is antigospel to its rotten core, justification takes on nationalistic and racist overtones, in which all evil can be imputed to those with more melanin.)

Let's return to Luther to better understand our culture's wide quest for justification. Luther claimed, "Although an impeccable monk, I stood before God as a sinner troubled in conscience, and I had no confidence that my merit would assuage him."[17] Today it would be "Although an impeccable activist, I stood before the woke as a sinner troubled in conscience, and I had no confidence that my merit would assuage them." At his first Mass, Luther felt "utterly terrified and terror-stricken . . . full of sin and speaking to the loving, eternal, and the true God."[18] Today people are terror-stricken less before the Creator and more before creatures.

Here is the difference. Luther read the first chapter of Paul's letter to the Romans: "For I am not ashamed of the gospel, for it is the power of God for salvation to everyone who believes. . . . For in it the righteousness of God is revealed from faith for faith, as it is written, 'The righteous will live by faith.'"[19]

In those words, Luther said he "grasped that the justice of God is that righteousness by which through grace and sheer mercy God justified us through faith. Thereupon I felt myself to be reborn and to have gone through open doors into paradise."[20] His tortured conscience found sweet relief in the gospel. The infinite God erased Luther's infinite guilt through the infinite grace offered in Jesus.

Social Justice B offers no grace, no forgiveness, no open doors to paradise. Why? Because it ignores the most important distinction there is—the Creator-creature distinction. At the top of a Christian worldview we find a Creator who is not only just—the ultimate standard by whom all our actions must be judged—but also the justifier of his creatures.

> The LORD is merciful and gracious,
>> slow to anger and abounding in steadfast love.
> He will not always chide,
>> nor will he keep his anger forever.
> He does not deal with us according to our sins,
>> nor repay us according to our iniquities.[21]

What happens if we erase the Creator-creature distinction? Instead of standing before a quick-to-forgive Creator, we stand before our fellow creatures. Instead of having a God willing to take the nails in our place, we face a quick-to-anger mob, ready to drive digital nails to crucify us for every sin against its ever-evolving standards of righteousness.

What we are slowly realizing as a culture is the impossible demands of justice and our irrepressible need for justification. Before grace found him, Luther lashed his own back bloody, slept without a blanket in the subzero German winters, and sat in a confessional booth six hours a day, all to earn status as "a Very Good Person." Today we virtue-signal, we hashtag our solidarity, and we self-censor lest we utter blasphemy. This is what penance looks like in the twenty-first century. We have become a sort of collective Martin Luther in our quest to be very good people. Oh, how I pray that we would experience Luther's sweet rebirth, walk through "open doors into paradise," realize the futility of trying to be good people, and trust Jesus as all the goodness we will ever need. We can never do enough justice to earn the not guilty sentence. Jesus can and did. Social Justice B obscures that great news.

There is a lot of doom and gloom in certain Christian circles about the rise of Social Justice B. But, what if, in God's providence, the rise of Social Justice B makes this a golden moment to be alive and proclaim the gospel?

Under postmodernism, recognizing any meaningful sense of guilt was extremely difficult for people. Under postmodernism, which championed moral relativism and prided itself on nonjudgmentalism, recognizing any meaningful sense of guilt was extremely difficult for people. Under the new rising cultural epoch of activism, what I have called "post-postmodernism," we are conditioned to judge the moral shortcomings of everyone all the time. Guilt is the world we all now inhabit. The West now feels the weight of "infinite responsibility" and "infinite guilt" in a way it hasn't in a long time.

God's law also brings "infinite responsibility" and "infinite guilt." Here is the difference. The impossibility of keeping Social Justice B's standards is cruel. There is no redemption. No grace. No salvation. It's a game we can't win. The impossibility of keeping God's standards is a mercy. It shatters our self-righteousness. In Luther's words, "God is trying us, that by His law He may bring us to a knowledge of our impotence."[22] Augustine echoes, "The law was given for this purpose: to make you, being great, little; to show that you do not have in yourself the strength to attain righteousness, and for you, thus helpless, unworthy, and destitute, to flee to grace."[23] Yes! Flee to grace. Run to the cross. Quit doing penance before creatures, and take your infinite guilt to the infinite Creator, who alone has the authority to declare us not guilty through the death and resurrection of Jesus. "There is therefore now no condemnation for those who are in Christ Jesus."[24] That is the good news we must declare as our first thing to this weary generation.

Is, in, or *from* the Gospel?

"But," comes the welcome objection, "aren't you copping out? Isn't all this gospel-first talk just a highfalutin way to shirk the Bible's justice commands? Wasn't the same logic used as an excuse to do nothing about Southern slavery and ten thousand other injustices?"

In case I haven't been clear, let me say it again, *justice is not optional for the Christian life.* Neither is telling the truth, honoring our parents, or loving our enemies. Yet as essential as these commands are, none of them is the gospel. Keeping those commands can't save you. Only Jesus can. None of them are what Scripture itself identifies as "of first importance." In my immediate family, my wife is "of first importance" to me, but that doesn't make loving my kids optional.

How, then, should we picture the relationship between the gospel and social justice? (I am speaking here of Social Justice A, the kind that is compatible with a Christian worldview). Instead of saying that social justice *is* the gospel or *in* the gospel, it is more helpful to say social justice is *from* the gospel. Let me clarify using Acts 2. Peter proclaims the gospel to the temple crowds on Pentecost. It's the same gospel Paul declares as "of first importance"—the good news of the death and resurrection of Jesus. Three thousand are saved.

In the first century, "only around two percent of the population of a Roman town would be genuinely comfortably off. The vast majority would be destitute poor."[25] Some historians estimate that upward of two-thirds of the Roman Empire was enslaved in the first century. In other words, there was no shortage of social injustice when Peter preached on Pentecost. Read Peter's gospel proclamation in Acts 2:14–40. You will find no imperative to do social justice. Nowhere does Peter expose systemic inequalities and rally the crowds to action. If we believe social justice is the gospel or part of the gospel, then we must conclude that Peter either (a) did not preach the gospel that day, making it a mystery how three thousand were saved or (b) preached a truncated gospel. The text itself makes it clear that the whole gospel was preached, and preached with astounding saving results.

Does this mean Peter and the early church shrugged their shoulders at injustice? No. Something astounding followed *from* Peter's gospel proclamation. By the end of Acts 2, we find the newly expanded community of believers "selling their possessions and belongings and distributing the proceeds to all, as any had need."[26] This action on behalf of the poor wasn't the gospel. It wasn't *in* the gospel. It was *from* the gospel. A second thing flowed from the first thing— the good news of Jesus's death and resurrection.[27]

This pattern repeats throughout church history. When Romans tossed their so-called blemished babies away like garbage—often simply because they were female—our ancient brothers and sisters went to those dumps and rescued and raised society's unwanted as their own cherished sons and daughters. They knew the gospel that God had rescued and adopted them, so, as an existential implication of that good news, they did the same until the human dumps were no more.

When a plague ravaged the Roman Empire, most people ran for the hills away from the sick and dying. But countercultural Christians, believing the good news that God had taken their sin-plague upon himself on the cross, ran to the bedsides of the plagued to treat them with dignity, often getting sick and dying right along with them. Likewise, William Wilberforce, John Newton and the Clapham Sect's efforts to abolish the British slave trade were not the gospel; they followed from the good news that God has redeemed us through the cross and empty tomb of Jesus.[28]

The White Man's Gospel?

Some may say, "Williams is just upholding a white European gospel, the gospel of Luther and Calvin and Spurgeon as if it were *the* gospel. He's pushing the western white man's religion, trying to colonize our brains with theological white supremacy." Here's the problem. The gospel I hold as the first thing is the same gospel that brings life, hope, and joy to unprecedented millions in Asia, Africa, South America, and the Middle East today. It is the same gospel championed by Augustine, and his fellow African church fathers like Clement, Tertullian, Cyprian, Athanasius, and Cyril over a thousand years before the Reformation in Europe. It is the same gospel the Ethiopian eunuch brought to Africa in the first century.[29] It is the gospel that Paul, a Benjamite Jew from Tarsus, preached all over Asia Minor. Most importantly, it is the good news that Jesus—hardly a white Western European or American—proclaimed throughout the red letters of the New Testament (See appendix G, "Good News to the Poor"). Did white Westerners like Luther and Calvin help bring clarity and depth to the gospel? Without a doubt. Simply read Luther's *On Christian Liberty* or Calvin's *Institutes* and let God's grace ease your heavy soul. But to think that proclaiming the good news of God's saving grace is an act of white supremacy is to rewrite history and sacrifice the best news in the world—the news so many weary and despairing souls need to hear—on the altar of identity politics.[30]

OJO'S STORY

Social justice is all the rage these days, especially among young adults coming of age in this current political climate. Whether we hear about social justice from the news, our coworkers, our friends, or social media streams, it is unavoidable. On one level, it is a welcome change that people these days seem to care more about justice for others. It beats the days when minorities and individuals from other marginalized groups were an afterthought, pushed to the bottom of society or treated as subhuman.

Yet the more I engage in social justice discussions with fellow millennials or gen Zers, the more disheartened I become. With this surge in social justice discourse there has been a steady increase in cynicism, aggression, and in some cases downright hatred toward people who are guilty of thinking about things in the "wrong way." Worse still is the unfortunate trend in people of my age group starting to see discussions and debates of social justice as an us-versus-them, zero-sum, winner-take-all battle. Instead of diverse perspectives being welcome at the table, daring to think outside the ideological confines runs you the risk of being "canceled," meaning declared null and void or having your career prospects erased. Disagreement is no longer taken as something that can be done respectfully and is seen instead as a rejection or attack on someone's personhood. The scary thing is that this is not happening just in the secular world but also within much of the church.

This reality has hit particularly close to home for me over the past couple of years. Friends in my inner circle have been strong Bible-believing Christians. They have unmistakably heard Scripture's call for justice, a call that has sadly been ignored in certain segments of the church. As I have engaged in conversations with my friends, a recurring theme has emerged. Their perception of the church's silence on matters of injustice such as explicit racism, homophobia, misogyny, or abuse has sent a loud and clear message that the church can't be trusted in matters of justice. Slowly but surely, young Christians begin looking outside the church and to the world for solutions to combat the injustice they see. When churches fail to live out biblical justice in a beautiful and compelling way, they turn rising generations into easy prey for social justice ideologues.

The results have been tragic, to say the least. Biblical morality is slowly replaced with the evolving moralism of progressive politics. Soon the Bible itself is deconstructed as an oppressive tool of the cisheteropatriarchy instead of the life-giving words of a loving Creator. The problem is that once we ditch biblical morality, we lose the concept of sin, and the gospel itself no longer makes sense. Then truth is seen as relative and socially constructed as opposed to defined by God. Again, we lose the gospel when we lose God as the sovereign standard of truth. In some cases, the idea of one God was considered as an oppressive case of "Christian supremacy." Universalism then becomes the default choice, and the uniqueness of Christ's saving work is abandoned. What started as a noble pursuit of justice becomes an erosion of a biblical worldview, and the gospel is lost.

Through God's grace, some of my friends' views on social justice changed only temporarily. Some have realized the fatal compromises being made in the name of social justice. But others have become nominally

Christian or in some cases no longer identify as Christians. My heart breaks for them, and I pray that they find their way back to the Lord. More than ever, I pray for revival and for the church to recommit itself to being a beacon to the watching world of what it means to act justly, love mercy, and walk humbly with God. To do that without succumbing to the ideologies of our age, we must make our highest priority what Scripture itself ranks "of first importance"—the gospel of the death and resurrection of Jesus.

—Ojo Okoye

Ojo has worked at Arizona State University and is currently training for lifelong ministry.

Questions for Personal or Small Group Study

1. Paul teaches that the gospel of God's saving grace through the death and resurrection of Jesus is "of first importance" and warns us with stern and passionate language against those who preach false gospels that seek to add human works to God's grace. In what ways might social justice become a false gospel?
2. Why is it important to clarify that justice flows from the gospel but is not identical to or part of the gospel itself? What is at stake?
3. What does it mean to keep the gospel as our first thing? What habits can we form to keep the gospel first in our daily lives? How can participation in a local church, taking the sacraments, investing in our prayer lives, and preaching the gospel to ourselves and others keep us from turning "the gospel first" into an empty slogan.

So You're Saying . . .

Given the power of the Newman effect in our day (see pp. 8–9), here are five points some may have heard me advancing in part 3, "Sinners or Systems? Three Questions About Social Justice and Salvation":

1. "So you're saying there's no such thing as systemic injustice."
2. "So you're saying that racism is a thing of the past, that there is no racism in policing, criminal justice, housing, or basically any other area of society in our day that we should work to reform."

3. "So you're saying, like those white Christians who opposed Martin Luther King Jr., that we should just preach the gospel and try to get people to heaven and not waste our time confronting oppression and social injustice here on earth."

4. "So you're saying that 'whiteness' has not been used as a justification, even by so-called Christians, to unleash unspeakable violence, dehumanization, and terror against people of color."

5. "So you're saying that the nice things white people have done throughout history and the mean things nonwhite people have done throughout history somehow excuse the vile evils done in the name of white supremacy throughout history."

No. I am not saying any of that. I don't believe any of that. If you are hearing any of that, then either the Newman effect is at work or I have simply done a poor job communicating, for which I pray you forgive me.

A Prayer to Redeem Sinners and Systems

God,

You are so holy and so committed to redemption that you oppose all sin—our individual sins as well as those we embed in systems whenever we "frame injustice by statute." Mark our hearts with that same commitment. As we seek to bring redemption to fallen systems, may we not fall into the traps of automatically assuming the most damning explanations for inequalities, ignoring evidence that may not support our ideologies, or telling self-serving narratives that pin all oppression on this or that people group. And most of all, make your first thing our first thing. The good news of Jesus's death and resurrection is "of first importance" according to your Word. Help us contend earnestly for the gospel and not try to add anything to the complete and sufficient saving work of Jesus. It would be easy to say we believe that gospel and then sit on our thumbs while people suffer. So please push us to do the kind of justice you command, the justice that is not the gospel itself but flows beautifully from that gospel. Amen.

PART 4

TRUTH OR TRIBES THINKING?

■ ■ ■

Three Questions about Social Justice and Knowledge

Love the LORD your God . . . with all your mind.

–Matthew 22:37

Every mind has what philosophers would call an "epistemology," what programmers might call an "operating system." How should we best decipher between a justified true belief and a falsehood? How should we best process and store the input and data of life? Should we feel, reason, experiment, trust, revolt, or Google our way to truth?

These aren't questions for pipe-puffing philosophers in rich mahogany offices with many leather-bound books. Everyone has an epistemology, and, as with computer operating systems, some are better than others. Some mental operating systems open our minds to new truths, while others are so riddled with bugs and viruses that they generate jumbled beliefs and crash cognitive systems.

If our mental operating systems are buggy, loving God and loving our neighbors will be difficult. If, for example, I seek truth at the psychic's shop—if palm readings, tarot cards, and Ouija boards are where I stake my trust—then my mind will not blossom into all that God designed it to be. My God-given capacities to know him deeply, reason well, weigh evidence, trust what is trustworthy, and see through propaganda—all of that God-given, intellectual potential will be squandered.

Again, the Bible does not merely say "do justice" but to "truly execute justice." Corrupted mental operating systems generate false beliefs that can easily dupe us into thinking we are doing great work for others, when in reality we are doing them damage. If we care about justice—giving both God and others what is due them—then we should care about epistemology.

Tribes Thinking

We must see Social Justice B for what it is. It is an epistemology, a mental operating system with a unique way of processing the world around us. Operating systems have names. A Mac might run on Mountain Lion, High Sierra, or Mojave. Epistemologies have names too. Some minds run on empiricism, others on rationalism, others on subjectivism. If there were a name for the mental OS of Social Justice B, it would be called "Tribes." According to Tribes thinking, reality is best interpreted as a story of oppressor groups versus oppressed groups. If you fail to see the oppression all around you, then you are sleepwalking through life. You are not "woke." You are unwittingly on the wrong side of history, the oppressors' side of history.

Why call it "Tribes thinking"? Because within the social justice epistemology, the story of oppression is typically told in one of six ways:

T, beware the **T**heocrats!
The oppressors are right-wing Christians trying to cram their outdated morality down everyone else's throats with the coercive powers of law.
R, beware the **R**acists!
The oppressors are those who marginalize and dehumanize people who do not share their skin tone or ethnic identity.
I, beware the **I**slamophobes!
The oppressors are those who fear that most if not all Muslims are hate-mongering terrorists rather than peace-loving neighbors.
B, beware the **B**igots!
The oppressors are those who use their heteronormative power to deny the rights and humanity of the LGBTQ community.
E, beware the **E**xploiters!
The oppressors are those whose capitalist greed leads them to use and abuse the poor for their own selfish, materialistic gain.
S, beware the **S**exists!
The oppressors are men who deny equal rights, equal access to power, and equal pay to maintain a patriarchal tyranny over half our species.

To a mind under this operating system, these six oppressor categories—theocrats, racists, Islamophobes, bigots, elitists, and sexists—combine to best explain the world around us.

What Tribes Thinking Gets Right

Can we say anything positive about Tribes thinking? Sure. Most epistemologies start with real insight before they go too far. The empiricists were right that our five senses can help us get at reality, just as the rationalists were right that logic and mathematics can help us get at reality. They went wrong when they ditched the countless truths that can't be tested in a lab or proved by an equation.

So the first thing to note about Tribes thinking is that there is a gut-wrenching measure of truth to it. There is no shortage of real-world examples of Christians taking political power to dangerous extremes, people being dehumanized for their skin color, moderate Muslims being treated like bloodthirsty jihadists, gays and lesbians being ousted from their homes and treated like subhumans, capitalists who have valued profits over people, and men who have trampled women. We must say, with tears, all of this is true. If we take the Bible seriously, we must strive to make all of this untrue. We must work toward a world in which the full humanity of everyone is respected and cherished, not only in theory but also in action.

This is what Tribes thinking gets right. Sure, not everything called "injustice" against such groups is automatically injustice simply because an anonymous mob says so in a collective Twitter rage. But that does not void the fact that there are real people bloodied and bruised from real injustice.

To ignore that fact is to become the priest and the Levite from the parable of the good Samaritan. We nonchalantly change lanes to pass the battered and abused who are curled up and moaning on the roadside. Ignoring the moans violates Jesus's second greatest commandment—to love our neighbors. If our mental operating systems function in accordance with the teachings of Jesus, then we should journey through our daily lives scanning the roadsides for anyone mangled by bandits. But if our epistemology keeps our eyes always fixed on the horizon—by focusing *only* on getting all our doctrinal i's dotted and t's crossed, or *only* on getting to heaven, or *only* on the triumph of our political party until the grimacing faces on the roadside become blurred—then *we* are the religious villains of Jesus's story. Of course, good doctrine matters immensely. Eternal destinies matter, well, eternally. Politics matter intensely (though not as much as the first two). We ignore them at our peril. But when our theology or politics give us a tunnel vision that bypasses those ravaged by real injustice, it's time to repent.

Tribes thinking can be helpful whenever it encourages those on fast-paced religious journeys to pull back the reigns and look, really *look*, to see broken people on the roadside as more than blurs. But if we are to *truly* execute justice for the battered, we must ask, "Can Tribes thinking go wrong? Is it possible that an epistemology designed to open our eyes to injustice might blind us to ways in which we unwittingly add to the net injustice in the universe? Is it possible to think we are the Good Samaritans of Jesus's story when, in fact, we have become the bandits?" Here are three questions we should ask if we don't want Tribes thinking to make bandits of us all:

Does our vision of social justice make one way of seeing some things the only way of seeing everything?

Does it turn the "lived experience" of hurting people into more pain?

Does it turn the quest for truth into an identity game?

Chapter 10

The Tunnel Vision Question

Does our vision of social justice make
one way of seeing something the
only way of seeing everything?

One of the most common ways mental operating systems crash is when they process the world in only one way. An entrepreneur believes it is good to make money. In its proper place, this belief yields more hard work than hedonism, more generosity than greed, and more industriousness than impulsivity. At its best, the belief that making money is good would not crowd out God, family, friendship, honesty, rest, caring for the poor, and the other good things in life.

Before long, our entrepreneur's belief becomes an idol that warps his mind. His mental space is overrun with thinking about how to build himself a Walter White bed of cash. He approaches others not as people but as suckers to take by the ankles and shake until everything he wants from the relationship falls out of their pockets. On account of his epistemological tunnel vision, he can no longer truly see a breathtaking stretch of beach. It hits his retinas. But he can't really *see* it. He can't see the lightshow produced by sunrays on the ocean ripples, which looks like ten million tiny cameras flashing. He can't see glassy sheets of water gliding up and sizzling down the sand. He can't see seagulls surfing the wind currents. All he sees is untapped beachfront property that could, with some investment savvy, go for billions. Given his epistemology, he can see the world in only one color—green.

To the old colonizers, the whole world became plunder. To the postmodernists, the whole world became a power play. The human mind has an uncanny way of finding a bit of knowledge, then turning it into a totalizing way of knowing everything. We need what Abraham Kuyper called a "unity of view," since "the question about the origin, interconnection and destiny of everything that exists cannot be suppressed."[1] We need grand, unifying stories. We need cosmic dramas with heroes and villains to make sense of life's head-spinning perplexities.

There is nothing wrong with our insuppressible need for grand stories. We are designed to live in big meaningful narratives. The problem occurs when our grand stories aren't as grand as they seem. Instead of prying the world open to us, they cram it into a tiny box and lock us inside. They make God's Technicolor world appear to us in monochrome.

Seeing What Is *Not* There

The Bible is clear. There is real oppression in the world. There is a big difference between believing this truth and downloading Tribes thinking as our mental OS. One helpful way to tell the difference is to honestly ask ourselves, "How do we process evidence that oppression may *not* be the best explanation in this or that case?"

When oppression—a true insight into *some things*—becomes the way of seeing *most things* or *all things*, then our story of the world ceases to be a grand story. Just as our tycoon couldn't really *see* a beach, he could see only dollars and cents, so we likewise lose our ability to see the world when we can see only oppression.

Take the hot-button issue of the gender pay gap. If I process the world through Tribes thinking, then I am left with one and only one interpretation— sexism. That totalizing answer forbids all kinds of important questions. Does the gender pay gap have anything to do with women voluntarily leaving the workforce or going part-time for a season because many find the prospect of raising babies to be more worthwhile than decades of overtime office drudgery? Could a gap exist because men, on average, are more disagreeable than women, and disagreeableness is a documented marker of negotiating bigger paychecks? Is it relevant that, in many fields, women make more than men when numbers are adjusted to account for overtime hours? Could the gap have ten or twenty or a hundred other contributing factors? Are we allowed to seriously ponder research into these factors, or should we simply write off the researchers as privileged members of the he-man woman-hater's club?

My point is *not* that factors other than sexism explain the gender pay gap. My point is that if our minds are programmed by Tribes thinking, then the question itself—"Do factors other than sexism help explain the gender pay gap?"—will likely never cross our minds. If the question does arise, then our mental OS will kick in and quickly suppress it. Why? Because, by the logic of Tribes thinking, the very act of questioning the sexist story of the pay gap is to commit the unpardonable sin of siding with the oppressor groups over the oppressed. If someone else poses the question to us, then our mental OS stores them away in our mental files under *S* for sexist, *M* for misogynist, or *P* for patriarchal oppressor. Those who do not accept Tribes thinking can be dragged into the trash bin for permanent deletion. The Tribes mindset trashes not only any meaningful relationship with that person but also any hope of meaningfully thinking about that person's perspective. In short, it makes us both closed-hearted and closed-minded.

Before long, we can barely scroll through our Netflix suggestions without righteous indignation kicking in. *Braveheart*—a three-hour celebration of toxic masculinity. *The Patriot*—shameless American exceptionalism. *Sleepless in Seattle*—heteronormative propaganda. *Lord of the Rings*—Eurocentric racism. *Argo, Zero Dark Thirty, American Sniper*—big budget Islamophobia. *Aladdin, Mulan, Princess and the Frog*—racial stereotyping. *Captain America*—more like Captain White Privilege.

I am hyperbolizing, but only slightly. In just the last week, the children's show *VeggieTales* has been criticized as racist for having colored vegetables with different accents play villains. The playground game of dodgeball has since been denounced at the annual Congress of the Humanities and Social Sciences as "miseducative" and a tool of "oppression" because it "reinforces the five faces of oppression."[2] Behind such headlines, though laughable to some, there is serious insight into how our psyches work.

We are talking about a well-documented phenomenon that psychologists call "concept creep."[3] Like spilling ink into a tub of water, a concept expands outward in all directions until the entire tub is clouded. One valid way of seeing something spreads into the only way of seeing everything. Concept creep is how someone can become so cloudy headed that they deconstruct *VeggieTales* as racist propaganda. Concept creep is how J. R. R. Tolkien's *The Lord of the Rings* can be read as racist Eurocentrism, despite the author's vocal antiracism.[4] Sociologist Melanie Dupuis in her book *Nature's Perfect Food: How Milk Became America's Drink* argues that "by declaring milk perfect, white northern Europeans announced their own perfection."[5] When a totalizing view of the world grips our minds, we experience things that are often not there. We start seeing racism in vegetable cartoons, tasting white supremacy in a glass of milk, hearing sexism in a holiday jingle, feeling oppression in the impact of a dodgeball, and smelling homophobia as it wafts from our chicken sandwiches.

Concept creep is particularly common in Social Justice B. It assumes that questioning sexism, racism, or any other evil ism as the best explanation is to side with the oppressors against the oppressed. This is exactly backward. If we care about ending actual sexism, then we should welcome the question of how much of the gender pay gap can be laid at the feet of actual sexism. Otherwise, we aren't fighting the real problem, but shadowboxing our own ideological projections. The extent to which we shadowbox our ideological projections of the problem is the extent to which we trivialize the victims of real sexism and racism. By diverting our finite injustice-fighting energies in every direction all at once, Tribes thinking unintentionally marginalizes the already marginalized. Calling most everything racism hurts the victims of actual racism. Calling most everything sexism hurts the victims of actual sexism, and so on.

Mechanics who care about cars and their owners, not merely trying to fleece their customers, will do everything in their power to ask questions, run diagnostics, and get down to the real problems. Mechanics who simply dump oil into every car without taking a serious look under the hood will create more broken-down cars and stranded drivers on the roadside. Maybe the problem is a worn timing belt, a busted transmission, or a dead alternator. Actually fixing problems requires more than one-dimensional diagnoses. Asking unpopular questions and openly gathering and assessing the facts is one of the most loving things we can do for our oppressed brothers and sisters. Contrary to popular opinion, questioning whether and to what extent sexism, racism, or any other antibiblical ism is the real problem is siding *with* the oppressed.

Yes, doing so is risky. You will not win any virtue awards or popularity contests. Online mobs are ever poised to pounce. They may call you names. They may flag you for hate speech and get your social media accounts deactivated. The question is, do we take the Bible's commands to truly execute justice seriously enough to endure the online mobs?

My point is not to deny the reality of racism, sexism, or economic exploitation. It is simply that caring about justice requires a commitment to truth. We can no more separate truth from justice than we can subtract one side from a triangle and still consider it a triangle. The extent to which Tribes thinking predetermines answers to hard questions is the extent to which it obscures truth and unintentionally leaves more people broken. If we are afraid to ask tough questions with open minds, if we equate asking hard questions with racism, bigotry, and sexism, if we aren't willing to follow the evidence wherever it leads, then we should ask ourselves, "What do we care about more, loving the oppressed in truth or marching to an ideological beat and saluting the onlooking culture so it does not brand us with a scarlet T, R, I, B, E, or S?"

Missing What *Is* There

Tribes thinking may not only cause us to see what is *not* there; it may also cause us to miss much of what *is* there. If we look at history and see no nuance or beauty, nothing to preserve or treasure, only a long brutal tale of oppressors exploiting and pillaging minority groups, then something has gone terribly wrong with our mental operating systems. We miss so much history. If we read great literature and see only dead white guys writing stories to push patriarchal oppression, then something has gone terribly wrong. We miss out on so much literary truth and beauty. When we pass someone on the street and don't see a unique person but an exemplar of an identity group, when we project all the historical transgressions of that group onto the flesh-and-blood person before us, we miss so much of who that person actually is.

Tribes thinking not only blinds us to a lot of truth, goodness, and beauty in the world; it also keeps us from seeing a lot of deception, injustice, and ugliness. It dupes us into seeing oppression where it isn't and keeps us from seeing oppression where it is.

In late 2015, I received my first branding with a scarlet *O*, for oppressor. Undercover videos had been released exposing Planned Parenthood leaders bargaining the body parts of aborted fetuses. Scrolling through my Facebook feed, I came across a student's post hailing the virtues of Planned Parenthood. The student had done a superb job of parroting Planned Parenthood's talking points. They are an "essential," "mammogram-providing" "advocate for women's health," with abortion as "only 3 percent" of its services, which have been unjustly "discredited" by "heavily edited" "fraud videos." I responded by fact-checking her points and exposing the $1.8 billion operation's long history of exploiting women, minorities, and their unborn children.[6] The student and I had a lively but charitable back-and-forth.

Then came a private message from another student. He was outraged that I would exploit the "power differential" between a professor and student by challenging a student's pro-choice arguments in a public forum. He expressed his disgust at my calloused act of online oppression. He took to social media to declare his "solidarity" with the student, whom I had apparently victimized, and his opposition to me and the historic patriarchal power I represented.

The outraged student expressed a grand total of zero outrage for the facts that surfaced in the public exchange—that Planned Parenthood aborts over 300,000 divine image-bearers a year, their historic targeting of minorities, their complicity in the sexual exploitation of minors, and their profiteering off people's bodies. There was no outrage for those victims. Who was all that outrage expressed for?

A university student with breath in her lungs and a brain that, instead of being sold to a bio research firm, had been challenged by a professor on social media.

Tribes thinking is neither as inclusive nor as concerned for the oppressed as its proponents claim. Its solidarity circle includes non-Christians, people of color, Muslims, people of the LGBTQ community, the economically poor, and certain people with two X chromosomes—that is, those who fall within the TRIBES acrostic. And, of course, we should care about all those people as divine image-bearers. However, if we care about the oppressed even more than we care about a particular political ideology, then . . .

Should we care about women exploited by the abortion industry? In 1973 seven powerful men rendered the *Roe v. Wade* decision, impacting millions. While hailed as a landmark decision for the liberation of women, 64 percent of women who seek abortions said they felt pressured by others to have abortions. Over half thought abortion was "morally wrong." Less than 1 percent said they felt better about themselves, 77.9 percent felt guilt, and 59.5 percent felt that "part of me died."[7] A massive fourteen-year study found that 81 percent of women who had an abortion were more likely to experience mental health problems.[8] That is not to speak of the physical toll that has been inflicted on them. Does our vision of social justice include these women or take their harrowing stories seriously?[9]

Should we care about the voiceless babies terminated by the abortion industry? According to the World Health Organization, abortion was the leading cause of death worldwide in 2018, tallying 42 million victims.[10] That is 42 million human beings who fell victim to the suction tubes, curette blades, and Mayo scissors of the abortion industry.[11] That is eighty image-bearers terminated in the last minute you have been reading, more than one per second. In places such as Iceland "the abortion rate for children diagnosed with Down syndrome approaches 100 percent."[12] In the United States, 90 percent of preborn humans diagnosed with Downs are terminated.[13] "In Asia, widespread sex-selective abortions have led to as many as 160 million "missing" women—more than the entire female population of the United States. Recent evidence suggests that sex-selective abortions of girls are common among certain populations in the United States as well.[14] In cities such as New York, more black babies are aborted than are born.[15] Human beings in utero literally cannot voice their oppression. How many Social Justice B advocates are willing to be the voice for those millions of divine image-bearers who do not enjoy the same size, developmental, locational, or breathing privileges they do?

Should we care about children who have endured split homes? There are mountains of research documenting the advantages of being raised by two parents. Mom and Dad sticking together, for all their imperfections, corresponds with higher levels of academic and career success for their children, along with lower rates of criminality and mental disorder. To achieve equality, should diversity committees work to dismantle two-parent privilege and ensure that candidates from broken homes are given more seats at the table? How often does what now brands itself "social justice" champion the cause of strong intact families as a justice issue? (Instead, one of the world's most popular Social Justice B organizations declares its "guiding principle" to "disrupt the Western-prescribed nuclear family" in its mission statement.[16]) If we care about justice, shouldn't we be deeply disturbed that the rate of black children born to unmarried mothers climbed from 25 to a heartbreaking 70 percent from 1965 to 2017, or the fact that white children born out of wedlock skyrocketed from 4 to over 28 percent over the same period?[17]

Should we care about the victims of the exploitative pornography industry? Pornography is a $97 billion industry.[18] In 2018 more than 5.5 billion hours of pornography were consumed on a single porn site, with 33.5 billion visits. According to the Internet Watch Foundation, recorded child sexual exploitation (otherwise known as "child porn") is one of the fastest-growing online businesses, with over 624,000 child porn traders discovered in the US.[19] Analysis of the fifty most popular pornographic videos found that 88 percent of scenes contained physical violence. Then there are the established links between pornography and human trafficking, rape, domestic violence, impaired brain function, broken relationships, and depression.[20] Why are repenting of pornography addiction and fighting to bring down the dehumanizing pornography industry so rarely mentioned in the same breath as "social justice"?

Should we care about the millions of Christians imprisoned or executed around the globe? The Social Justice B narrative often uses a broad brush to paint Christians as the oppressors, the driving force behind the theocracy, racism, Islamophobia, bigotry, exploitation, and sexism in the world. To many with the Tribes mindset, it is obvious which side of the oppressor-oppressed equation Christians fall on. Yet according to *Newsweek* in 2018, "Christian persecution and genocide is worse now than 'any time in history.'"[21] This includes being targeted, imprisoned, beaten, raped, hung, crucified, and bombed for claiming Jesus as Lord. Every month an average of 345 Christians are killed for faith-related reasons, 105 churches or Christian buildings are burned or attacked, and 219 Christians are detained without trial.[22]

Should we care about the desperately oppressed victims of far-left systems like communism and socialism? According to the international bestseller *The Black Book of Communism*, the quest to achieve economic equality between the rich and poor through communist and socialist policies has resulted in over 100 million casualties in the twentieth century alone.[23] Nevertheless, several studies show that support for socialism is trending high in the United States, particularly among younger generations. These are the same generations in which one-third believe that more people perished under George W. Bush than Joseph Stalin, almost half are "unfamiliar" with Mao Zedong and the 50 million victims of his plan for economic equality.[24] If social justice is truly about ending oppression, why are so many Social Justice B advocates quick to fall for the lofty rhetoric of "compassionate" political visions that led to the oppression and termination of more people in the last century than any other system? Can they state with clarity why their version of socialism would not yield similar catastrophic results as the socialist regimes, past and present?

The distinguishing mark of the political left, one that is particularly attractive for young generations, is its care and compassion for the "others." Frankly, I don't buy it. Do "others" include oppressed women, terminated babies, home-split children, those exploited by the pornography industry, the religiously persecuted, or socialism's victims? The tunnel vision of Social Justice B tends to leave these millions of oppressed people in the dark.

Of course, we must not commit the same error in the opposite direction. This is where Tribes thinking serves as a helpful reminder. Scripture does command us to love our neighbors. That certainly includes our non-Christian, ethnic minority, Muslim, poor, and female neighbors. Given the political polarization of our day, seeing our side as caring about others and the other side as cruel is easy and self-serving. But it is not so black-and-white. Often the left and right simply have different "others." If we are shaped by Scripture instead of the culture wars, then we will not become the priests and Levites galloping past bodies on the side of the road. Christians should be known less as culture warriors and more as Good Samaritans who stop for battered neighbors, whether they are black, white, brown, male, female, gay, straight, rich, poor, old, young, Muslim, Christian, Jewish, atheist, capitalist, socialist, Republican, Democrat, near, far, tall, short, or smaller than a peanut.

> Christians should be known less as culture warriors and more as good Samaritans who stop for battered image-bearers.

Tribes thinking, for all its claims of inclusivity, is clear about who is *not* worth stopping for. While it may help us see hurting people we may have otherwise missed, it also redefines "oppression" in a way that leaves far too many people bleeding out on the roadside.[25] The church must show the world a better way.

Missing the Main Thing

There is one final thing that Tribes thinking leaves outside its field of vision. It is the main thing—the gospel. Sadly, every one of my friends, colleagues, and students who has continued down the road of Social Justice B has ended up in the same place, a place where they no longer evangelize. They no longer tell people the truth about how supremely holy and satisfying God is. There is no talk of the scandalous reality of sin in every human heart or the sweet redemption that comes only through crucifixion and empty tomb of Jesus. They offer no loving calls to repent of sin and self-righteousness to trust completely in the righteousness of Christ. It's sad to watch the best news in the universe fade from view in a fog of rhetoric about pay gaps, cisheteropatriarchal privilege, and the evils of capitalism. It's sad to watch the cultural revolution eclipse the Great Commission. It's sad to watch political "wokeness" become their message and mission with less and less concern for seeing the spiritually dead reborn by the Holy Spirit, redeemed by the Son, and declared righteous by the Father.

If you find yourself moving toward Social Justice B, ask yourself honestly, "When was the last time I shared the good news of God's saving grace through the death and resurrection of Jesus with anyone?" "Do the justice causes I care about throw gasoline or water on my desire to proclaim Christ crucified?" Of course, working against racism, misogyny, and other sinful forms of oppression is important to the Christian life. Christianity should never be reduced to fire insurance or floating off to the clouds after we die. But if we no longer share the gospel, then there is a problem.

Let's face it. Evangelizing is risky (though far less risky than *not* evangelizing). Telling the truth about the godhood of God makes you a heretic in the eyes of those who are their own moral authorities. Straight talk about the sinfulness of sin is offensive to those convinced that their own hearts are unfallen and worth following. Proclaiming Jesus as our only hope for salvation will step on toes. So we take the safe road. A recent study revealed that nearly half of "practicing Christian millennials" believe "it is wrong to share one's personal beliefs with someone of a different faith in hopes that they will one day share the same faith."[26] (It is good for the eternities of millions that the apostles, the Jim and Elizabeth Elliots, the Lottie Moons, the Amy Carmichaels, the Hudson Taylors, the David Brainerds, and the William Careys of history did not share this opinion.) The same study found that 40 percent of millennials believe "if someone says they disagree with you, it means that they're judging you." Given this cultural climate, it is far less risky to baptize trending visions of social justice in Christian terminology than to share the gospel that Jesus and the apostles proclaimed. And let us not forget, they were beaten and executed for it.

The problem is that this shift, no matter its payoff for our public image, leaves people in profound oppression. When we don't share the gospel, we leave people shackled to soul-crushing ideologies, enslaved to sin, and captive to forces of darkness. The oppression unleashed by the world, the flesh, and the devil is real. The tunnel vision of Tribes thinking blinds us to such oppression. It shouldn't surprise us, then, that Christians who adopt this mindset eventually stop sharing the gospel, and in many cases end up rejecting the gospel altogether. If our vision of social justice reduces evangelism to an offense or an afterthought, then we don't care about the oppressed the way Scripture calls us to care for them.

NEIL'S STORY

I became a Christian in graduate school at UC Berkeley while obtaining a PhD in theoretical chemistry. Because I wanted to reach my fellow academics with the gospel, I plunged headlong into the world of apologetics, learning how to address topics like the relationship between science and Christianity, the reliability of the Bible, and the evidence for Jesus's resurrection. I tried to avoid "political issues," believing that Christians should center their faith on the life, death, and resurrection of Jesus and the authority of Scripture.

But a few years ago, I noticed a theological drift in certain Christians, both public figures and people I knew personally. This drift began with an interest in "social justice," which I wrongly assumed meant the application of biblical principles to our laws and institutions. But these same Christians then began to express other views that were harder and harder to reconcile with orthodoxy. They moved from conservative denominations to progressive ones and sometimes left the Christian faith altogether. Why?

Not until I read Anderson and Collins's *Race, Class, and Gender* did I understand what was happening. People were not merely adopting a few new beliefs about politics; they were adopting a new worldview that was gradually displacing their Christian worldview. I began reading voraciously and discovered that contemporary "Social Justice B" is rooted in a comprehensive ideology that emerged from a discipline known as "critical theory." Social justice scholars see reality as divided between oppressed groups and oppressor groups along lines of race, class, gender, sexuality, physical ability, and age. Oppression has been redefined to refer not merely to overt acts of cruelty and coercion but also the ways in which dominant groups impose their ideologies ("patriarchy," "heteronormativity," etc.) on everyone else. Because of their "social location," oppressors are blinded by their privilege, while oppressed people have special insight into social reality.

This framework has devastating effects on our theology. First, a Christian's primary identity is not in their race, class, or gender. It is in their union with Christ. To see our brothers and sisters as "oppressors" solely because of their demographic group is to re-erect the dividing wall of hostility that Christ tore down (Eph. 2:14). Second, while unbiblical values oppress, God's values are ultimately liberating. God is our Creator, and his design for us frees us. We dare not haphazardly dismantle all society's dominant values. Instead, we must ask which values are consistent with Scripture and which are not. Third, while Christians should be concerned with giving a voice to the voiceless, our ultimate authority must always be God's voice in Scripture. Someone's membership of a marginalized group does not make them an infallible interpreter of reality. Finally, our primary problem is sin, and the solution is redemption, God reaching into history through the work of Jesus to rescue us from our rebellion and restore us to himself. Yes, Christians should be concerned with biblical justice. But that concern flows out of a heart that has been individually transformed by the work of Christ and the power of the Holy Spirit.

Many Christians are unconsciously adopting a comprehensive framework that inevitably unravels basic Christian doctrines. How can you be committed to a biblical view of gender or sexuality if you view gender and heteronormativity as oppressive social constructs? How can you be committed to the authority of the Bible when it claims that Christianity is true and that other religions are false? How can you celebrate the deep truths in confessions of the Reformation if they are hopelessly "Eurocentric"? How can you be committed to centering "voices of color" while rejecting liberation theology? These are serious issues. Don't just coast along with the cultural zeitgeist. Test all things. Think critically and think biblically.

−Neil Shenvi

Neil is a PhD in Theoretical Chemistry from UC Berkeley who researches and writes extensively about social justice and critical theory from a Christian worldview perspective at www.shenviapologetics.com

Questions for Personal or Small Group Study

1. What is the kernel of truth in Tribes thinking, an insight Christians should take seriously?
2. State three ways Tribes thinking distorts our vision of justice.
3. What are three ways Tribes thinking conflicts with a biblical worldview? How might you winsomely explain those conflicts to a brother or sister in Christ who may have embraced Social Justice B?

Chapter 11

The Suffering Question

Does our vision of social justice turn the
"lived experience" of hurting people into more pain?

S ince I'm a speck on a blue dot in a gigantic universe, my perspective is often *way* off. I leap to wrong conclusions. I make snap judgments about other people and their motives. I can take my own experiences and my own interpretation of those experiences as far more authoritative than they actually are.

That is one reason the Bible is so important to me. It keeps me from taking my own conclusions and feelings too seriously. It is a two-thousand-page reminder that I am not the final word on reality. I am, indeed, a speck on a blue dot. That's why I try to take the words of the One who made this speck and this blue dot more seriously than I take myself.

This realization brings us to a second aspect of Tribes thinking. It encourages us to make our own "lived experiences" authoritative, a view known as "standpoint epistemology." When applied to questions of justice, this means that anyone who claims that theocrats, racists, Islamophobes, bigots, exploiters, or sexists have hurt them must not be merely heard, but taken authoritatively. Lived experiences must, in turn, become the foundations on which we rebuild everything from public policy and school curriculum to theological systems and church ministry. Questioning the narratives of the oppressed and the policies or theologies derived from them makes *you* the oppressor.

Listening

Lived experiences do matter. The Bible commands us to "be quick to hear,"[1] "bear one another's burdens,"[2] and "weep with those who weep."[3] These commands fit together. It is impossible to bear someone else's burdens without really, truly listening to them as they bravely unbandage their wounds for us to see. In our post-Genesis 3 world with billions of firsthand experiences with evil, listening with open ears and hearts is our Christian duty. Any "Christianity" that plugs its ears is not worthy of the name.

The easy response is to roll our eyes and chalk others' experiences up to snowflakery or a Marxist conspiracy. Eye-rolling comes particularly easy to us if we have no personal experience of being mistreated because of our skin, sex, or status. We must fight the temptation to take that easy road. There really is something to the firsthand way in which truly oppressed people understand oppression that must never be sloughed off if we care about justice. Would we understand the true horrors of communism without Solzhenitsyn's *The Gulag Archipelago*, of Nazism without Anne Frank's *Diary*, of American racism without Solomon Northup's *Twelve Years a Slave*?

Consider the story of hip-hop artist Shai Linne:

This is about how being a black man in America has shaped both the way I see myself and the way others have seen me my whole life. . . . It's about being handcuffed and thrown into the back of a police car while walking down the street during college, and then waiting for a white couple to come identify whether or not I was the one who'd committed a crime against them, knowing that if they said I was the one, I would be immediately taken to jail, no questions asked. . . . It's about the exhaustion of constantly feeling I have to assert my humanity in front of some white people I'm meeting for the first time, to let them know, "Hey! I'm not a threat! You don't need to be afraid. If you got to know me, I'm sure we have things in common!" . . . It's about having to explain to my 4-year-old son at his mostly white Christian school that the kids who laughed at him for having brown skin were wrong, that God made him in his image, and that his skin is beautiful—after he told me, "Daddy, I don't want brown skin. I want white skin."[4]

Why should we listen to such heartbreaking lived experiences? Why take them seriously? Because we are Christians. Because we worship the God who told Moses at the burning bush, "I have surely seen the affliction of my people who are in Egypt and have heard their cry."[5] This is the same God who says of the oppressed, "I will surely hear their cry" and "If he cries to me, I will hear, for I am compassionate."[6] God listens, and so should we. This is where Tribes thinking becomes attractive to many Christians today. It markets itself as stepping into the painful lived experiences of the oppressed. But genuine Christian listening is not the same as hearing "lived experiences" in a Social Justice B kind of way. There are important differences. Here are two.

Rewiring Brains for Breakdown

Ponder how phobias work. A trio of brain regions—our amygdalae insulae, and anterior cingulate cortexes—function together as what doctors have called "the uh-oh center" or "the fear reflex" (one famous brain researcher calls it the "Oh s***!" area of the brain). At the genesis of many phobias we find lived experiences that light up the brain's uh-oh center like a Christmas tree. A scary childhood sickness, a panic attack in a tight space, or a humiliating social moment can rewire a brain for germaphobia, claustrophobia, or social phobia.

The psychological literature is clear that exposure therapy has tremendous healing effects for phobics. Why? Because the arachnophobe who dares to pet a tarantula may learn that not all spiders are out to kill him. The germaphobe eating chips from the communal party bowl learns that she won't drop dead from Ebola. The claustrophobe in a closet comes to realize that his heart won't explode in closed quarters.

As with exposure therapy, rational cognitive therapy also has a solid clinical track record of helping people heal. When our brain's uh-oh center ignites and freaks us out, our brain's assessment center goes dark. Assessment centers are found in the lateral prefrontal cortex, "which is involved in voluntarily modulating the responses from your Uh-Oh Center."[7] Cognitive therapists help people spark their assessment centers so we can challenge the catastrophic signals of our uh-oh centers.

Good psychologists help phobics *ungeneralize.* Whether through exposure or cognitive therapy, good psychologists help people internalize that specific trauma should not be generalized in a way that the whole world begins to feel more traumatic than it already is. Trauma from *this* spider does not mean *all* spiders are out to kill you; trauma from *this* sickness does not mean the whole microscopic world is plotting your death from every doorknob. Good psychologists help rewire phobic brains to realize the world is not, in fact, as terrifying as their brain's uh-oh center would have them believe.

Tribes thinking does the exact opposite of what good psychologists do. It *generalizes.* That spider bit you. Listen to all these other stories of lethal spider bites. Here are some Facebook groups, podcasts, public protests, and college courses to remind you daily that the spiders—*or rather the theocrats, racists, Islamophobes, bigots, exploiters, and sexists*—are out to get you! The brain's assessment center is bypassed. *People questioning whether the spiders are out to get you are probably spiders themselves!* The uh-oh center is ignited, and Tribes thinking allows for nothing that might stop the flames from spreading until the whole brain turns to ash.

This is where "lived experience" comes in. If a little boy, call him Johnny, has been convinced that most if not all spiders are out to get him, then imagine what Johnny will experience the next time he spots a daddy longlegs under his bed. He will experience fear from an arachnid that is clearly an existential threat. He really, truly feels it is out to get him. Johnny's lived experience is *his* reality. The only problem is that Johnny's reality is not reality. Daddy longlegs spiders are harmless to humans.

Next comes the confirmation bias. Imagine I tell my son, "Women in this world will hate you because you're a boy. Beware the vicious feminists!" What will happen when he hears what virtually every little kid hears from some other kid at some point: "I hate you" or "You're dumb"? These words sting for any kid. But my son will not hear just that he is hated or dumb. He will hear "You're hated or dumb *because you're a boy.*" That will be his lived experience, even if he is the victim of standard childish jabs and not *gender-motivated* childish jabs. How can he tell the difference? If he is sufficiently indoctrinated, he can't. He will deeply feel more boy-hatred in the world than actually exists.

Little Suzy, who has been indoctrinated to believe that an evil patriarchy is out to crush her feminine spirit, is taunted by Billy on the playground. Granted, little Billy is a walking, mudslinging case for original sin. But Suzy will experience his verbal assaults not as a fallen boy doing what fallen boys do, and what fallen boys do to other boys no less. She will experience it as confirmation of her mother's propaganda to beware the all-pervasive patriarchy. To the extent that ideology takes root in her soul, she will *experience* Billy as the incarnation of patriarchal oppression, the living, mouth-breathing, snot-nosed, insult-hurling proof that Western culture is indeed a grand conspiracy against her and her XX chromosomes. How can Suzy tell whether she is a victim of sexism—gender-motivated meanness—or run-of-the-mill meanness? Again, if she is sufficiently indoctrinated, she can't tell the difference. She ends up deeply feeling far more girl-hatred in the world than actually exists. The indoctrination of little Suzys around the world ends up having an ironic effect. More girls than boys will end up bearing the weight of perceived hatred under this ideology, which is a form of male-privilege that *the ideology itself* brings into reality.

Some will read me as saying there's no such thing as gender discrimination or racism; they're a grand illusion, a conspiracy fobbed on us by leftwing media or the Marxist infiltrators. That is *not* what I'm saying. There are real creepy spiders with venomous bites in the world. There are real misogynists and real racists. When they strike, it is the Christian mandate to listen and love the struck. My point is that to love people well—especially people who bear the wounds of racism, sexism, or any other sinful ism—we must be careful not to inadvertently pour salt in their wounds with an ideology that generalizes their trauma. If we care about people, we shouldn't turn them into festering balls of suspicion and anxiety.

I have seen it happen and it's heartbreaking. A twenty-one-year-old is reasonably happy, socially connected, creative, curious, and kind. Her professors fill her head with Tribes thinking, deconstructing Shakespeare as patriarchal propaganda. Before long, every male in her life becomes a conniving power-hungry Iago plotting her demise. Her indoctrinators perhaps believed they were turning a soft "yes-girl" into a fearless warrior woman to join their just cause. I do not see a fearless warrior woman. I see a fear-racked, perpetually triggered, cynical, seething, paranoid, isolated person with the light snuffed out of her beautiful eyes. I've seen it happen more times and to more precious souls than I care to recount. As one former Tribes thinker describes his experience, "We . . . saw insidious oppression and exploitation in all social relationships, stifling our ability to relate to others or ourselves without cynicism. Activists anxiously pore over interactions, looking for ways in which the mundane conceals domination. To see every interaction as containing hidden violence is to become a permanent victim, because if all you are is a nail, everything looks like a hammer."[8]

If Tribes thinking has us seeing ourselves primarily as oppressed, then most everything around us will look like oppression. What effect did such nail-and-hammer thinking have on this young radical's soul? It left him "exhausted and misanthropic, because any action or statement can be shown with sufficient effort to hide privilege, a microaggression, or unconscious bias."[9]

Note his words: "a permanent victim," "exhausted and misanthropic." In short, Tribes thinking is mean. It adds psychological oppression to those already suffering. The more we come to think that reality is best understood as the oppression of theocrats, racists, Islamophobes, bigots, exploiters, and sexists, the more our brains are rewired for a chronic state of fear[10]—a kind of "oppressi-phobia." The oppressi-phobic's brain can't stop seeing "every interaction as containing hidden violence."

They will believe they have been retraumatized by the person who made a thoughtless comment. They will see that person as the embodiment of all the evils of the West. But the true culprits of their daily retraumatization are those who indoctrinated him with Tribes thinking in the first place—professors, journalists, and entertainers who fancy themselves liberators. Rarely do such influencers stop to look behind the bars they have built in young brains to behold their disciples wallowing in self-pity and fear instead of enjoying the world God made. There is such a thing as *psychological* oppression. If we train brains to see oppression everywhere and never question "lived experience" then we, the self-appointed liberators, have become the oppressors. Consider the insights of sociologist Musa al-Gharbi:

> There is *abundant* research demonstrating harm caused by heightened *perceptions* of racism, discrimination, racialized violence, and racial inequality. There are very well-established and highly-adverse impacts of the psychological (and even physical) well-being of people of color when they perceive more racism, racial inequality, and discrimination.... We have ample reason to believe that sensitizing people to better perceive and take greater offense at these "slights" actually *would* cause harm.[11]

Do you see al-Gharbi's point? If we teach along with Robin DiAngelo that "the societal default is oppression; there are no spaces free from it," that the question should be "'*How* is it manifesting here?' rather than '*Is* it manifesting here?'"[12] then we aren't defending the oppressed; we are adding to their number. We are inadvertently adding to the net anxiety, depression, anger, and fear in the universe.

Psychological oppression is not just a risk for those on the left. For Christians on the right, be careful not to play the same cruel game in reverse, raising generations to live in chronic fear of those evil "secularists," "liberals," "Marxists," "evolutionists," "immigrants," "homosexuals," or whatever. As Christians, we must do better. Fear must never be a prime motivator in any thoroughly Christian justice. We must not teach any ideology—left or right—that pumps enough wattage into people's uh-oh Centers to light up Times Square. That would be mean. That would not be loving our neighbors. That would be oppressive. Especially in an age of social media, which capitalizes on fear in both directions, Christians must be radically countercultural.

The Bible is as anti-fear as it is anti-oppression.

Think of such fear biblically. The Bible is as anti-fear as it is anti-oppression. God commands us to "fear not" over a hundred times. God is not only pro-justice; he is also pro-fearlessness, and we should be too. It is not enough to merely be on the side of the oppressed. If we aren't *for* the oppressed without also being antifear—if we advance ideologies that generalize people's painful experiences, leave them chronically triggered, and set their uh-oh centers ablaze—then we should not pretend that we are doing the kind of justice Scripture commands.

Hurtful Experience and Helpful Evidence

This leads to a second way in which elevating lived experience can end up inadvertently hurting people we care about. As I pointed out at the beginning of the book, no one is pro-injustice. No one waves "Boo Justice!" or "Hooray Oppression!" signs. We all like to believe we're on the "right side of history." We can't all be right. The difference between those who *do* justice and those who merely *think* they do comes down to the question of truth.

Imagine a scenario in which the president can give the thumbs up to drop bombs on a compound that may be a terrorist headquarters. Half the White House situation room is convinced there are only terrorists inside. The other half believes it is a school packed with innocent children. One half says, "Fire away!" The other half passionately objects. Which half believes they are doing justice? *Both.* Which half, if they had their way, would *actually* be doing justice? It all comes down to the facts, the evidence, and the reality of the situation on the ground. If it is, in fact, a school, then the pro-bomb crowd would be committing a terrible injustice no matter how just they believed their actions to be. If it is, in fact, a terrorist headquarters, then the anti-bomb crowd would be accomplishing nowhere near the amount of justice they believe they are. It's the *facts* that matter.

Perhaps we should be less concerned about being on the so-called right side of history—a phrase so easily deployed to feel good about ourselves and demonize our opponents—and more concerned with being on the right side of *truth*. If we're on the wrong side of truth, then no matter how virtuous we believe ourselves to be, we are adding to the net injustice in the world.

Herein lies the problem with Tribes thinking. Our lived experiences can be wrong. Mine often are. Just this morning I had a lived experience of my wife being annoyed at me. My sense of injustice kicked in. It turned out to have nothing whatsoever to do with me. I figured it out eventually, but only by questioning my own feelings long enough to take the facts seriously (facts like our three-year-old biting our five-year-old's finger and our eight-year-old ignoring several requests to practice basic hygiene).

There is often a big difference between feelings and facts, between lived experience and objective reality. That difference matters, and we should take both seriously if we want our quest for justice to lead to real justice.

Yet we hear something very different from many Social Justice B scholars.

We hear that the lived experiences of the oppressed should be paramount over and against oppressive notions like objective truth, facts, research, and evidence. According to Shay-Akil McLean, "The idea of objectivity in western intellectual traditions is problematic for many reasons. . . . And to think there are universal truths perpetuates a particular kind of able-bodied white cisgender male logic."[13] In her diversity curriculum used by some of the biggest companies in the world, one of the seminal works of "anti-racism," Judith Katz argues that "objective, rational, linear thinking," "controlled emotions," "the scientific method," and "quantitative research" are all defining marks of racist "white culture" (Katz includes such values as "Individual has primary responsibility," "Working hard brings success," "Plan for future," "Delayed gratification," "Value continual improvement and progress," "Written tradition," "Owning goods, space, property," "Nuclear family is the ideal social unit," and "Belief in Christianity" as "Components of White Culture"). [14] Another professor argues that requests for evidence of oppression is itself a form of "epistemic exploitation," "epistemic injustice," and "epistemic oppression."[15] Still another adds that to free ourselves from oppressive ideologies, "we must learn to trust our own senses, feelings, and experiences, and to give them authority."[16]

This kind of thinking has swept through universities around the West. We have generations raised on a steady soundtrack of "always believe in yourself" and "follow your heart" anthems sung by cartoon characters and pop stars. Many then go off to college, already well primed to accept their professors' encouragement to treat their own feelings and experiences authoritatively, while questioning facts, evidence, and the search for objective truth as the tools of white cisgender racist male oppression.

As Jonathan Haidt has noted, this leads to a shift in higher education from "Truth University" to "Social Justice University." Truth U exists for the open-minded pursuit of knowledge. It is a place where "all become smarter" through "a process in which flawed individuals challenge each other's biased and incomplete reasoning" with a shared goal in mind—truth. The ultimate reason Social Justice U exists is "changing the world in part by overthrowing power structures and privilege."[17] One university encourages students to question their lived experiences and actively seek out contrary evidence. It welcomes diverse viewpoints. Why? Because its commitment to truth recognizes how biased, incomplete, and off base our understandings and experiences often are. It recognizes our shared need for a standard of reality higher than our fallible selves.

There are important questions we might ask, like: On which campus— Truth U or Social Justice U—are we more likely to find students caught in downward spirals of fear, suspicion, and resentment? On which campus are we more likely to find students inspired by the literary beauty of Shakespeare, Dostoyevsky's probing insights of human nature, or the Western world's hard-won triumphs over global slavery in the eighteenth and nineteenth centuries? On which campus are we more likely to find open-mindedness or humility among the student body?

For the purposes of this chapter, there is a still deeper question. *Which campus is more likely to produce the kind of students who will go out into the world and help make it a more just place?* Since truth is the decisive factor between *doing* justice and merely *thinking* we are, it is no mystery which university's students would bring more justice to the world.

Making the lived experience of the oppressed authoritative and writing off counterevidence as oppressive adds oppression to the world. Counterevidence may be the very thing that helps most. I offer one example.

Pretend you are in Chile in 1970. Outspoken socialist Salvador Allende is running for president. Socially concerned church leaders weigh in. Priests rooting for Allende from the parish in Santiago declare, "Socialism . . . offers a possibility for the development of the country for the benefit of all, especially the most neglected."[18] Leaders from the Workers' Catholic Action Movement supported Allende because his "Socialism generate[s] new values which make possible the emergence of a society of greater solidarity and brotherhood."[19] Why were they so committed to Allende's socialism? "The profound reason for this commitment is our faith in Jesus Christ."[20]

You raise questions but are told you are cancelling the lived experiences of the poor, siding with the Western capitalist oppressors. This is where things get problematic. Allende wins. He begins implementing socialist policies, collectivizing land and agriculture to reduce the unjust disparities between rich and poor. Inflation skyrockets 600 percent, and poverty rates spike 50 percent. What occurred wasn't "the development of the country for the benefit of all, especially the most neglected" but the further destitution, scarcity, and even more people forced into the sad ranks of the neglected. There wasn't "greater solidarity and brotherhood;" there was more protesting and strife.[21]

It is common to use people's tragic lived experiences to push a political vision, advertise that vision with winsome words such as *solidarity*, compassion for "the neglected," and even "faith in Jesus Christ," then assume anyone who doesn't accept our political vision is anti-solidarity, anti-"the neglected," and anti-"faith in Jesus." Here's the problem. A mother endures the lived experience of seeing her family torn apart by immigration enforcement agents. That happens and it's horrible. Another mother has the lived experience of seeing her family torn apart by a homicide committed by an illegal immigrant. That also happens and it's horrible. I am not taking sides on the immigration debate here. I am simply pointing out that both of these women's lived experiences can be used to advance opposite political visions. Both visions can use noble language to market themselves. Both can charge anyone who questions these visions with failing to show "solidarity" with these "neglected" mothers and failing to represent their "faith in Jesus." But which mother's lived experience should be made more authoritative than the other's if we want to use their experiences to promote this or that public policy? It's not so easy to highlight one without erasing the other in such a way that one mob or the other won't come after you for your utter lack of compassion.

To end where we began, everyone thinks they are on the right side of history. The difference between those actually making the world better and those who only *think* they are has everything to do with the facts. Lived experiences matter. They matter in working for important social changes, as Alexander Solzhenitsyn, Anne Frank, Solomon Northup, and many others have proved. We should never write off people's pain but should instead listen with open ears and "weep with those who weep."[22] But using the lived experiences of the oppressed to push noble sounding visions of social justice and insulate those visions from factual criticisms is not compassionate. It is cruel to the oppressed. It exploits their pain. It adds to their number. Again, as Christians commanded to *truly* execute justice, we have to do better.

BELLA'S STORY

Raised in a Christian home, I knew the gospel years before I wanted it. I wanted life on my own terms; I wanted love I could deserve. By the time I started college, I had all but "deleted" God from my life. I chased the mirage of love through fraternity houses, down bottles of liquor, and into the beds of strangers. Soon I was empty, afraid, and aching. I made new friends who had a "solution" to my pain: fighting injustice with anger. I learned that all men are predators, that religion is oppressive, and that "truth" and "morality" are only constructs. If I just converted fear into anger and rejected all these institutions, I would be free.

What I didn't know is that when you choose an anger-fueled life, you choose a fear-controlled life. I feared men and anticipated abuse constantly. I saw social injustice everywhere, and it appeared to be winning.

And scariest of all, I didn't know where to find my self-worth. If morality didn't exist, how could I ever hope to be "good"? After two years of living this way, I was a mess. I desperately needed to recalibrate and decided to take a year off from school.

I took an internship with an anti-sex-trafficking organization in Germany. I tolerated that it was a Christian organization. I wanted to be enough to save these women but was no match for this evil—women sold for consumption, men addicted to dehumanizing abuse, and pimps using sex as a weapon. Absolute evil really did exist, and I was looking at it. How were my Christian coworkers not drowning in this darkness as I was? In that stillness, I heard a whisper. It said this darkness wasn't the end of the story, that without a good God, this would be all there was, but God cannot be deleted. I remembered Jesus and how his promises to heal this world finally made sense. And so, on a cold spring morning, I walked outside and cried out to him. The heart transformation was immediate; God released me from anger and fear. Years of shame slid off me and I was clean. While I was still a sinner, Christ died to purchase my heart, and I was made whole.

I transferred to Biola University to pursue God. I had no idea of the pain that awaited me in California. A week after moving, I ventured off campus to go dancing in LA with my new roommates. A group of young men drugged me and gang-raped me until five in the morning. When I woke up, there was no denying the black bruises covering my body or the flashbacks of cruel violence. I told my roommate, who sobbed with me and went with me to the police station.

As we drove to the station, I expected to feel hopeless, dirtied, and lost. Instead, I felt perfect peace. My Father was holding me in his arms, and I could feel it. I played "In Christ Alone," singing and worshiping God with deep joy. I can't put into words how deeply I understood his love that day. Though I could never earn his love, he pours it into my heart. I am his precious, beloved daughter; no evil could ever change that. Even through horrible flashbacks and anxiety attacks, I stand firm in this confidence. The final chapter of my story is already written and waits for me; it ends with me running into the Father's open arms. No power of hell or scheme of man could ever pluck me from his hand.

I have a new heart, one that sees every human as a precious creation of God's love. I do not hate anyone, not even my rapists. I know those men are responsible for their wrongs, but I also know God longs for their hearts as recklessly as he longed for mine. Jesus paid my full debt on the cross, and anyone who turns to Jesus has theirs paid too. I still care deeply about justice for victims of sexual violence, now more than ever. However, I no longer use hatred and fear as fuel for revenge. Instead, I draw on God's perfect love for restoration. Fear can't drive out fear, nor hate drive out hate, only love can do that. And God's love can and will heal the pains of this world a thousand times over, just as it healed mine.

–Bella Danusiar

Bella is a student at Biola University and is currently training for lifelong gospel ministry and justice work.

Questions for Personal or Small Group Study

1. Lived experiences matter. It would be easy to write off people's stories if we immediately associate them with political ideologies we disagree with. How can we resist this urge and be more present with people in their pain? How can we bring the gospel to bear on their pain?
2. God commands us to be fearless. In what ways can we end up inadvertently making people more fearful and easily triggered in the name of "social justice"?
3. Why is the pursuit of truth so essential to the biblical pursuit of justice, and how does Tribes thinking derail us in that pursuit? How can serious thinking and research, even if our conclusions go against the political orthodoxies of our day, make us more effective in loving the oppressed?

Chapter 12

The Standpoint Question

Does our vision of social justice turn the
quest for truth into an identity game?

Tribes thinking can make us see things that aren't there and miss things that are. It can elevate lived experience in ways that make oppression worse. It can also make its own conclusions unfalsifiable by turning the quest for truth into an identity game.

We must first understand what philosophers mean by the clumsy term *unfalsifiable*. If no amount of logic, evidence, experience, or Scripture could possibly change our outlook, then our beliefs are unfalsifiable.

A man sitting next to you on a train clutches your arm and whispers, "The KGB is after me." You politely explain that the security arm of the Soviet Union has been disbanded since 1991. "That's exactly what a clandestine organization would *want* you to think," he replies. "The devil's greatest trick was convincing the world he doesn't exist. Trust me, red devils are everywhere!" He motions with his eyes to a man reading a newspaper across the aisle. "That's one there," he whispers.

"Looks like a businessman in a suit to me," you reply.

"That's how disguises work, dummy! You think he'd wear one of those furry ear hats while reading the Communist Manifesto and humming *Slav'sya, Otechestvo nashe svobodnoye?*"

Just then the stranger across the aisle interrupts, "Excuse me. Which way to the dining car? Caffeine time, if you know what I mean."

You point him the right direction. "Not much of a Russian accent," you remark.

"Of course! Foreign agents are trained to master every voice inflection of the people they're infiltrating. No doubt, he's probably gone to alert one of his comrades to my presence, probably an assassin."

Your paranoid travel companion's problem is that an *unfalsifiable* belief consumes him. No matter how much counterevidence you supply, he can always find a way to jimmy that evidence into his own theory. "Friend," you say sympathetically, "here he comes with his coffee and no assassin in sight. You're in the clear."

After a long, tense pause, your travel companion turns and stares you down with a look of shock and betrayal. His quivering voice swells into a rage, "Y-y-yooouuu. You're one of, of, them! You're the red devil's assassin!" That you have questioned his conspiracy only proves that you are part of the conspiracy. Only a clever KGB agent, after all, would try to lull an innocent man into a false sense of security and friendship.

A good belief system, unlike that of our unfortunate traveler, can spell out the ways in which it could be proved false. Take Christianity, for example. In 1 Corinthians 15, Paul says that if Jesus died and stayed dead, if his bodily resurrection turned out to be a legend or hoax, then the Christian faith would crumble into falsehood.

By contrast, Tribes thinking comes complete with programmed responses that safeguard its core beliefs from any system-crashing virus of contrary evidence. If a man tries to say a preborn human being is more than a clump of cells, then the Tribes OS quickly generates the response, "No womb, no say." A white woman attends a conference on peace-making where she is informed that her "whiteness is wickedness." If she disagrees, the Tribes OS says she suffers from "white fragility." (Bestselling race educator Robin DiAngelo, who coined the term, clarifies that white fragility can be identified by defensive emotions like feeling "judged," actions like "denying," or words like "I disagree."[1] Yes, simply saying "I disagree" is evidence of white fragility.)

A white scholar questions the Social Justice B narrative of vast systemic racism. She is seen as proving her own racism, protecting her privilege, or complicit in white supremacy. If she uses logic and evidence, then she is using white constructs like logic and evidence to oppress or erase people of color.

Black scholars write dozens of books with rigorous evidence that challenges the Social Justice B narrative. The Tribes OS neatly files them away under "internalized racism," perhaps even labeling them "race traitors," "coons," "Oreos" or "Coconuts" for being black on the outside and white on the inside.

None of these examples are fictional, nor are they uncommon. If you spend much time on the digital battlefields of social media (which I don't recommend), you know that this style of thinking has skyrocketed in recent years.

Sixty years ago, under the sway of modernism, ideas were typically criticized in the West if they lacked evidence. Ten to twenty years ago, as postmodernism broke mainstream, ideas were criticized not so much because they lacked evidence but because they lacked "tolerance." If a view claimed to be *the* truth instead of *a* truth, it was dismissed as intolerant. Today, as we have entered what I have called the "post-postmodern" era,[2] it is not a lack of evidence or a lack of tolerance but a lack of melanin or a lack of a second X chromosome that makes someone's ideas wrong.

Melanin over Merit

Critics will point to my melanin, gender, sexual orientation, economic status, or faith to attack the ideas I am setting forth. There will likely be charges of fragility, blaming the victim, and protecting my privilege.

Any basic logic text would tell us that attacking people for their personal traits or perceived motives instead of their ideas themselves is a fallacy known as *ad hominem*, Latin for "to the person." Instead of seriously engaging ideas we disagree with, which requires mental energy, we can simply shift focus to the person, citing skin tone or gender, or assuming bad motives, which requires no mental energy. "You disagree with me? Clearly you are motivated by hate, bigotry, phobia, white supremacy, or white fragility." The problem with such Tribes thinking is that it erases the Creator-creature distinction, assuming we have an X-ray vision into others' hearts, an omniscience about people's true motives that only God has.

The more under the power of Tribes thinking we become, the less we will care whether we violate the laws of logic with *ad hominem* fallacies. Why? Because we are told that "objective, rational, linear thinking" is a mark of "whiteness" and that "the idea that objectivity is best reached only through rational thought is a specifically Western and masculine way of thinking."[3] One activist tells us we must "accept the grievances of faculty of color *without question*."[4] And what if you do raise questions? "We are inflicting harm asking for evidence . . . to ask for evidence of racism is racism with a capital R."[5]

Do you see how Social Justice B makes itself unfalsifiable? It shifts our focus from "isms" to "ists," from ideas to people, from evidence to people's external identity markers. This is attractive to many. Why? It offers a way to become irrefutable authorities on extremely complex issues. All we have to do is memorize a handful of condemning buzzwords—white fragility, white privilege, male privilege, toxic masculinity, internalized racism, epistemic exploitation—and at no point do we have to do the hard work of engaging any evidence that contradicts our worldview. Why? Because if anyone challenging us is an oppressor, by definition, then there can be no such thing as a reasonable challenge to our doctrines. In short, Tribes thinking is too easy. We can process ideas as true or false based purely on *melanin* rather than *merit*, *private parts* over *persuasiveness*, and *economic status* over *evidential substance*.

The problem is that ideas don't have melanin, private parts, or bank accounts; people do. Jesus wasn't a white European but a brown Middle Easterner who used logical arguments such as *modus ponens, reductio ad absurdum, argumentum a fortiori* as part of his stated life mission to "bear witness to the truth."[6] He used empirical evidence such as restored bodies, empty tombs, and nail-scarred hands to substantiate his extraordinary claims. With logic and evidence, Dorothy Hodgkin did pioneering work with X-rays, penicillin, vitamins, and insulin that has blessed countless lives. NASA's "hidden figures"— Katherine Johnson, Dorothy Johnson Vaughan, and Mary Jackson—used logic and evidence to smash through barriers in space exploration. Shinya Yamanaka's breakthroughs in mature cell pluripotency paved the way to save countless lives with stem cell research that doesn't require the destruction of human embryos. Charles Octavius Boothe made great theological leaps forward with his keen eye for biblical interpretation. This is just a tiny sampling of millions of image-bearers of all stripes and shades who used their God-given intellects to make the world a better place. Why should we deconstruct logic and evidence as trademarks of malevolent whiteness?

If the argument is simply that appeals to logic and evidence have been used to justify oppression through history, then sure. Tragically, that has been true, and we must work to make it untrue for future generations. Just a hundred years ago, notable high-brows of British Society—H. G. Wells, George Bernard Shaw, Julian Huxley, and Neville Chamberlain—supported eugenics, the pseudoscience used to justify racism and the involuntary sterilization of genetic "undesirables." In America, such pseudoscience was all the rage in universities.[7] It was embedded in the founding mission of Planned Parenthood. It was particularly devastating for black communities. Surely, such oppressive visions of genetic inferiority claimed to have logic and evidence on their side, just as slave owners and segregators through American history claimed to have Scripture on their side. The antidote to oppressive pseudoscience and racist theology is *better* science, *better* biblical interpretation, and *more* logic and evidence. The more truth we find, the less dark corners racist ideologies have in which to hide.

The way to avoid repeating the sins of the past is by letting truth shine forth from whatever source we find it. It is not by making truth a matter of group identity. Take the arguments I have set forth in this book. It is not hard to find them articulated from thinkers in virtually every social demographic I don't belong to. The points I have made have been articulated far better than I ever could by thinkers such as Rosaria Butterfield, Sidney Callahan, Elizabeth Corey, Walter Williams, Glenn Loury, Voddie Baucham, Shelby Steele, Neil Shenvi, and many others. Do arguments magically become true or false by putting them in someone else's mouth? No. Writing off someone's viewpoint because of their melanin levels makes us actual racists. Dismissing someone's argument because of their gender makes us actual sexists. Silencing someone's ideas because of their sexuality, their economic status, or any other quality of their lives rather than the quality of their ideas does not make us a voice of justice for the marginalized; it makes us actual bigots.

Take the laws of aeronautics, for example. We have the Wright brothers to thank for pioneering many breakthroughs in aviation. Their ideas helped propel humans through the air not because the Wright brothers were *white* but because their ideas were *true*. Had it been a different set of brothers or sisters with different coloring, their breakthroughs would still be true. And if we flew over a region that rejected the aeronautical laws they discovered, we would not suddenly plummet from the sky. Why? Because the laws of aeronautics are *objectively* true. They remain true even if people disagree with them and regardless of the color, gender, or ancestry of the people articulating them. This is the way physical laws work. It is why penicillin works whether or not you think it will. If the laws of justice are like the laws of nature, if justice is a real thing and not an imaginary construct, then we should expect statements about justice to be true regardless of the color, gender, or social status of those who articulate them. We wouldn't write off an aeronautical engineer's research because of his or her skin tone, and we shouldn't resort to playing such identity games as we seek a more true justice together.

Tribes thinking plays that identity game, leaving its vision of justice severely distorted. James Cone, for example, tells us, "If there is one brutal fact that centuries of white oppression have taught blacks, it is that whites are incapable of making any valid judgments about human existence."[8] Don't bother reading Isaac Newton, Fyodor Dostoyevsky, C. S. Lewis, John Calvin, Dorothy Sayers, William Wilberforce, Flannery O'Connor, Jane Austen, J. K. Rowling, or others who are pigmentally challenged. You won't find any "valid judgments about human existence." Their color makes that quite impossible because they are the same shade of pale as those who unleashed "centuries of white oppression." It is irrelevant whether people with the same color historically stamped out slavery around the globe or cured polio. To keep the game of identity politics going, focus only on the "white oppression." And we mustn't think too seriously about the nonwhite casualties of Templo Mayor, Genghis Khan, Mao Zedong, Idi Amin, Pablo Escobar, the Taliban, or other countless examples of oppression.

There is a related problem with Tribes thinking. If old white guys represent an oppressive patriarchy we must abolish, then we may ask, Why does so much Social Justice B doctrine sound so close to the economic theories of Marx, Engels, or Bernie Sanders? Why does it advance Rousseau's vision that institutions, not fallen human hearts, are the source of evil? Why does it often defend the abortion ruling of seven powerful robed men, embrace the expressive sexual ethics crafted by Herbert Marcuse and Wilhelm Reich, espouse an oppressor versus oppressed narrative championed by Antonio Gramsci and the all-white male Frankfurt school, employ the deconstructionist tactics invented by Foucault and Derrida, and practice the political tactics of Saul Alinsky? These architects of Tribes thinking share something fascinating: they were well-off white guys.[9] The epistemological color game is played in only one direction—namely, against those of lighter shades who question the doctrines of Social Justice B.

There is a deeper point here we should care about, particularly as Christians. That is, the more we start weighing ideas on the *melanin* of the idea-speaker rather than the *merit* of the idea itself, the more difficult it will become for us to love God with all our minds the way Scripture commands. If we care about the greatest commandment and the pursuit of truth, we must actively resist the identity games of Tribes thinking. We must weigh ideas based on Scriptural fidelity over social status.[10]

The Infallible Poor

Tribes thinking works in two directions. As we have seen, your appearance tells the Tribes thinker virtually all they need to know about whether you have any insight to offer. If you happen to share identity markers in common with those in any of its featured oppressor groups, then it matters very little how much love you display for atheist, minority, Muslim, gay, lesbian, poor, or opposite gendered people. You will be treated as what Thomas Sowell calls "an intertemporal abstraction," what Shelby Steele calls "a cipher" or "non-individuated member of your group."

But Tribes thinking works the other way too. Those on the oppressed side of the equation are often granted automatic authority. One way this bit of Tribes thinking makes its way into Christian circles is with the oft-repeated mantra that "God is on the side of the poor and oppressed."[11] That's certainly true, depending on what we mean. We could mean one of two things. First, it could mean something like I meant two weeks ago when my six-year-old daughter was stung by a bee. My wife and I had special concern for her not because we love her siblings any less but because she was especially in pain and distress. We find such special concern for the poor all over Scripture. God is in such deep solidarity with those in the pains of poverty that the Proverbs say, "Whoever oppresses a poor man insults his Maker," and "Whoever is generous to the poor lends to the Lord."[12] God speaks judgment against those who cheat the poor.[13] God's law mandates special protections for widows and orphans. The essence of true religion, according to Scripture, is "to visit orphans and widows in their affliction."[14] Philosopher Nicholas Wolterstorff sums up the Scriptures well: "God's love for justice is grounded in his love for the victims of injustice. And his love for the victims of injustice belongs to his love for the little ones of the world: for the weak, the defenseless, the ones at the bottom, the excluded ones, the miscasts, the outcasts, the outsiders."[15]

There is another way to read "being on the side of the poor and oppressed." In Tribes thinking, taking the poor's side sometimes includes taking the poor's lived experience as authoritative in everything from biblical interpretation to public policy.

However, God's solidarity with the poor and oppressed in Scripture never means that he elevates their perspective to sacred, unquestionable status.[16] Sin afflicts both the poor and the rich, and both need salvation. The "all" of "all have sinned and fall short of the glory of God"[17] includes rich, poor, privileged, underprivileged, haves, and have-nots. The oppressed in Egypt were hardly infallible. They bowed to the golden calf. The paralyzed man in Luke 5 was far from rich. And Jesus says, "Man, your sins are forgiven."[18] God is "not wishing that any should perish, but that all should reach repentance."[19] "Any" and "all" includes the oppressed. We all need repentance. God does not suggest but commands that we not "be partial to a poor man in his lawsuit."[20] Scripture puts strong standards of evidence for accusations of injustice.[21] It never encourages to take people's word for it if they claim to be victims of oppression. The Bible is far too realistic about the human potential for deception to let justice rest on such a shaky foundation. The biblical quest for justice is simply incompatible with the Social Justice B identity game of making truth a matter of social status, color, or gender.

Anthony Evans argues that the black experience must be seen as "real but not revelatory, important but not inspired."[22] Tom Skinner agrees: "There are some black theologians who seek to make their frame of reference purely the black experience, but this assumes the black experience is absolutely moral and absolutely just, and that is not the case. There must be a moral frame of reference through which the black experience can be judged."[23]

This objection may come: "Williams is asking us to interrogate the oppressed, while the oppressors seemingly get a free pass." No. Our Lord preached the gospel of salvation to the poor, and he preached the same message to the rich.[24] We are all fallen. We are all fallible. We all need grace. No one's perspective, including my own, is free from the truth-blurring power of sin, except God's perspective. Granting unquestionable status to the poor and oppressed or to anything other than the Word of God is to erase the Creator-creature distinction. And when we erase the difference between God and his creatures, what we call "justice" is sure to become injustice.

FREDDY'S STORY

I was born in rural Appalachia with flickering electricity and no running water. We bathed in the cool gray-shale water of a turn-of-the-century metal wash tub. We had a two-seat outhouse as primitive as any you've ever seen in a TV Western. I've heard people say, "We grew up poor, but we never knew it." Well, *we knew it*. And nobody would let us forget it.

Raised by our single mom, my brother and I were "half-breeds," or so we were told. I honestly didn't know what I was—except *different*. My dominant genes drew more melanin. In the rugged mountains of Tennessee, my twin and I were the only people of color. We scored the social-pariah trifecta: poor, fatherless, and dark-skinned.

These factors were immediately evident in visible ways, including my clothing, grooming, vocabulary, and social graces. I suffered daily harassment, frequent attacks by young gangs, and verbal terrorism from adults. The piercing stares, nods of dismissive disapproval, and being called every racial pejorative in existence, regardless of the inaccuracy of nearly all the terms, was a way of life.

In my early teens, as these forces increasingly impacted me, I met Christ. A divorced white lady reached out to disciple me two hours a week, for two years. It was a death knell for her social life. After that, a young white part-time minister discipled me. Then later, an older white pastor. Then, in my duress, a wealthy white church member provided me with much-needed clothes. Generous white widows in the church helped me pay for Christian summer camp.

Ultimately, God called me to ministry. I ended up going to a majority-Anglo Christian university known for its fundamentalism. I was met with nearly universal support. I was challenged, called to high standards, and expected to perform. I didn't receive scholarships or anything resembling equal opportunity perks. Instead, I was given dignity, community, and accountability. These imparted me self-respect that was earned. God has been faithful. I became the first in my family to go to college. I have served for two decades in pastoral ministry. I have an earned PhD and serve as the dean of both a college ministry school and a graduate theological seminary. I'm an author, a good father, and an "amazing husband" (just ask my wife). Best of all, I have an intimate, personal walk with Jesus.

Over the years, I've pieced together the fact that those who wounded me were not racists and bigots *because they were white*; they were racists and bigots who *happened to be white*. I've learned that real racism is a product of sinful hearts, something that has nothing to do with the color of one's skin. I've learned that identity must be based in Christ, not rooted in ethnicity, heritage, or culture.

Sadly, because of these convictions and the direction of culture under the sway of Social Justice B, I've had several ironic experiences. Tribal identity has not only infected society; it is insidiously working its way into many Christian institutions, including Christian higher education. Christian academics have generally failed to do the hard work of Christian integration. As a result, many are seduced into unbiblical versions of social justice. The shocking twist is this. Although I am a minority who has encountered unmitigated racism in the past, I have become a pariah in many circles. Why? Because I reject today's trending justice ideologies. The intensity of attacks on people who reject identity-based tribalism has become a spiritual pathology in many Christian institutions. Even so, biblical justice exposes today's social justice as little more than a resounding gong or clanging cymbal. Lord, give us the courage to stand for your justice and against its counterfeits, no matter the threats to our reputations or livelihoods. You are worth it!

–Freddy Cardoza
Freddy serves as dean of Grace Theological Seminary, writes extensively,
and hosts multiple podcasts at www.freddycardoza.com

Questions for Personal or Small Group Study

1. God commands us to grieve with those who grieve, and feeling some-one else's grief is impossible if we don't listen well to their pain. What steps can we take as Christians to be better listeners, both to the pain of our brothers and sisters and to those who have yet to call God "Father"?

2. Scripture commands us to "truly execute justice," which implies that there are untrue ways to execute justice. Why is weighing ideas based on their merit rather than melanin, their credibility over chromosomes, and their scriptural fidelity over social status so important to doing true justice?

3. According to Scripture, God exhibits deep solidarity with the poor and commands us to care for them. What are three practical habits we can form to help us live these Scriptures well?

So You're Saying . . .

Given the power of the Newman effect in our day (see pp. 8–9), here are five points some may have heard me advancing in part 4, "Truth or Tribes Thinking? Three Questions About Social Justice and Knowledge":

1. "So you're saying that oppression in today's world is mostly a delusion, with zero factual evidence."

2. "So you're saying that anyone who cares about the oppression of non-Christians, people of color, Muslims, people of the LGBTQ community, the poor, or women is guilty of endorsing Social Justice B."

3. "So you're saying sinful discrimination doesn't cause any disparities in today's world."

4. "So you're saying that people's lived experiences don't matter, that people's encounters with injustice should be swept under the rug, and that we shouldn't grieve with those who grieve."

5. "So you're saying that we should not side with the poor and oppressed as God does."

No. I am not saying any of that. I don't believe any of that. If you are hearing any of that, then either the Newman effect is at work or I have simply done a poor job communicating, for which I pray you forgive me.

A Prayer to Pursue Truth over Tribes Thinking

God,

You command us to love you with our minds. You are the God of both justice and truth, and you call us to seek both together. When we replace the pursuit of truth with extrabiblical epistemologies, we begin seeing oppression in places where it isn't and overlooking it in places where it is. We push fear-inspiring narratives that inflict pain on those already aching. We assess ideas more on melanin than merit, project the worst motives onto those who disagree with us, and ignore evidence that contradicts our ideologies. We grant people's lived experiences an authority that belongs only to you and your Word. Help us be more like Jesus, who does "not judge by what his eyes see, or decide disputes by what his ears hear, but with righteousness he shall judge the poor, and decide with equity for the meek of the earth."[25] Sharpen our minds to obey Christ's command to "not judge by appearances, but judge with right judgment."[26] Match our justice-seeking with truth-seeking, that we may better reflect who you are to the watching world and more truly execute justice. Amen.

12 Differences Between Social Justice A and B

Now that we have asked our twelve questions, it should be clear that Social Justice B and Social Justice A are not two different political persuasions; they are two fundamentally different religions. I capture twelve of their clashing doctrines in the following chart:

	Social Justice A	Social Justice B
1.	. . . brings us to our knees before Jehovah as supreme and seeks a justice that begins with giving God his due. "You shall have no other gods before me" is where Social Justice A starts.	. . . erases the Creator-creature distinction and downplays the divine image in everyone. As with Jezebel turning ancient Israel to false gods, it lays us prostrate before the false gods of self, state, and social acceptance.
2.	. . . brings unity by acknowledging our shared blame in Adam and our new identities "in Christ." Jesus destroyed the wall of hostility between Jew and gentile to make for himself "one man," uniting people from every tongue, tribe, and nation and making them ambassadors of reconciliation. Family and reconciliation, not intergroup warfare, is the Bible's model for Christian living.	. . . leaves us in a state of uproar, breaking people into group identities, telling the most damnable edited histories of certain groups, making every individual of that group an exemplar of that evil, and blaming our current troubles on them. The predictable result is tribal warfare, one of the worst ideas in human history and with a staggering body count.
3.	. . . offers us the fruit of the Spirit, such as joy, peace, patience, kindness, goodness, gentleness, self-control.	. . . generates a spirit of mutual suspicion, hostility, fear, labeling, and resentment.

(cont.)

	Social Justice A	**Social Justice B**
4.	. . . champions a love that "is not easily offended."	. . . inspires in its followers a quickness to take offense.
5.	. . . sees evil not only in "systems," where we ought to seek justice, but also within the twisted hearts of those who make those systems unjust. All the external activism in the world will not bring lasting justice if we downplay our need for the regenerating, love-infusing work of God in the gospel.	. . . blames all evil on external systems of oppression, often assuming that any disparity is damning evidence of discrimination. It then makes activism against that discrimination a "gospel issue," often downplaying our need for repentance and saving grace.
6.	. . . assesses everyone of every ethnicity as guilty because of our group identity "in Adam." This guilt can be erased not by oppressed group affiliation but only by finding our new and deepest group identity in Jesus, "the second Adam." Rather than condemning people for ethnic or gender group identity, "there is now no condemnation for those who are in Christ Jesus" (Rom. 8:1).	. . . credits guilt on the basis of one's skin tone, condemning people because of their group identity. Individuals must then work off their "infinite guilt" by confessing their privilege and joining the Social Justice B mission to end all oppression as its leaders define "oppression."
7.	. . . confronts us with the humbling reality that our self-righteousness is like filthy rags and Christ is the only ground for our righteous standing.	. . . inspires self-righteousness; i.e., enables us to think, "I am not a bigot because I hold these particular views on social justice or am a member of this or that cultural identity group."
8.	. . . calls us to love God with our whole minds. This includes evaluating ideas on the basis of their biblical fidelity and truth value. It also includes acknowledging real oppression and listening well, while refusing to interpret all of God's world as a mere power play of oppressors vs. the oppressed.	. . . interprets all truth, reason, and logic as mere constructs of the oppressive class, encouraging us to dismiss someone's viewpoint on the basis of their skin tone, gender, or economic status.
9.	. . . teaches that the Creator defines our telos. The refusal to live within that telos brings oppression to ourselves and those around us. Real authenticity and freedom don't come from defining yourself and "following your heart" but from letting God define you and following his heart.	. . . teaches that the human telos (i.e., ultimate purpose and meaning) is defined by the creature and that anyone who challenges our self-defined telos is an oppressor.

	Social Justice A	Social Justice B
10.	... envisions the male-female differences as "very good"– distinctions that can't be erased without losing something precious. It highlights the male-female sexual union within the covenant of marriage as the only proper and life-giving context for human sexual expression.	... sees "heteronormative" sexual and gender distinctions as oppressive and seeks to liberate all forms of sexual behavior and gender expression from such "cisgender constructs."
11.	... accepts the full humanity and worth of unborn image-bearers of God and calls us to love and protect women and their offspring who are exploited or terminated by the abortion industry.	... celebrates abortion as an expression of female liberation from patriarchal oppression, excluding the preborn from its circle of justice.
12.	... celebrates family and upholds the rhythms of self-giving within family as a beautiful and God-ordained signpost of Jesus and his relationship to the church.	... interprets the nuclear family as an unjust patriarchal system of oppression, a construct that must be abolished.

From the previous chart, it is clear that Social Justice A and Social Justice B are both concerned about the oppressed, but in very different ways. *When we hear someone express concern about the way blacks or women are treated, we must be especially careful not to immediately lump them into the Social Justice B category.* As I have repeated throughout this book, there is real, sinful racism and sexism in the world. Assuming that a brother or sister who draws our attention to such injustice is automatically a Social Justice B advocate is hardly a way to advance church unity or true justice in the world.

Then there are some Christians who embrace perhaps one or two of the Social Justice B doctrines mentioned. We must also be careful not to project the entire system onto our brothers and sisters who may be wavering on a few points. That would not be helpful. There is, however, a predictable pattern: one Social Justice B doctrine tends to lead to another, then another, until many Christians end up abandoning their faith. I have watched this play out more times than I care to recall. With love as our motive, rather than dominating a political battle, we must winsomely point out to fellow Christians how Social Justice B makes it much harder for us to live the Scriptures together.

Its view of worship will make it harder to live out the first commandment, "Have no other gods before me."[1]

Its approach to community will make it that much harder to live out the beautiful truths of these verses:

> There is neither Jew nor Greek, there is neither slave nor free, there is no male and female, for you are all one in Christ Jesus.[2]

> He himself is our peace, who has made us both one and has broken down in his flesh the dividing wall of hostility.[3]

> Live peaceably with all.[4]

> The Lord's servant must not be quarrelsome but kind to everyone.[5]

> Walk in a manner worthy of the calling to which you have been called, with all humility and gentleness, with patience, bearing with one another in love, eager to maintain the unity of the Spirit in the bond of peace. There is one body and one Spirit—just as you were called to the one hope that belongs to your call—one Lord, one faith, one baptism, one God and Father of all, who is over all and through all and in all.[6]

Its approach to salvation will make it harder to take these passages seriously:

> All have sinned and fall short of the glory of God, and are justified by his grace as a gift, through the redemption that is in Christ Jesus.[7]

> Repent therefore, and turn back, that your sins may be blotted out.[8]

> If we confess our sins, he is faithful and just to forgive us our sins and to cleanse us from all unrighteousness.[9]

Its approach to knowledge will make it difficult to obey these divine commands:

> Love the Lord your God with all your heart and with all your soul and with all your mind.[10]

> [You] shall not be partial to a poor man in his lawsuit.[11]

> My brothers, show no partiality.[12]

Do not judge by appearances, but judge with right judgment.[13]

The more that Christian brothers and sisters get wrapped up in Social Justice B, the harder it becomes to live out these beautiful Scriptures.

Save the World from Suicide

This leaves us with one final question. *How do we best engage those who have been swept into the flow of Social Justice B?* We do so with the same tried-and-tested method the church has used for millennia. We preach "the faith that was once for all delivered to the saints."[14] We herald the good news that only Jesus can define the human telos in the deeply meaningful ways that we cannot. We offer the good news that we no longer have to pretend, and force others to pretend, that we are perfect. Jesus is perfect, and through his substitutionary death for our evil, he offers a new identity as infinitely beloved sons and daughters of God. We preach the good news of his bodily resurrection, by which he launched the age to come, with all its shalom and justice. We preach the same gospel that was able to bring real racial reconciliation to first-century Jews and gentiles and real liberation to the slaves of American and British history. We preach the only gospel that offers real meaning to our generation created to know and enjoy God. To those gasping for air under the crushing weight of Social B, we preach the gospel.

But that is not all. If we don't want to see more of our brothers and sisters abandon the gospel for Social Justice B, then we must show them through our words and actions just how compelling, beautiful, and liberating social justice can be when we do it God's way, by his grace, through his power, for his glory, and for the good of his image-bearers. We can't simply knock Social Justice B, then take a seat and fold our arms as if our work is done. We must take action and show our brothers and sisters, and indeed the watching world, what it means to "truly execute justice." I leave you with the words of T. S. Eliot: "The world is trying the experiment of attempting to form a civilized but non-Christian mentality. The experiment will fail; but we must be very patient in awaiting its collapse; meanwhile redeeming the time: so that the Faith may be preserved alive through the dark ages before us; to renew and rebuild civilization, and save the World from suicide."[15]

Acknowledgments

First, I'd like to thank my parents. They taught me how Christianity inspires justice not only in the Bible but also in potato fields and orange orchards, in food co-ops, in Tijuana shacks and jails. Thank you, Mom and Dad, for making serving the poor such a defining mark of my childhood. I'd also like to express gratitude to

... the living legend and civil rights hero John Perkins who never ceased to inspire me in our long chats about the gospel, justice, dignity, and how—with the Holy Spirit's help—to answer hate with love.

... my friend, mentor, and colleague J. P. Moreland whose ongoing encouragement (bordering at times on harassment) kept me motivated through the many times I felt like throwing in the towel on such a soul-taxing project.

... my closest "work proximity associate," Uche Anizor, for being an insightful sounding board for virtually every idea in this book and for keeping the laughs going amidst long days in the office and classroom.

... great friends Aron McKay, Joe Mellema, Paul Ruggiero, Oscar Navarro, Joshua Scott, Sean McDowell, and Sean Maroney for their wisdom and humor, along with Taylor Landry, who "in the absence of any indicators to the contrary," did a phenomenal job, yet again, editing this project.

... sharp colleagues Leon Harris, Brad Christerson, Rick Langer, Tim Muehlhoff, Kent Dunnington, William Lane Craig, Scott Waller, Darren Guerra, Michelle Lee-Barnewall, Greg Ganssle, James Petitfils, Fred Sanders, and Patrick Sawyer. Each in your own way, you helped expand my thinking about social justice.

... my strong leadership team at Biola University, Erik Thoennes, Doug Huffman, Scott Rae, Clint Arnold, and Barry Corey, for constant support and forming my dream team of caring bosses.

... the world-class Zondervan team, especially Ryan Pazdur, Stan Gundry, Brooke Brycko, Joshua Kessler, and Kim Tanner, for believing in this project and bringing the full weight of their expertise to it.

... my stellar team of TAs, Josiah Solis, Abner Aguilar, and Jake Ekstrom, for handling much of the grunt work that made this book possible.

... my beloved Biola students. Serving you is one of the greatest joys and privileges of my life.

... my thoughtful coauthors, Eddie, Walt, Becket, Edwin, Suresh, Michelle, Samuel, Monique, Ojo, Neil, Bella, and Freddy, for sharing your extraordinary stories of the power of the gospel in your lives.

Last and most of all, thanks to the love of my life, Jocelyn, for the patience, the laughter, the love, the feedback, the prayer, the support, and especially for mothering the four living, breathing proofs of God's goodness—Gracelyn, Holland, Harlow, and Hendrik.

All my love,
Thaddeus Williams

Abortion and the Right to Life[1]

In 2018 abortion was the leading cause of death worldwide, with 42 million victims.[2] That is roughly seven holocausts in a single year, more than one victim per second sacrificed on the altar of "choice." In Iceland, which many consider a progressive utopia, "the abortion rate for children diagnosed with Down syndrome approaches 100 percent."[3] In the United States, 90 percent of preborn humans diagnosed with Downs are terminated.[4] In New York City, more black image-bearers are aborted than are born.[5] "In Asia, widespread sex selective abortions have led to as many as 160 million 'missing' women—more than the entire female population of the United States. Recent evidence suggests that sex-selective abortions of girls are common in the United States as well."[6]

For many Social Justice B advocates, these millions of unwanted image-bearers don't fit into their definition of "the oppressed." For many who don't embrace Social Justice B, this calloused "sizeism" and "spaceism" (believing we have a right to life because we are bigger and more developed or because spatially we are outside the womb) makes Social Justice B's claim to care about the vulnerable ring hollow.

How, then, do pro-choice Social Justice B activists reconcile what seems like such a gaping inconsistency? Let's explore six of the most common arguments for abortion using the acrostic CHOICE.

Coat Hangers

This first argument has been around for over fifty years. Without legalized abortion, women will be forced to revert to the dangerous pre-*Roe v. Wade* days, dying from coat-hanger abortions at the hands of back-alley butchers, rather than being safely in the care of licensed medical professionals.

I offer two responses. First, *the coat hanger argument inflates the facts.* Before *Roe v. Wade* in 1973, 90 percent of illegal abortions were performed by licensed physicians in good standing with their medical boards,[7] according to Mary Calderone, former president of Planned Parenthood, not "back-alley butchers." According to the US Bureau of Vital Statistics, thirty-nine women died from illegal abortions the year before *Roe v. Wade* (with 133 in 1968 and 120 in 1966), not thousands.[8] Dr. Bernard Nathanson, one of the fathers of America's pro-choice movement and cofounder of the National Abortion Rights Action League (who later became a pro-life advocate), admits that he and others within the early pro-choice movement intentionally fabricated the numbers. Says Nathanson,

> How many deaths were we talking about when abortion was illegal? In N.A.R.A.L. we generally emphasized the drama of the individual case, not the mass statistics, but when we spoke of the latter it was always "5,000 to 10,000 deaths a year." I confess that I knew the figures were totally false, and I suppose the others did too if they stopped to think of it. But in the "morality" of the revolution, it was a useful figure, widely accepted, so why go out of our way to correct it with honest statistics. The overriding concern was to get the laws eliminated, and anything within reason which had to be done was permissible.[9]

Second, *the coat hanger argument misses the point: whether or not the preborn are people.* If the unborn are human people, this argument leads us to the false conclusion that society must make it safe and legal to kill people. If the preborn are people, then we are talking about roughly 1.5 million deaths per year since 1973. Even if we grant the pro-choice movement's admittedly inflated five to ten thousand deaths per year, this number pales in comparison. Pro-choice advocate Mary Anne Warren admits, "The fact that restricting access to abortion has tragic side effects does not, in itself, show that the restrictions are unjustified since murder is wrong regardless of the consequences of prohibiting it."[10] The coat hanger argument ignores the quintessential question: Are the preborn people?

Hardships

A second argument for abortion says that women should not be forced to bring into the world disabled children who would be genetically reduced to lives of extreme hardship and unhappiness.

I offer four replies. First, *people with disabilities are vehemently opposed to this argument.* There is not a single organization of disabled people in favor of abortion of those who may have disabilities. As one group put it,

> Sirs: We were disabled from causes other than Thalidomide, the first of us having two useless arms and hands; the second, two useless legs; and the third, the use of neither arms nor legs. We were fortunate . . . in having been allowed to live and we want to say with strong conviction how thankful we are that none took it upon themselves to destroy us as useless cripples. Here at the Debarue school of spastics, one of the schools of the National Spastic Society, we have found worthwhile and happy lives and we face our future with confidence. Despite our disability, life still has much to offer and we are more than anxious, if only metaphorically, to reach out toward the future. This, we hope will give comfort and hope to the parents of the Thalidomide babies, and at the same time serve to condemn those who would contemplate the destruction of even a limbless baby.[11]

Second, *the hardships argument makes a false correlation between deformities and unhappiness.* Former Surgeon General C. Everett Koop worked for years with severely deformed infants as a pediatric surgeon at Philadelphia's Children's Hospital. He has this to say:

> It has been my constant experience that disability and unhappiness do not necessarily go together. Some of the most unhappy children whom I have known have all of their physical and mental faculties, and on the other hand some of the happiest youngsters have borne burdens which I myself would find very difficult to bear. Our obligation in such circumstances is to find alternatives for the problems our patients face. I don't consider death an acceptable alternative. With our technology and creativity, we are merely at the beginning of what we can do educationally and in the field of leisure activities for such youngsters. And who knows what happiness is for another person?[12]

Stephen Krason echoes, "No study . . . has found that handicapped persons are more likely than non-handicapped persons to want to be killed or to commit suicide. . . . Of 200 consecutive suicides at the Baltimore Morgue . . . none had been committed by people with congenital anomalies."[13]

Third, *who are we to determine when another life is not worth living?* In 1982 "Infant Doe," an Indiana infant with Down syndrome and correctable spina bifida, was born. At the request of her parents, the physician withheld food and water from Infant Doe until she died. This course of action was upheld by an Indiana court. George Will comments on this case:

> When a commentator has a direct personal interest in an issue, it behooves him to say so. Some of my best friends are Down's syndrome citizens. (Citizens are what Down's syndrome children are if they avoid being homicide victims in hospitals.) Jonathan Will, 10, fourth-grader and Orioles fan (and the best Whiffle-ball hitter in southern Maryland), has Down's syndrome. He does not "suffer from" (as newspapers are wont to say) Down's syndrome. He suffers from nothing, except anxiety about the Orioles' lousy start. He is doing nicely, thank you. But he is bound to have quite enough problems dealing with society—receiving rights, let alone empathy. He can do without people like Infant Doe's parents, and courts like Indiana's asserting by their actions the principle that people like him are less than fully human. On the evidence, Down's syndrome citizens have little to learn about being human from people responsible for the death of Infant Doe.[14]

Fourth, *the hardships argument misses the big point—whether or not the preborn are people*. If the preborn handicapped are people, nothing in this argument keeps us from executing handicapped who are already born, unless of course the arguer contends that adults with deformities are subhuman. As bioethicist Francis Beckwith observes, "If the unborn are fully human, homicide cannot be justified simply because it relieves one of a terrible burden."[15]

Overpopulation and Poverty

A third argument for abortion goes like this. Banning abortion forces poor women to continue their pregnancies, putting them under a crushing financial burden, while simultaneously contributing to the problem of overpopulation. Here are three responses.

First, *this argument contradicts the pro-choice position that abortion is an inherent right that all women possess during all nine months of pregnancy*. If there were no overpopulation or economic hardship, would this right go away? All this argument could possibly validate is abortion in cases of overpopulation and financial stress, not a *carte blanche* right to abortion.

Second, *it confuses "finding a solution" and "eliminating a problem."* We could eliminate the problem of poverty by executing the poor, or the AIDS crisis in Africa by committing mass genocide against those with the disease.

But those methods undercut our moral axiom that people have great value and should be treated with dignity regardless of their predicament, thereby failing to find a solution.

Third, *the overpopulation and poverty argument overlooks the question of whether the preborn are people.* Only by assuming that the preborn are not people does the argument hold any weight. After all, if the preborn are people and the threats of overpopulation justify taking their lives, then the argument also justifies infanticide (killing postbirth babies) and the elimination of anyone else who may be financially burdensome or contribute to crowding the planet. As bioethicist Scott Rae says, "Only if the fetus is not a person can we say that financial burdensomeness is a criterion for elimination."[16] Baruch Brody of Baylor University echoes,

> In an age where we doubt the justice of capital punishment even for very dangerous criminals, killing a fetus who has not done any harm, to avoid a future problem it may pose, seems totally unjust. There are indeed many social problems that could be erased simply by destroying those persons who constitute or cause them, but that is a solution repugnant to the values of society itself. In short, then, if the fetus is a human being, the appeal to its being unwanted justifies no abortions.[17]

Incest and Rape

The fourth argument for abortion is a popular one: a woman should not be forced to endure the trauma of bringing an unwanted pregnancy to term in cases in which she was profoundly violated, such as incest and rape.

First, we must *acknowledge the immense pain endured by women who have been victimized by incest or rape.* These are grievous evils. We must weep with those who weep and do everything in our power to help women who are pregnant due to the selfishness of and sin of others.

Second, it is important to *gain perspective to clarify the real reason abortion is supported.* Such heartbreaking cases make up around 1 percent of abortions.[18] You may ask the pro-choice advocate, "Does this mean we can agree that the other 99 percent of abortions are morally wrong?" They aren't likely to agree, in which case it becomes clear that such tragic cases aren't the underlying reason they support abortion. Women who have already been used and abused should not be turned into pawns to win a political argument.

Third, *the argument does not justify the abortion-on-demand position, which holds up abortion as an inherent matter of "reproductive justice," a right that all women possess during all nine months of pregnancy.* Like our last three arguments, it conveniently bypasses the essential question. As Rae points out, "How the pregnancy was conceived is irrelevant to the central question of the personhood of the fetus."[19]

Choosing for *My* Body

The fifth argument is perhaps the most common and the most persuasive for many: a woman has the right to do whatever she chooses with her own body without interference from either the government or other people's personal moral beliefs, so abortion should be legal.

First, *the fetus is not part of the woman's body but is attached to it in a biologically intimate way.* Scientifically speaking, the fetus is not a clump of cells like a tumor. "It is simply biologically incorrect to say that they are 'mere tissue' or 'part of the mother.'"[20] A preborn fetus is a distinct human being with its own unique genetic code, heart, circulatory system, brain, and more. To grasp this fact, we need only ask simple questions: Does a woman have four legs, four feet, and four arms? Does she have two brains, two hearts, and two livers? In roughly half of pregnancies, we should ask, does she have a penis? The answer to all three questions is no because there's a big difference between being just another body part and having your own body, as preborn humans do. There is a profound connection between these two bodies. One undeniably affects the other in life-changing ways. But it is simply not true, scientifically, that the fetus is a mere part of the woman's body.

Second, *our rights over our bodies aren't absolute as far as the law is concerned.* Prostitution is illegal in most states, and nowhere in the US can you legally pour drugs into your body as an exercise of bodily freedom. These rights are overridden in cases when your exercise of bodily rights presents a clear harm to yourself or others.

Third, *the choosing for my body argument is often combined with the slogan "No Womb, No Say" to say men have no business weighing in on the abortion question.* But as we saw back in chapter 12, we shouldn't evaluate someone's ideas on the basis of their private parts but on their persuasiveness, because arguments don't have private parts, people do. But if we want to play that game, I highly recommend the work of the great pro-life feminist scholar Sidney Callahan. She makes the case far better than I can that abortion hurts women—physically, psychologically, and politically. Her famous essay "Abortion and the Sexual Agenda: The Case for Pro-Life Feminism" is a good entry point to her work.

Fourth, *the "choice" is hardly as autonomous and liberating as it's cracked up to be.* Sixty-four percent of women who sought abortions said they felt pressured by others. Over half thought abortion was "morally wrong." Less than 1 percent said they felt better about themselves, 77.9 percent felt guilt, and 59.5 percent felt that "part of me died."[21]

Fifth, *the choosing for my body argument misses the question on which millions of lives depend: Are the preborn people?* In the case of abortion, roughly half of those preborns are male. We can't say abortion is exclusively a women's issue unless we beg the question about the humanity of the preborn.

Economic Discrimination

This leads us to a sixth and final argument for abortion. In the days before legalized abortion, wealthy women would simply travel to have legal abortions in other countries. Banning abortion would leave poor women, the ones who often need abortions most because of their economic stresses, without any options.

First, *this argument adds pain to the already aching.* Living in poverty, worrying about where the rent money or the next meal will come from is a terrible burden. Christians should join the historic church in caring for women who find themselves in such straits. Yet abortion is hardly a solution to such suffering. A massive fourteen-year study found that 81 percent of women who had an abortion were more likely to experience mental health problems.[22] That is not to speak of the physical toll that has been inflicted on women by the multibillion-dollar, profit-maximizing abortion industry. Why add even more pain and trauma to women already languishing in poverty?

Second, *the argument assumes what it is trying to prove—namely, that abortion is a moral good.* Consider that rich women have the means to hire a hit man, whereas poor women don't have financial access to such "professionals." Does it follow logically that we should legalize the murderer-for-hire industry simply to resolve this inequality?

Third, *it fails to seriously consider the personhood of the preborn.* If the unborn are human people, this argument is equivalent to saying that society must make murder equally accessible to rich and poor.

We have engaged six of the most common justifications for abortion. Obviously, there are other arguments and much more to be said than can fit in an appendix. I point readers to two of the best books on the market that go far deeper. Charles Camosy's *Beyond the Abortion Wars* makes a brilliant and compassionate case for moving beyond polarization to advance the rights of preborn people and their mothers, who are often exploited by the abortion industry. Though it is highly academic, Francis Beckwith's *Defending Life* lays out a superb "case for human inclusiveness." This book is a *tour de force*. Beckwith engages the world's brightest pro-choice philosophers and activists.

The Pro-Life Argument

We turn now to the argument for life in four simple steps:

> Step 1. It is wrong to take the life of a human person, since people have the right to life.
> Step 2. Preborns are human people with a right to life.
> Step 3. Abortion takes the life of a preborn.
> Step 4. Therefore, abortion is wrong.

The watershed issue of the pro-choice versus pro-life debate is Step 2. Are preborns human people with a right to life? Pro-choice advocates offer a number of explanations as to when human personhood begins in order to make abortion consistent with the moral axiom of premise 1. It's important to realize that, ethically speaking, pro-life advocates and pro-choice advocates agree it is wrong to take the life of a human person (with few exceptions, like Peter Singer, Judith Jarvis Thomson, David Boonin, and Eileen McDonough). Most people are on the same page. It is not a pro-life versus pro-murder debate, but a debate about the nonmoral question of when human personhood begins. When is that "decisive moment" when the right to life kicks in? Here are four common pro-choice answers to that question:

1. *Birth* (40 weeks): A human becomes a person with full rights to life the moment he or she is outside the mother's womb.

However, the only difference between a baby five seconds prior to and a second after is birth is one thing—location, which seems like an arbitrary foundation for personhood. Pro-choice advocates Peter Singer and Helga Kuhse point out, "Pro-life groups are right about one thing: the location of the baby inside or outside the womb cannot make such a crucial moral difference.... The solution, however, is not to accept the pro-life view that the fetus is a human being with the same moral status as yours or mine. The solution is the opposite: to abandon the idea that all human life is of equal worth."[23]

2. *Viability* (24–26 weeks): A human becomes a person with full rights to life the moment he or she is capable of surviving independent of the mother's body.

Yet viability is contingent on the advancement of technology, with newer, better technology pushing viability back. The level of technological sophistication in a given society seems like a strange criteria for when personhood begins. Moreover, a strong case could be made that the more dependent, the more vulnerable, the more helpless a human being, the more we should do as a society to protect it. As Cardinal Roger Mahony put it, "Any society, any nation is judged on the basis of how it treats its weakest members—the last, the least, the littlest."[24]

3. *Brain function and sentience* (6–14 weeks): A human becomes a person with full rights to life the moment its brain begins functioning and it becomes capable of experiencing pain.

This "decisive moment" contradicts the position that abortion is a fundamental woman's right through all nine months of pregnancy. It also fails to recognize that humans retain the right to life even when they aren't in a sentient state, whether sleeping or comatose.

4. *Agnostic individualism* (?): We don't really know when human life begins, so we should leave it to individual women to decide for themselves.

Not knowing when human personhood begins does not justify a pro-choice position—quite the opposite. If you're hunting in the woods and hear a rustling in the bushes and you're uncertain as to whether it's your friend or a deer, morality and common sense dictate that you don't pull the trigger, given the risk of murder. French geneticist Jerome Lejeune sums it up well: "To accept the fact that after fertilization has taken place a new human has come into being is no longer a matter of taste or opinion. The human nature of the human being from conception to old age is not a metaphysical contention, it is plain experimental evidence."[25]

In conclusion, human beings *in utero* literally cannot voice their oppression. Are we willing to be the voice for the millions who do not enjoy the same size, developmental, locational, or breathing privileges we do? If we don't speak up for the tiny image-bearers and their mothers exploited by the multibillion-dollar abortion industry, then we should stop pretending that we care about justice for the oppressed and marginalized.

Appendix B

Black and White

C hristianity is about truth. The Father, whose "every word ... proves true," seeks to be worshiped in "truth."[1] Jesus identifies himself as "the truth" and tells Pilate that the purpose he was incarnated was "to bear witness to the truth."[2] "Truth" according to Jesus, "will set you free."[3] The Holy Spirit is "the Spirit of truth."[4] The Bible commands us to seek, speak, walk, and rejoice in truth.[5] The church is to be "a pillar and buttress of the truth."[6] The Greek word *aletheia* does not describe what we feel to be true or what a trending political ideology says is true. *Aletheia* denotes objective reality as God defines it. Real Christianity is not about deception, propaganda, or wish-fulfillment; it is about reality.

Because reality is so massively important, Christianity has a long history of taking words and the definitions of words extremely seriously. We could fill libraries with Christian works arguing about the definitions of words like *homoousia* and *homoiousia* (same nature vs. similar nature), *justification, free will, kingdom*, and many other words. Is this because Christians throughout history have been word sticklers and dictionary snobs? No. It is because Christianity is a religion of truth. Since words have tremendous power to illuminate or obfuscate truth, definitions should be a big deal for Christians.

Redefinitions

Redefining words is one of the trademarks of Social Justice B. Over the course of my lifetime, it has successfully changed the meanings of a great many words.

Tolerance and *intolerance*: Tolerance used to mean treating people with dignity and respect even when you disagree with them. Social Justice B redefines tolerance as agreement with or celebration of certain viewpoints. On this new definition, thinking someone else is wrong and saying so is intolerance. But the new definition of tolerance is incoherent because in reality the only way to be truly tolerant of someone else is to think they are wrong but still treat them with respect. If, for example, you believe In-N-Out is the best burger joint in Southern California, then it is impossible for me to *tolerate* you. Why? Because I *agree* with you, and agreeing is different from tolerating. If you say Five Guys, The Habit, or McDonald's, then it becomes possible for me to be truly tolerant; that is, I can continue treating you with respect and give you a fair hearing despite your preference for inferior burgers.

Marriage: Marriage used to mean a lifelong, sexually exclusive union between a man and a woman. With ideas like polyamory and open marriages (sex with multiple partners within or beyond the marriage bed), "throuples" (a union of three), "wedleases" (a contract that expires and may or may not be renewed), and gay marriage (unions with either no husband or no wife), every essential feature of the historic definition has been changed.

Bigot: Bigot used to mean "a person who is obstinately or intolerantly devoted to his or her own opinions and prejudices; especially: one who regards or treats the members of a group (as a racial or ethnic group) with hatred and intolerance."[7] *Bigot* has been redefined to mean anyone who questions the doctrines and policies of Social Justice B. It becomes inconceivable that those who disagree have reasonable counterpoints or truly love those on the other side. Bigotry becomes the default explanation for those with a different perspective. If bigotry is the only reason we can imagine for why people disagree with us, then perhaps we are the real bigots.

The list could go on. Believing that preborn image-bearers of God have a right to life has been redefined as a "war on women." Articulating the biological and biblical facts that males and females are different has been redefined as "transphobia." Disagreeing with Social Justice B's redefinitions of words has been redefined as "hate speech." Thomas Sowell carefully traces the ways in which words like *diversity*, *privilege*, *violence*, and *change* have been hijacked by an ideology by which "the hardest facts can be made to vanish into thin air by a clever catchword or soaring rhetoric."[8]

Redefining Racism

A major source of tension over race has been a new definition of racism that was invented in the 1970s. This new definition has since gone mainstream. It has become the definition presupposed without question in the social science and humanities departments of many universities. It has become an unquestioned starting point in many Christian conversations about racism, generating a lot of unnecessary confusion and division. Racism used to mean, and for many who hear the word slung around today it continues to mean, discriminating against people on the basis of their race. It says, because you are black you are property, not a person. You must sit at the back of the bus, you can't eat here, vote, go to school, or buy a home here. The historic fact that many claiming allegiance to Jesus practiced such racism is a scandal and tragedy we must never repeat. Such race-based discrimination is appalling and utterly antithetical to a Christian view of the world.

But some powerful segments of our society have added something significant to the historic definition of racism. For them, racism is defined as *prejudice plus power*, a definition invented in 1970 by a white social scientist named Patricia Bidol-Padva.[9] Only those "in power" can be properly deemed racist. Thus, it is impossible for any person of color to be racist because they aren't in power. Only white people can be truly racist because white people, it is claimed, hold all the power.

In the 2014 movie *Dear White People*, we learn that "racism describes a system of disadvantage based on race. Black people can't be racist since we don't stand to benefit from such a system."[10] On the MTV show *Decoded*, Franchesca Ramsey enlightens America's youth with the insight that "if you want to understand racism, you need to talk sociology, and sociology explains racism as a combination of prejudice and power."[11] Sociologist Michael Eric Dyson informs us that "racism presupposes the ability to control a significant segment of the population economically, politically, and socially by imposing law, covenant, and restriction on their lives. Black people ain't had no capacity to do that. Can we be bigoted? Yes. Can we be prejudiced? Yes. Can we be racist? No."[12]

The Bidol-Padva redefinition forms the unquestioned premise of such bestselling books as Robin DiAngelo's *White Fragility* and Beverly Tatum's *Why Are All the Black Kids Sitting Together in the Cafeteria*. It has made its way into bestselling Christian books[13] and the social science departments of major Christian universities.

This new definition is rarely defended so much as it is stipulated, followed swiftly with charges of "racism" against millions of people who have never heard a solid case for the Bidol-Padva redefinition. Predictably, the net impact of simply stipulating a new definition, one that indicts millions of fellow Christians, is not real racial reconciliation, but greater division in the body of Christ. Suppose that the new definition is better than the old. If we care about church unity, we should do our best to appeal to our brothers and sisters that the new definition makes more rational, factual, and biblical sense than the standard definition. Sadly, that is not what is happening at the moment. Instead, the new definition is being assumed and then imposed on the church in a way that creates rifts and resentments. We must do better.

Is there anything true or helpful about this new definition? Yes. Racism is not just something that individuals express. It can't be reduced to using the n-word, harboring personal animus or fear toward people who are different, or believing that a skin tone makes some people superior over others. As Nazism, apartheid, American slavery, and segregation have taught us, the sin of racism can be supersized to monstrous proportions through powerful systems of oppression. Systems can take racial prejudice to diabolical depths, and the Bidol-Padva redefinition is correct to draw our attention to that fact so the church can take a more broad-shouldered stand against racial sin.

Is there anything problematic about this new definition, or should Christians adopt it wholesale? If we care about the lasting unity of the multiethnic body of Christ, then we shouldn't be afraid to ask hard questions about racism as prejudice plus power.

Four Questions about the New Racism

1. *Does this new definition of racism generate false conclusions?* Let's assume, with Bidol-Padva, that power is a necessary condition of racism. What follows? It follows that Hitler, as he sat powerless in a prison cell before the rise of the Third Reich, was not racist when scribbling away the anti-Semitic screed of *Mein Kampf.* By making power an essential feature of racism, something astounding happened to Nazis when the Allies successfully dismantled the power of the Third Reich. With each Allied victory, with each degree of Nazi power lost, the Nazis, by definition, became less racist. Once liberation came to the last concentration camp, once Hitler's Berlin fell, once the Fuhrer himself took a self-inflicted bullet to the head, something magical happened to the Nazis. Those on trial at Nuremberg, those who fled to South America, despite their unrepentant anti-Semitism, were miraculously no longer racists.

Today's Ku Klux Klan, which has less institutional power in our century than, say, the Congressional Black Caucus, is not racist when it spews white supremacist propaganda in some backwoods barn meeting. Under the new definition, by which "black people can't be racist" because "racism is a matter of power" and "white people have the most influence," it follows that Nation of Islam leader Louis Farrakhan was not racist when he declared, "White folks are going down. And Satan is going down. And Farrakhan, by God's grace, has pulled the cover off of that Satanic Jew and I'm here to say your time is up, your world is through!"[14]

Do you see the point? Institutional power is not a requirement for other sins to count as sin. Why should such power be a requirement for racism to count as sin? George is greedy. His every waking moment is consumed with accruing more money and more material luxuries for himself. How might we cure George of the sin of greed? Don't take him to the cross. Simply drop him into socialist Venezuela in 2020 under a socialist regime that wields its systemic powers to achieve "economic equality." George can't express his greed through the prevailing institutions, so his greed ceases to be greed. Perhaps he merely struggles with financial overambition or a materialistic fixation.

When you can show animus toward others on account of their race and not count as a racist, we have entered a 1984 world of Newspeak.

2. *Does the new definition of racism change the meaning of the word so radically that we are no longer talking about the same reality?* Take the word *violence*. For most people the word means "physical force used to inflict injury or damage" or "the use of physical force so as to injure, abuse, damage, or destroy." By this definition, the church has been guilty of violence throughout its checkered history. Roman Catholics resorted to violence during the Inquisitions and Crusades. Catholics and Protestants used violence against each other for decades on the streets of Northern Ireland. Such bloody moments in church history are difficult to reconcile with Jesus's commands to love our enemies.

Today's Christian churches are certainly far from perfect. Nevertheless, there is stark contrast between church sanctioned violence in history and today's church. There has been real repentance, a change of mind, a substantial turning away from using physical force to injure, abuse, damage, and destroy others. But suppose we see protestors waving "Speech is Violence!" signs. We read Lisa Feldman Barrett's *New York Times* article entitled "When is Speech Violence?" Barrett argues, "If words can cause stress, and if prolonged stress can cause physical harm, then it seems that speech—at least certain types of speech—can be a form of violence."[15]

Churches around America use speech that may cause stress levels to spike—speech like "You are a sinner," "God is just and pours out holy wrath on sinners," or "An eternity of conscious torment awaits those who reject Jesus as God's solution to sin." Under the recent redefinition of violence, the charge comes—*the American church is violent!* Books with titles like *Can the Violent Church Be Saved?* hit the market. It doesn't matter how vehemently churches oppose the use of physical force against others or prove their antiviolence beliefs by their words and actions. By the new definition, they are "violent."

Imagine we explore the bloodiest moments in church history, moments so gory that no Christian can hear the facts without tears streaming and blood boiling. Then we the deploy the new definition of violence without making any case that it is better than the old definition. Advocates of Social Justice B say violence doesn't go away; it morphs, it adapts, it shape-shifts into new forms. Any Christian who stands condemned under the new definition is then saddled with the blame of those who were guilty under the old definition, and are called to repent for their ancestors' violence and their complicity with church-sponsored "violence" today.

Something like this happens when Christians with good intentions embrace the new definition of racism without interrogating it first. They offer appalling historic examples of racism under the old definition. This is helpful insofar as it reminds us never to repeat those egregious sins in the present. Then comes the bait-and-switch. Then word *racism* is subtly filled with the new definition, and we are told that this sin is the same old sin; it just looks different today than it did in the 1750s or the 1950s. In this way, we can use the new definition to heap historic guilt of racism under the old definition on our Christian brothers and sisters in the present tense. This leads to the body parts of Christ's church turning to scratch and beat one another instead of celebrating together that "there is now therefore now no condemnation for those who are in Christ Jesus."[16]

3. *Does this new definition of racism blur the meaning of power?* Who says who holds the power or how much power is enough for one's prejudices to cross the line and become racism? Was it suddenly possible for black people to be racist when Barack Obama was leader of the free world for eight years? Did it magically become impossible for them to be racist once Trump took the Oval Office? Ta-Nehisi Coates, a darling of the media and a fixture in America's sociology department curricula, wields lots of power, as do Jesse Jackson, Al Sharpton, Maxine Waters, Eric Holder, Kamala Harris, Cory Booker, and many other black influencers. Is it possible for them to be racist? The black hip-hop industry has massive culture-shaping power. One could argue that in many cases the values they promote in their music surpass the influence of many parents to shape their own children. That is power. The so-called black vote in America has hardly been powerless in the outcome of national elections.

I am not arguing that any of these people are racist. I am simply pointing out that they (rightly) are not powerless. The reality of their power makes it difficult to sustain the claim that racism is only a white-folk problem because they hold all the power.

This creates a strange irony. People who advance this new definition of racism are quick to denounce Western imperialism, Eurocentrism, and American supremacy. They are critical of "centering" conversations around white people. But doesn't the new definition of racism do precisely that? There are longstanding racial tensions in South America between lighter and darker shades of people, those of more Spanish and those of more Mayan descent. In North American history, there has been a lot of tension between lighter and darker shaded people within the black community.[17] Globally, there is clear racism in places where white faces are few and far between. The new definition of racism ironically imposes a Western conception on everyone else. Sowell says it well: "Often it is those who are most critical of a 'Eurocentric' view of the world who are the most Eurocentric when it comes to the evils and failings of the human race."[18]

There is another problem with the way the new definition of racism decides who has power and, therefore, who can be racist. It is deeply politicized. Think of those in power who pour millions upon millions of dollars into funding organizations such as Planned Parenthood, which has terminated hundreds of thousands of small black image-bearers. Is targeting poor mothers and eliminating their offspring while turning billions in profit enough power to count as racist by those who invoke the new definition? If we vote for candidates who support Planned Parenthood funding, are we complicit in systemic racism? What about the welfare system, which offers financial incentives for not having two parents in the home? Back in 1965, before the exponential growth of welfare systems in the US, about one in four black children were born in single parent homes. By 2017 that number had nearly tripled, leaving a heartbreaking 70 percent born without a married mother and father in the home. Is that system powerful enough to count as racist for the harm it has inflicted on black communities? That those who redefine racism are often quick to defend such systems tells us that political biases are often smuggled in with the new definition.

4. *Does this new definition of racism obscure the gospel?* I believe this is the most important question we can ask about racism as prejudice plus power. Let us run a quick thought experiment. Imagine a bunch of white people who harbor prejudice against black people. They board a flight bound for Uganda. When the wheels hit the tarmac, do their prejudices no longer count as racism because, presumably, they are no longer in a social context where whites hold the institutional power? Yes, they may still be guilty of prejudice, but thanks to their new geography, they no longer have to confess their racism to their Creator. Such logic would be a cop-out. *All racism* must be confessed and taken to the cross of Jesus. By making power essential to racism, we keep many forms of racism from being called out for what they are and brought into the light of

God's grace. We give sinners a way of achieving a not guilty sentence based on longitude and latitude rather than the cross of Jesus.

Consider a final example. When the *New York Times* hired Asian American Sarah Jeong to their editorial board, despite her tweets including "#WhiteMenAreBull****" and "#CancelWhitePeople," her defenders invoked the new definition of racism to prove Jeong's blamelessness. As an Asian woman in a white male–dominated society, the argument went, she lacked the power necessary for her actions to count as racist.

It would be easy to point out that serving on the editorial board of one of America's most influential media outlets is a power most people never possess, or that Asians are among the top tier of economic status holders in America. It would be even easier to filter Jeong through a political culture-war mindset with which we could make her an exemplar of leftist hypocrisy to score ideological points. But what happens if we interpret Jeong's animosity not through the lenses of power or politics but through a biblical worldview?

When we do that, we find ourselves caring about Sarah Jeong herself as a fallen image-bearer of God like the rest of us. When she's viewed through biblical lenses, we should pray fervently for her to experience the single greatest joy, meaning, and fulfillment possible for any human being—the privilege of being in a life-giving relationship with her Creator. Our Creator is holy and has made it clear that knowing and enjoying him forever requires us to be honest about our unholiness, to turn from our sin, and receive his free forgiveness, free for us only because the punishment we deserve was paid in full by Jesus on the cross.

To enjoy her Maker—her Maker who "shows no partiality,"[19] and who cares about "every tongue, tribe, and nation"—Sarah Jeong needs to repent of her sin.[20] Branding an entire color and gender of people "bull****" and calling for their cancellation is a sin, a sin that would keep Ms. Jeong from enjoying the most meaning and joy she could possibly experience, a relationship with her Maker.

Under the Bidol-Padva redefinition of racism, our "not guilty" sentence no longer comes by being in Christ but by being in this or that ethnic group. It is justification apart from Christ, which, sadly, is a false gospel. A false gospel—such as innocence by being nonwhite—cannot save. It leaves billions of people missing out on the only real way of being declared righteous—salvation by God's free grace through the death of Jesus. Your femaleness can't make you innocent and your Koreanness can't make you innocent, any more than being white or male can render you innocent. The new definition gets racists off the hook much too easily. It is by the blood of Jesus and only by the blood of Jesus that sinners of every color can find true blamelessness from any sin, including the sin of racism. When it comes to justification, it is not black or white, but only *red* that counts.

Appendix C

Capitalism and Socialism

There is a tidal wave of concern about justice among the 87.2 million Americans born between 1978 and 1995, aka "the millennials," and the 82.1 million born between 1996 and 2016, aka "generation we."[1] Like their millennial forbearers, *Forbes* reports that gen we is "passionate about equality and justice of every kind."[2] There is a documented shift in values from the boomers (the 79.2 million born between 1945 and 1964) and gen X (the 63.4 million born between 1965 and 1977). The individualized quest for personal affluence has morphed into a more collective vision, a quest for a better world for everyone.[3] Among generation we, "77 percent feel businesses should make 'doing good' a central part of their business" and 76 percent are concerned about human impact on the planet and believe they can operate as change agents.[4]

Fast-Food Knowledge

Taken by itself, this rising concern for justice is inspiring. But there is a second factor that makes it less inspiring. It is what we might call "fast-food knowledge." This last Sunday, I drove my family through (try to hold back your gasp of moral revulsion) McDonald's. The smiling window worker made me pull up the minivan twenty feet to await our order. About three minutes and two cars passed before I began protesting the injustice of our plight.

Fast-food knowledge is what happens when we want grand conclusions about the world with the same speed and convenience with which we want a Big Mac. We want it *now*, and so we bypass the traditional means of truth-seeking. We rarely immerse ourselves in the great thought traditions of human history. We rarely wrestle with the best arguments of the other side (as John Stuart Mill famously said, "He who knows only his own side of the case, knows little of that."[5]) We rarely spend time in distraction-free space to ponder the nuances and complexities of big issues. We prefer knowledge all boxed up and handed to us through a window, or a glowing screen, in a matter of seconds. No doubt, the "knowledge" we can now gain with ease in the Google age is abundant and more accessible than at any prior age in history. But prepackaged, expedient answers, especially when they involve deep human questions, have the same nutritional value for our heads that a daily diet of Big Macs would have for our hearts.

Put those two factors together—a rising zeal for a better world and a widespread aversion to the intellectual disciplines required to achieve knowledge worth having—and you have the makings of an epically tragic future. Among the generations that are "passionate about equality and justice of every kind,"

> ... one-quarter think more people were killed by George W. Bush than Joseph Stalin.[6]
> ... 42 percent are "unfamiliar" with communist leader Mao Zedong, whose over fifty million casualties make him the greatest mass murderer of the twentieth century.[7]
> ... 49 percent of millennials couldn't name a single one of the over forty thousand concentration camps and ghettos operating during the Holocaust. Two-thirds were unable to identify what Auschwitz was.[8]
> ... 22 percent of millennials said they haven't heard of the Holocaust or aren't sure whether they've heard of it.[9]

With a lack of real meat and substance in our knowledge of injustice, how can we work for a better world? A National Study of Youth and Religion found that 60 percent of millennials believe they'll simply be able to "feel what's right."[10] As the old Proverb says, "Desire without knowledge is not good."[11]

By modest estimates, the quest to achieve economic equality through communist and socialist policies has resulted in a catastrophic 100 million fatalities in the twentieth century alone. Nevertheless, several studies show that support for socialism is trending high in the United States, particularly among younger generations. Let us make an effort to add knowledge to our desire for a better world by taking a deeper look at Socialism and Capitalism.

The Allure of Socialism and Spotted Owls

There is a renewed zest for socialist ideas not just among college students but particularly among many Christian college students. In long conversations with many of them, I have found that a core motivator is the perceived resonance between socialism and biblical commands to lift up the poor. The logic runs something like this: (1) The Bible tells me to care for the poor. (2) Socialism, unlike greedy capitalism, cares for the poor. (3) Therefore, I like socialism.

The first premise is deeply Christian. We should take God's commands to love the poor seriously. The crucial link is premise 2, which rests on several problematic assumptions that many Christians with big hearts for the poor have never seriously reckoned with. Simply put, socialism smuggles in assumptions about human nature that are fundamentally incompatible with how God defines us in Scripture. Bad ideas about people have bad effects on people. If we get human nature wrong, then no matter how golden and noble our intentions, the very policies we endorse to help people will end up hurting them.

Allow me to illustrate through well-intentioned efforts to help northern spotted owls in the forests of the northwestern US. Environmental legislation significantly restricted the lumber industry with the aim of preserving the owls' natural habitat. As loggers struggled to cope with unemployment, the forests they once cut grew denser. Northern spotted owls, with an average wingspan of six feet, had an increasingly difficult time navigating the crowded trees to reach the forest floor, where wood rats, their primary food source, scurried freely. With less accessible sustenance, the spotted owl populations continued to dwindle in the very forests where they were intended to thrive.[12] How could efforts toward spotted owl thriving achieve such ironic results? The answer is: *an inadequate understanding of spotted owls*. Bad "owl-ology" led to a false concept of owl flourishing, which in turn led to bad policy, and, finally, the harm of the very animals that people sought to help.

The implications for how we think about socialism are clear: true anthropology is a necessary condition of good economic policy. Where, then, does socialism go wrong on human nature? I briefly highlight five problems in hopes of breaking the spell that socialist ideologies increasingly hold over Christian minds. None of what follows implies that capitalism is without problems. Charges include: it's *unbiblical*,[13] a contradiction of Scripture's commands against wealth accumulation; it's *oppressive*,[14] making the rich richer by making the poor poorer; it's *greedy*,[15] rewarding ruthless selfishness; and it's *soul-sucking*,[16] making endless material consumption the be-all, end-all of existence. Since this is a book about social justice, and social justice is often used synonymously with socialism, it is here that we will set our sights.

Five Problems

1. *Socialism takes the joy, charity, and humanity out of helping the poor.* God loves a cheerful giver.[17] According to the Old Testament, we should "give to him [our poor brother] freely, and your heart shall not be grudging when you give to him. . . . You shall open wide your hand to your brother, to the needy and to the poor, in your land."[18] The New Testament commands us to "remember the poor" and "contribute to the needs of the saints and seek to show hospitality."[19]

Socialism champions the government-enforced redistribution of wealth. Faceless programs replace the humanity of seeing a brother or sister in need and sacrificing your own resources to ease their burden. Instead of voluntarily opening our hands to the poor, our hands are pried open by law on threat of prosecution. It's not charity if the government has a hand in your wallet and a gun to your ribs. Coerced giving is the opposite of cheerful giving. How many people pays taxes cheerfully? How many people who distribute those taxes do so out of the goodness of their hearts, out of cheerfulness, out of true compassion?

With 36 percent of practicing Christians in America endorsing Marxist ideas, according to Barna research,[20] perhaps we need to reckon more seriously with the difference between free, cheerful, biblical giving and coercive government wealth redistribution. We should not buy into ideologies that claim to care for the poor but undermine the way Scripture commands us to care for the poor—that is, by giving *freely*.

2. *Socialism often confuses **its way** to help the poor with **the way** to help the poor.* It is common to hear that Christians who don't support big government programs intended to help the poor don't really care about the poor. I heard that charge today, in fact. This charge is often combined with the claim that Christians are so fixated on getting people's souls to heaven that they don't care how impoverished people's bodies are on earth. But what are the facts?

In a 2018 Barna study on global poverty, we learn that

- . . . 75 percent of practicing Christians in the United States provided food to a poor person or family, compared with 58 percent of all US adults.
- . . . 72 percent of Christians directly donated resources such as clothing or furniture to the poor, compared with 64 percent of all US adults.
- . . . 62 percent of Christians spent a significant amount of time praying for poor people, versus 33 percent of all US adults.
- . . . 47 percent of Christians gave of their personal time to serve the needy in their community, compared with 29 percent of all US adults.

. . . nearly twice as many Christians compared with all US adults volunteered for an organization to serve the poor in other countries or traveled outside the US to help the disadvantaged.[21]

A 2010 study from a nonreligious research group looked at a dozen faith communities around Philadelphia—ten Protestant churches, one Catholic parish, and one Jewish synagogue. Researchers used a fifty-four-point metric to determine the economic impact these congregations had on their surrounding communities. The results were astounding. These twelve congregations brought $50,577,098 in economic benefits to their neighborhoods in a single year.[22]

There is a big difference between not caring for the poor and thinking that government-enforced redistribution of wealth is a bad way to help the poor. Equating the two is a convenient way to feel like we're on the side of the angels and those who disagree are in league with the Devil.

Is it possible to be opposed to government-enforced redistribution of wealth precisely *because* we care about the poor? The welfare state had noble intentions of helping the poor. Yet it denied government checks to intact households, effectively incentivizing homes without married parents, thereby making poverty even worse in communities that were already suffering. In the last twenty-five years, 1.25 billion people have risen above extreme poverty. That's about 475 people who have broken away from extreme poverty over the last five minutes while you've been reading.[23] The major factor in this historically unprecedented rise from poverty, according to economists, has been the spread of free market economies, particularly in countries like India, China, and Nigeria. The "Asian tigers"—Singapore, South Korea, Taiwan, and Japan—have become prosperous despite a lack of natural resources as they have encouraged free markets, while resource-rich Russia and Brazil remain poor with big government systems that claim to help the poor. Endorsing government wealth redistribution is simply not the same as caring for the poor.

3. *Socialism overlooks the world's complexities, offering simple noble-sounding solutions that often inflict unexpected harm.* The more I listen to Christian friends who are excited about the prospects of socialism, the more I hear a familiar line of logic. It runs like this: (1) Here is a problem so we must do something. (2) *This* sounds noble. (3) Therefore, we must do *this*. (4) If you oppose *this*, then you must be antijustice. (5) If you oppose *this*, then you don't understand Jesus's kingdom.

The problem with this line of thinking is that it rarely makes room for the complexity of our fallen world, how solutions often generate new, unforeseen problems. I offer three quick cases to illustrate the potential for unintended consequences.

Case 1: Forgiveness for Tanzania

Here is a problem: abject poverty in Tanzania. We must do something. Forgiving the national debt of Tanzania is something that sounds noble. Therefore, we must forgive the national debt of Tanzania. If you disagree, you are antijustice and out of sync with Jesus's kingdom. But economist Dierdre McCloskey asks, "Who gets the benefit? If the poor in the countryside get it, good; if the thieves running the government get it, no poor person has been helped. So forgiving debt may not accomplish its ethical intention. . . . Will big banks continue to make loans to poor countries if the debts are forgiven? Is a lack of access to international capital market a good thing for the poor of Tanzania?"[24]

Case 2: Nikes for Nigeria

Abject poverty in Nigeria is another problem. We must do something. Let's wear new shoes to church this Sunday, then leave in our socks, leaving our shoes to show our solidarity with the poor. We can ship our new Nikes and Converse in giant crates to Nigeria. That sounds noble.

After much adversity and innovation, some Nigerian cobblers have reached a point where they can provide footwear to their communities and support their own families at the same time. Here come the red, white, and blue crates with tens of thousands of shoes, *free* shoes. The market value of Nigerian shoes instantly plummets. As the Americans walk in socks to their cars, feeling the buzz of caring, little do they know that their actions, however well intentioned, have set the Nigerian cobblers and their families back ten years.

Case 3: Egg-Quality for All

Here's a third problem: poor people can't afford eggs. We must do something. Some kind-hearted politicians have just the thing. Let's pass a law that caps the price of eggs at a dollar a dozen, about a dollar below current market value. Now the poor can enjoy omelets and quiche like everyone else. Mid- to low-level egg producers wake up the next day to find they are hemorrhaging money as chicken feed, electricity, gasoline, and transport costs now exceed their profit. Many will sell their chickens to the big guys and have to start from scratch in a new industry. As more farmers leave the egg business, eggs become more scarce than before all the "justice" efforts kicked in.[25] If those good-hearted politicians intervene again to cap the chicken feed prices to help sustain the poor egg farmers—or more accurately, the egg farmers they made poor—then the grain farmers will find themselves in the same plight as the egg farmers. To alleviate their poverty the benevolent bureaucrats can pass more economic regulations until, lo and behold, we have reached total state control over an entire industry and people keep getting poorer. Several unintended consequences later, our noble intentions have left more people in poverty than there were before we started working for "economic justice."

The moral of these cases is obvious. We are often unwitting morons when we try to fix broken systems. Most broken systems are incredibly complex and require more than good intentions and noble-sounding solutions.[26]

Of course, this insight should never become a cop-out to throw up our hands in defeat. We must also beware of the opposite error of the activist fallacy—that is, the apathy fallacy: (1) There's an extremely complex problem. (2) Doing something will probably make it worse. (3) Therefore, we shouldn't do anything.

Our planet would be worse off today if Martin Luther King Jr. had said, "Racist systems in America have a lot of moving parts. It's probable that by trying to fix this bit over here I will only make matters worse over there, so perhaps it's better to just take a nap." What if Wilberforce decided to give up the fight against slavery because, well, it's tied to the British economy and it could have all kinds of unforeseen consequences?

Inaction is hardly the right answer to misguided activism. Knowledge without zeal is hardly the solution to zeal without knowledge. The solution is for us to take the Bible's commands to be discerning just as seriously as we take its commands to do justice. Look at the great justice agents of church history—the discarded-infant-rescuing early church, the slavery-abolishing Brits and Americans of the eighteenth and nineteenth centuries, the white-supremacy-subverting believers of the twentieth century, and more. What made them great was not only their countercultural courage to obey the Bible's justice commands but also their unwillingness to settle for skin-deep justice. They wanted the real thing. They had not only courage but also clarity about the issues behind the issues. Let's follow their example as we seek to love the poor.

4. *Socialism tends to reduce humans to* homo economicus, *elevating the government to God status.* These last two problems focus particularly on secular forms of socialism. Christians who gravitate toward socialist ideas would be quick to reject the atheistic premises of historic socialism. Yet I have seen it happen over and over. Christians with great intentions welcome socialist ideas into the gates of their faith, only to have their Christian worldview—their doctrines of Scripture, sin, and salvation—plundered from the inside out.

According to historic socialism, *a la* Marx and Engels, humans aren't the creative workmanship of God, whose image we bear and who offers us salvation in Christ. In the absence of God, humanity is reduced to *homo economicus*. As humans are reduced to material-economic categories, socialism diagnoses our deepest problem not as a broken relationship with our Creator, but a material economic problem. This leads to an inflated emphasis on the saving power of external socio-political-economic remedies, while the internal human propensity to evil and selfishness goes undiagnosed and untreated.[27]

Who, then, in this new economic gospel, does the "saving"? As Chesterton observed, "Once we abolish God, the government becomes God."[28] Before Soviet communism went wrong with economic policies that drastically exacerbated the problems of poverty, it had already gone wrong on the deeper questions of human nature. Moreover, it went wrong on human nature because it denied the existence of God, who defines us, paving the way for a God-sized government and the false gospel of economic equality that mistakes symptoms for the disease.

Historically, such a false gospel carries a zero-tolerance policy for the actual gospel. Under Joseph Stalin, "The Society of the Godless" (also known as the "League of Militant Atheists") took form in the Soviet Union. Russian churches and synagogues were bulldozed. Atheism became a state-enforced dogma. Did this produce the godless utopia of peace and economic equality that the Soviet leaders dreamed of? On the contrary, worship was redirected to a new deity—Lord Stalin—while tens of millions of heretics who refused to bow were starved or executed. We see a similar phenomenon in China and North Korea today. As Roger Trigg notes, "Religion is always a target of totalitarian regimes. . . . Dangerous for would-be dictators, is the appeal to transcendent norms, and a supernatural authority beyond this life."[29]

5. *Without God, we lose the transcendent moral reference point we need to make an accurate and humble assessment of our own moral powers—or lack thereof.* According to Harry Schaffer, "Socialists and Communists of all shades and leanings believe in the perfectibility of all mankind. Man is basically good and capable of being master of his own destiny."[30] From this sin-less anthropology it follows that human effort combined with the right economic policies can usher in heaven on earth. But as Darrell Cosden points out, "Rationalized labor and advancing technology were meant to free us from the need for religion by bringing a new kind of paradise to earth now. Yet this modern salvation has more often than not ended up creating hell instead for many people around the world."[31]

By downplaying the depth of human corruption, socialism becomes a counterfeit gospel. It relies on corrupt human authorities with no room for God's heart-regenerating grace. Socialism seeks Christ's kingdom, minus the Christ, and becomes a destructive parody of God's *shalom*. The harder it tries to create heaven on earth, the more hell it unleashes, particularly on the poor whom Scripture commands us to love.

Appendix D

Defining Sexuality

There is an important question I'd like to ask you about sexuality, but first a true story. In the second century a mysterious plague broke out in the Roman Empire. It was catastrophic, wiping out as much as one-third of the population in many regions of the empire. Most Romans ran for the hills away from the plagued. "If this life is all I've got, then I'll be damned if you're going to take that from me" was the mindset of the masses. The Christians who believed God bore their sin-plague on the cross and defeated the power of the grave took a different approach. As society ran away from the sick and dying, our ancient brothers and sisters ran to the bedsides of the sick to care for them, dignifying them as divine image-bearers, and often getting sick and dying right alongside them. Their care wasn't conditional on the plagued first embracing a biblical worldview or a Christian sexual ethic. It was love, like God's love, freely given.

Now fast-forward from the second to the twentieth century. A mysterious plague breaks out. Immune systems are shutting down. Doctors are baffled. This new disease seems to be particularly devastating to gay men. Where was the church of the late twentieth century when the AIDS crisis hit? The answer ought to bring us to our knees. More often than not, it was right where the nonchurched were in the late second century—running for the hills away from the sick and dying.

I share this tragedy to remind us that we do not debate sexuality in a vacuum. There is a painful context to such conversations. Where we have failed to treat people as image-bearers and failed to embody the gospel, we must say sorry. People who disagree with us over sexuality must know we love them so much we'd be willing to die right alongside them in the twenty-first century, just as our ancient brothers and sisters did in the second century.

"Ranting Homophobes"

If we realize we must lead with love, then we are ready for that important question I wanted to ask you: Have your views of sexuality been shaped more by Jesus and Paul or by two people you have likely never heard of named Kirk and Madsen?

In 1987 a neuropsychiatrist named Marshall Kirk and a public relations consultant named Hunter Madsen teamed up to write "The Overhauling of Straight America." This article would later balloon into the four hundred–page tome *After the Ball: How America Will Conquer Its Fear and Hatred of Gays in the 90s.* Kirk and Madsen lay out a six-phase strategy.

First, "talk about gays and gayness as loudly and as often as possible." Why? Because "almost any behavior begins to look normal if you are exposed to enough of it. . . . The way to benumb raw sensitivities about homosexuality is to have a lot of people talk a great deal about the subject in a neutral or supportive way."[1]

Second, "portray gays as victims, not as aggressive challengers."[2] Third, "give protectors a just cause."[3] Kirk and Madsen clarify, "Our campaign should not demand direct support for homosexual practices, [but] should instead take anti-discrimination as its theme."[4] Fourth, "make gays look good;" that is, "the campaign should paint gays as superior pillars of society."[5] Fifth, "make the victimizers look bad."[6] This is a crucial step to their strategy. They explain:

> At a later stage of the media campaign for gay rights . . . *it will be time to get tough with remaining opponents.* To be blunt, *they must be vilified. . . .* Our goal here is twofold. First, we seek to replace the mainstream's self-righteous pride about its homophobia with shame and guilt. Second, *we intend to make the anti-gays look so nasty that average Americans will want to dissociate themselves from such types. . . .* The public should be shown images of ranting homophobes whose secondary traits and beliefs disgust middle America. . . . [Show them as] bigoted southern ministers drooling with hysterical hatred.[7]

The sixth and final step of their strategy is simple: "Solicit funds. The buck stops here."[8]

I offer the following six questions to help us more honestly answer whether our understanding of sexuality is influenced more by Jesus and Paul or Kirk and Madsen.

1. *Is our view of sexuality an expression of Creator- or creation-worship?* It is no accident that Paul connects sexual sin with idolatry.[9] There is no such thing as sex that is not simultaneously an act of worship. Sexuality is an inherently religious matter; the way we think about it and the way we engage in sexual acts will be a fundamental expression, consciously or not, of either Creator-worship or creation worship. Philip Yancey observes, "If humanity serves as your religion, then sex becomes an act of worship. On the other hand, if God is the object of your religion, then romantic love becomes an unmistakable pointer, rumor of transcendence as loud as any we hear on earth."[10]

Non-Christians increasingly make this connection between sexuality and worship in ways the church often does not. Chris Hinkle argues that "homosexuality must make its moral case, not merely its civil-social rights. It must show the deep spirituality of homosexual love."[11] Paula Ettelbrick adds, "Being queer is more than setting up house, sleeping with a person of the same gender, and seeking state approval in doing so. . . . Being queer means pushing the parameters of sex, sexuality, and family, and in the process transforming the very fabric of society."[12] It shouldn't surprise us to find homosexuality hailed for its spiritual and saving power. When Paul describes the move from Creator- to creation-worship, one of the first places this self-destructive exchange expresses itself is in the realm of sexuality.[13]

When we acknowledge the godhood of God, our view of sex starts with the Creator, who infused his cosmos with "exceedingly good" differences. With astounding artistic brilliance, God structured the universe with beautiful distinctions, separating day and night, the waters above from the waters below, the sea from the dry land, different animal and plant species, and more. Six times in the Genesis account of creation, God looked at his creative works of contrast and declared "it was good." As I have argued elsewhere, this is not like saying the boy who ate his vegetables "was good" for obeying Mommy, or the Magna Carta "was good" for society, or the Hadron particle accelerator "was good" for quantum research. God's declaration was more like someone beholding a Titian canvas or a sunset over the Pacific and saying, "It is good." It is a declaration of beauty. It is not a moral, legal, political, or prudential claim. It is an aesthetic claim.

Between the sixth "good" and the seventh in which God calls his creation "exceedingly good" there is but one more addition to his masterpiece—sexuality, including the wondrous distinction between male and female. The ultimate meaning of sexuality, therefore, is not determined in a boardroom, a bedroom, or a courtroom but in the garden where it was first designed and deemed "exceedingly good"—that is, exceedingly beautiful.

As with everything else in God's good creation, this beautiful distinction can and has been twisted. It can and has been warped and mangled into gender confusion and sins like sexism. The solution, however, is not to erase the difference between male and female but to affirm the original and sacred beauty of loving male-female relationships. Gender distinctions are a gift from God to be celebrated, not obliterated. Men can't simply replace women, or women replace men, without something exceedingly beautiful being lost.

When we get swept up in Social Justice B, our understanding of sexuality comes less and less from Scripture and more and more from the ideological architects and ancestors of the sexual revolution. Most of us have never heard of Herbert Marcuse, Paul Goodman, Norman Brown, Michel Foucault, and Judith Butler. We may have never read Marcuse's *Eros and Civilization*, Goodman's *Growing Up Absurd*, Brown's *Love's Body*, Foucault's *The History of Sexuality*, or Butler's *Undoing Gender*. But if we have smartphones, Netflix accounts, or haven't buried our heads in the sand for the last ten years, we are already familiar with their ideas. They are to today's popular understanding of sexuality what Matthew, Mark, Luke, and John are to our understanding of Jesus: our authorities even if few bother to read them.

What these pioneers of today's new sexual orthodoxy have in common is that they all are avowed atheists. But if you've been paying attention, does that mean they were not worshipers? No. Each and every one of them was on their knees. They simply worshiped creation rather than their Creator. That should tell us something. Unless we think the godhood of God has no implications for the meaning of sexuality, we should not simply go with the flow but should instead question the sexual dogmas of our day. As Philip Yancey observes, "I might feel more attraction towards a reductionistic approach to sex if . . . I sensed that the sexual revolution had increased respect between the genders, created a more loving environment for children, relieved the ache of personal loneliness, and fostered intimacy. I have seen no such evidence."[14]

2. *Does our view of sexuality redefine love and hate?* Westboro Baptist excepted, few people wave signs explicitly advocating hate. Everyone thinks they are pro-love. Yet one side sees itself championing love and the other side as pro-hate, and vice versa.

Abraham Kuyper provides the theological clue we need to make sense of this bizarre standoff. Our definitions of love and hate don't spring into existence from some quantum vacuum. They come from our deeper worldview commitments, what Kuyper calls "two absolutely differing starting points."[15] It all comes down to the question of whether we see man "in his present condition as normal, or as having fallen into sin, and having therefore become abnormal."[16] For abnormalists, like Jeremiah, Solomon, and Paul, the human heart is desperately sick, full of moral insanity, and dead in transgressions and sins.[17] Those who recognize such abnormality "maintain the miraculous as the only means to restore the abnormal; the miracle of regeneration; the miracle of the Scriptures; the miracle in the Christ, descending as God with His own life into ours; and thus, owing to this regeneration of the abnormal, they continue to find the ideal norm not in the natural but in the Triune God."[18]

If, however, we are unfallen, then humanity "moves by means of an eternal evolution from its potencies to its ideal."[19] This clarifies ways in which #loveislove and #lovewins have become defining slogans of Social Justice B. What is presupposed and then *imposed* is a normalist account of human nature. You must corroborate and celebrate my happiness *as I currently conceive of happiness in all my unfallen perfection*. Anything less is bigotry. From an abnormalist perspective, by contrast, love is not constricted to always say "be who you are." It can also say "*become* who you are" when that needs to be said. It is a love, like God's, that can passionately and zealously pursue the beloved's redemption and flourishing. Love can be redemptive only if we need redemption.

Kuyper's normalist-abnormalist distinction captures one of the deepest rifts in contemporary faith, why we often talk past one another. Consider the driving thesis of evolutionary zoologist Alfred Kinsey in the mid-twentieth century. Every sexual drive and behavior becomes justified as "normal mammalian behavior." The scientific community eventually rejected Kinsey's spurious research. But his normalist worldview assumptions about human sexuality have risen over the last fifty years to become cardinal dogmas of the Western mainstream. This occurred largely through the work of twentieth-century thinkers such as Marcuse, Goodman, and Brown. "We knew that at bottom their gospel was a sexual one," says one scholar of Marcuse, Goodman, and Brown, "that sex was their wedge for reorienting all human relations."[20] If creation is our standard, then whatever sexual drives I find within myself are "normal," and the loving thing to do is to celebrate them. If the Creator is our standard, then our sexual drives are far from perfect. They are broken, and the loving thing to do is to work by God's grace toward redemption and the recovery of the beauty of our sexuality as God designed it.

The same thing happens with our definition of *hate*. Recall our madness machine from the opening chapter, the set of core convictions inside us. Into one end you feed a question—What is hate?—and from the other end pops an answer. If our madness machines are structured around the sovereign self—I am the standard of truth, my emotions are unquestionable, and my pleasure is the chief end of existence—then the conclusion pops out: Anyone who questions my sexuality can be motivated by only one thing: hate. If our worldview is structured around the sovereign God, then quite a different conclusion pops out: It is hardly loving to tell other sexually fallen people that they have no need for grace, redemption, and healing.

3. *Does our view of sexuality resort to worldview coercion disguised as courtesy?* I believe that by God's grace I am an adopted son of God. I have been welcomed into God's family thanks to the work of Jesus on my behalf. This is not some superficial opinion. It is the core of my identity as I understand it in light of Scripture.

Imagine I ask people to address me as "Thaddeus Williams, adopted son of God." The problem is that such an address makes sense only within a Scripture-informed Christian worldview. Many people I interact with don't share my belief system in which a claim to be the adopted son of the Creator of the universe makes sense. Such a notion would be nonsense to a Muslim, a Buddhist, an atheist, and those with many other worldviews. Demanding that Muslims, Buddhists, and atheists address me as an adopted son of God would be a form of worldview bullying. I would, in effect, be telling people who don't interpret the world the way I do that they must accept my worldview—act and speak as if my beliefs are truer than their own—as a precondition of having a conversation with me. Otherwise, they will be called mean names. A non-Christian might respond to my demand, "Respectfully, no. You may believe those things to be true about yourself. But I don't share your worldview, and you can't force the words out of my mouth that endorse your worldview over mine. I refuse to play your game of social coercion." And they would be right to say so, no matter how offended I may feel that they refuse to accept my core identity as I understand it.

There has been an increasing demand, at times mandated by force of law, to use the pronoun of choice for transgender image-bearers. Here is the issue behind the issue. There are only certain worldviews in which the claim "I can define my gender by an act of will" makes sense. It is only within a worldview that separates gender from biological sex, only a worldview in which gender is purely a social construct, only a worldview in which we consider the subjective feelings of individuals to be authoritative and unquestionable, only a worldview in which there are no important and even beautiful distinctions between male and female that the pronoun issue becomes an issue. So underneath the request "Please call me by my desired pronoun" is an implicit demand— "Disavow your own worldview, and embrace my understanding about sex, gender, and the authoritative role of subjective feelings." The same could be said for the redefinition of marriage as a wife-optional or husband-optional institution. Such redefinitions make sense only under certain worldview presuppositions. It is precisely this form of worldview coercion that lies behind much of the legislation and litigation facing Christian schools, businesses, and churches in our day. Such coercion is incompatible with a Christian view of how to treat others.

4. Does our view of sexuality include self-deification? Imagine a man who fancies himself a theological innovator who says, "I believe God is good, kind, loving, forgiving, and all that, but I don't believe God is some kind of supreme power ruling over the entire universe." Our so-called theological innovator is more of an a-theological innovator. He has, in a peculiar way, denied the very existence of God. Why? Because the God who actually exists really is the ultimate power over the universe. Rejecting a supreme God is the same act as rejecting the God who actually exists. A. W. Pink comments, "In reality, they are but atheists, for there is no other possible alternative between an absolutely supreme God and no God at all."[21] In other words, strip God of his supremacy—or any of his attributes for that matter—and you are no longer thinking about God but a projection of your imagination.[22] Divine attributes can't be sprawled out like meats, veggies, and condiments at a sandwich bar for us to custom craft a deity to our own tastes.

This is a big difference between who God is as Creator and who we are as creatures.[23] Because he is the Creator, to deny any truth about God is to deny his very existence. But we are not God. Nevertheless, in Social Justice B thinking, if someone has the gall to question our chosen gender identity or our sexual acts, we hear "You're cancelling my existence!" No doubt, the person in this scenario feels genuinely rejected, like someone is trying to erase their very being. But underneath that profound offendedness lies a hidden rejection of the Creator-creature distinction, a belief that we are sovereign self-defining selves. Colin Campbell clearly captures this dogma:

> The "self" becomes, in effect, a very personal god or spirit to whom one owes obedience. Hence "experiencing," with all its connotations of gratificatory and stimulative feelings becomes an ethical activity, an aspect of duty. This is a radically different doctrine of the person, who is no longer conceived of as a "character" constructed painfully out of the unpromising raw material of original sin, but as a "self" liberated through experiences and strong feelings from the inhibiting constraints of social convention.[24]

To clarify Campbell's point, if someone denies my identity as an adopted child of God, if they refuse to address me as such, that is fine. I am not a perfect or authoritative standard on my identity, and neither is the person who rejects that identity. We are both made of "the unpromising raw material of original sin." God is the standard on who I am. His verdict about me is infinitely more trustworthy than either how I feel about myself or who others say I am. And, oh, how liberating that is!

If, however, I turn my "self" into a kind of "personal god or spirit to whom I owe obedience," if I make my own feelings and choices authoritative, then anyone who denies any part of my self-defined self becomes an offense and threat to my very being, a bigot or hater who must be silenced for sinning against my sovereignty.

Just as God's feelings in traditional theology are expressions of his nature, so our feelings—particularly our sexual feelings—come to define our identities. As I unpack elsewhere, the first sin of our ancient ancestors in the garden, with the serpent's temptation to "be like God," was the sin of saying we get to be the authoritative definers of reality.[25] Once we take the fruit, getting everyone to accept and celebrate our sexuality as we autonomously define it becomes a matter of social justice. We must fight the oppression of cisgender and heteronormative culture for threatening our self-defined selves. Such "social justice" becomes a double injustice. It refuses, on the one hand, to give God his due, and on the other hand gives creatures a divine status we are not due. From there it quickly becomes a triple injustice because, under the delusion of our own divinity, we become tyrants to those around us.

5. *Does our vision of sexuality promote the kind of authenticity and freedom that leaves people confused and enslaved?* Social Justice B sees being true to ourselves—specifically, being true to our sexual drives and feelings—as a mark of authenticity and freedom. This popular line of thinking is challenged in, of all places, the Pixar film *The Incredibles.*

An aspiring crime-fighter named Buddy Pine says something profound to his superhero idol Mr. Incredible. "You always say 'be true to yourself,' but you never say which part of yourself to be true to!" As the plot unfolds, Buddy becomes a super villain named Syndrome who will stop at nothing to make a name for himself. In becoming a megalomaniacal villain, Buddy was indeed taking Mr. Incredible's advice. He was being true to himself, or, more accurately, he was being true to the part of himself (which is inside all of us) that is malevolent and self-centered. The advice to be true to ourselves and follow our hearts only works on the assumption that our selves are thoroughly good, that our hearts aren't filled with dark, twisted desires.

C. S. Lewis made the point in *The Abolition of Man*: "Telling us to obey Instinct is like telling us to obey 'people.' People say different things: so do instincts. Our instincts are at war. . . . Each instinct, if you listen to it, will claim to be gratified at the expense of all the rest."[26]

The advice to "follow your heart," in the estimation of Buddy Pine and C. S. Lewis, is lousy advice because our hearts are not simple. They are divided. The heart is an epic war of imperialistic drives and contradictory instincts. Which ones, then, should we follow?

What sounds like a call to captain your own soul, chart your own course, and be authentic and free turns out to be the opposite. "Follow your heart" is actually a call to be slavishly devoted to the ideologies of others. Let me explain. Picture a Northern Irish teen called Jon, coming of age in 1970s Belfast in an Irish Republican Army heavy neighborhood. In that context, the desire to unleash aggression against the Brits would beat strong in Jon's heart, especially after "Bloody Sunday," when British paratroopers opened fire and killed thirteen Catholic civil rights protestors. Should Jon follow his heart? Now let's pick up Jon by the back of his shirt and drop him in an American university in 2018. Here Jon is warned over and over by those in authority about the dangers of what has been branded "toxic masculinity." He once found a military career to be an adventurous life path but has found a new competing desire in his heart to unleash his inner interpretive dancer, a desire his gender studies professor strongly encouraged. Should Jon follow his heart?

Do you see the problem? In both scenarios, whether in the streets of Belfast or the halls of the gender studies department, telling Jon to follow his heart is hardly the call to unfettered self-definition that it's cracked up to be. If he takes the advice, he will end up a walking paradox, thinking he's strolling freely when he's really just marching to the beat of a drum that someone else is beating.

Let's bring it closer to home. If a teenager has competing sexual desires—to experiment sexually or to hold up sex as something sacred and reserved for marriage—it is obvious which set of desires those telling her to follow her heart would consider to be her real heart. She will believe she is being true to herself and free from social constraints, when she is really just a pawn in a sexual agenda invented by Alfred Kinsey, Herbert Marcuse, Judith Butler, and other ideologues she's never heard of.

One of the cruelest things you can do to young people is tell them to follow their own hearts. Slowly but surely the driving moral of our stories has shifted.[27] It was no longer, don't be self-centered like the witch from *Snow White*, Captain Hook from *Peter Pan*, Jafar from *Aladdin*, or Scar from *The Lion King*. Instead, be courageous for the sake of others, like Pinocchio taking on Monstro or Prince Charming slaying the Dragon. Defeat malevolence with kindness like Cinderella or Snow White. Those timeless truths were replaced with a disorienting false gospel of be true to yourself, follow your heart, and don't let anyone tell you who or how to be. Jesus said, "Whoever causes one of these little ones who believe in me to sin, it would be better for him to have a great millstone fastened around his neck and to be drowned in the depth of the sea,"[28] where Pinocchio won't be on his way to save you.

Think again of justice as giving others what they are due. What are children due? They are due a rich, beautiful, and compelling vision of a moral reality that's bigger than their feelings. They are due the exhilarating offer not of trying to craft their own identities out of thin air but of being authored by Someone infinitely smarter, stronger, and more loving than they are. Creating and sustaining an identity—including a sexual identity—is a Creator-sized task. Heaping that weight on the shoulders of young creatures, using "sexual freedom" and "gender identity" to deprive people of the joy of being authored, is not social justice; it is cruel. This leads to our sixth and final question.

6. *Does our vision of sexuality undermine the best news anyone could ever hear?* In his classic work *Evangelism and the Sovereignty of God*, J. I. Packer sets out to define the gospel from the pages of Scripture. Drawing from Paul's gospel declaration to the Athenian philosophers on Mars Hill, Packer makes a keen observation: "The gospel starts by teaching us that we, as creatures, are absolutely dependent on God, and that he, as Creator, has absolute claim on us. Only when we have learned this can we see what sin is, and only when we see what sin is can we understand the good news of salvation from sin. We must know what it means to call God Creator before we can grasp what it means to speak of him as Redeemer."[29]

The gospel becomes gobbledygook the minute we separate it from the godhood of God. If we go with the cultural flow—celebrating creatures' sexual drives as if they are authoritative and unquestionable, with no need for repentance or redemption—then we aren't upholding the godhood of God. We become complicit with the lie that the creature is the measure of sexual truth. In the name of social justice, redefined to jive with the sexual orthodoxy of our day, we commit a double injustice. We rob the Creator of the honor he is due, and we rob creatures of the gospel that makes no sense apart from the supremacy of God over all of life, including sex. How horrifying would it be to find out that just when we think we are at our most loving we had actually been depriving those we claimed to love of the most liberating, life-giving news in the universe?

I hope these six questions help us better discern whether our vision of sexuality is shaped more by Kirk and Mattson or the Scriptures. I hope they help us better love those we have failed to love in the past. Obviously there is far more to be said than can fit into an appendix. What about those who argue that Scripture supports gay and lesbian behavior? What about the redefinition of marriage? How do we best love those struggling with same-sex attraction or gender dysphoria? To those who want to go deeper or who may be struggling, I recommend some of the best resources from those who have found true freedom and identity in Christ from the false sexual freedom and identity promised by Social Justice B. I recommend *A Change of Affection: A Gay Man's Incredible Story of Redemption* by Becket Cook, and *The Secret Thoughts of an Unlikely Convert: An English Professor's Journey into the Christian Faith* by Rosaria Butterfield. Nancy Pearcey's *Love Thy Body: Answering Hard Questions about Life and Sexuality*, Peter Jones's *God of Sex: How Spirituality Defines Your Sexuality* and Preston Sprinkle's *People to Be Loved: Why Homosexuality is Not Just an Issue* are also profoundly helpful.

Appendix E

Ending the Culture War

I was raised in a church world in which "culture war" was a favorite metaphor of how the church relates to the nonchurch. We were God's courageous, moral infantry doing battle against those cunning cultists, those hateful homosexuals, those lying liberals, and those devilish Darwinists. If we listen with tuned ears to Christian radio, Christian literature, Christian blogs, and Christian conversations, it becomes clear: we Christians love the language of war. Over the last thirty years it has become our dominant metaphor for relating to culture; it saturates our vocabulary, shapes our politics, and soaks our worldview. But is culture war helpful? Is it biblical? Should we be jarheads for Jesus?

I offer two reasons we need to permanently jettison the culture war metaphor as the church moves into the future:

1. *Culture war blurs important biblical distinctions regarding evil, moving us to battle the wrong "enemy."* What if the Allies of World War II had declared war against Holland, marching on the Hague to dethrone Queen Wilhelmina, while the rampaging Fuhrer of Berlin continued his vicious Blitzkrieg unopposed? Such a witless Allied blunder would have been cataclysmic. As Sun Tzu observed in *The Art of War*, you must "know your enemy."

When looking through biblical lenses, we begin to see evil not in monochrome but in three dark hues. We behold what we might call an "anti-Trinity" of forces ambushing the triune God's good mission for his universe. In the Trinity we have God, the Father of Lights; in the anti-Trinity, the Devil, who is the Father of Lies. In the Trinity we find Jesus, the Word made flesh; in the anti-Trinity, we encounter our internal sin drive, which Paul calls "the flesh." In the Trinity we meet the Holy Spirit, called the Spirit of Truth; in the anti-Trinity, the world, or "the spirit of the age." These important distinctions are captured in the following chart:

The Trinity		The Anti-Trinity	
The Father	**"The Father of Lights"**	**"The Father of Lies"**	**The Devil**
Jam. 1:17 Eph. 4:6 1 Pet. 1:3 Matt. 5:45 John 4:23 John 10:29-38	The Father is God, "The Father of Lights" on a redemptive mission in the world for his glory's sake. Narrow focus on this truth may lead theologically to Arianism and a practical failure to worship and enjoy the Son and Holy Spirit.	The Devil is evil, "The Father of Lies" on a destructive mission in the world for his glory's sake. Narrow focus on this truth may lead to blaming self-caused blunders on the devil and often unhealthy obsession with or fear of demons.	John 8:44 1 Pet. 5:8 John 17:15 Eph. 6:10-16 John 10:10 James 4:7
The Son	**God Who "Became Flesh"**	**"The Flesh"**	**The Sin Nature**
John 1:1, 14 Isa. 9:6-7 Heb. 1:3-13 Col. 1:15-17 Rom. 9:5 John 20:28	The Son is God who "became flesh," lived flawlessly, died as our substitute, and rose bodily to give us life. Narrow focus on this truth may lead to "Jesus only" theology and a practical failure to worship and enjoy the Father and Holy Spirit.	The sin nature is evil, "the flesh" as an internal driving force toward selfish action and away from God, leading to death. Narrow focus on this truth may lead to morbid introspection and ignoring the need for spiritual warfare.	Rom. 8:1-17 Gal. 5:16-25 Ps. 51:1-12 1 Pet. 2:11 Col. 3:5-10 Matt. 15:8-20
The Holy Spirit	**"The Spirit of Truth"**	**"The Spirit of the Age"**	**The World**
John 14:16-17 Ez. 36:26-27 Acts 5:3-9 2 Pet. 1:21 Gal. 5:22-23 John 16:8-14	The Holy Spirit is God, "The Spirit of Truth" who moves people deeper into the reality of God and his glory. Narrow focus on this truth may lead to "Charismania" and a practical failure to worship and enjoy the Father and Son.	The world is evil, "The Spirit of the Age" that moves people deeper into the illusion of our own godhood and glory. Narrow focus on this truth may lead to an us-them xenophobia and failure to acknowledge or fight against internal evils.	1 Cor. 2:12 Rom. 12:2 James 4:4 Titus 2:12 1 John 2:15-17 Eph. 2:1-5

The Bible's distinctions between the world, the flesh, and the Devil are massively important to the question of whether we should engage in culture war. Should we war against the Devil? Yes. Paul calls us to prayerfully armor up "against the schemes of the devil" and "extinguish all the flaming darts of the evil one," wielding the Word of God to assault God's ancient enemy.[1] As Calvin put it in his commentary on 2 Corinthians 10, "The life of a Christian, it is true, is a perpetual warfare, for whoever gives himself to the service of God will have no truce from Satan at any time."[2]

Should we war against the flesh, those internal anti-God propensities that "wage war against your soul,"[3] "making me captive to the law of sin"?[4] Again, the Bible issues a call to war: "Put on the armor of light ... [and] put on the Lord Jesus Christ, and make no provision for the flesh, to gratify its desires."[5] With violent language, Paul calls us to "put to death" the flesh by the Holy Spirit's power, to execute or "crucify" it.[6]

So is Christianity a religion of war? If our enemies are the flesh and the Devil, then, yes, onward Christian soldiers! If, however, our enemy is the world, then the Bible has something else to say. First, we are commissioned not to live in a bubble like a world-phobic tribe but to go into the world to herald the good news of Jesus.[7] Second, we don't go as chameleons absorbing into our skin any Christless colors of the broader culture but as nonconformists, unstained from the world, shining as lights in the midst of a crooked and twisted generation.[8] We refuse to become slaves, victims, friends, or lovers of an oppressive system in which greedy consumption, radical self-glorification, and constant pleasure-center brain stimulation are hailed as virtues.[9] Third, as we go, the Bible warns that the world might very well take an aggressive posture of hatred toward those who refuse to conform to its values.[10]

When the hatred comes, should the church beat its plowshares into swords and counterattack with culture war? On the contrary, Jesus commands (not suggests) not that we retaliate or even merely tolerate but that we "love our enemies."[11] Jesus prayed for the salvation of the very men hammering spikes through his wrists and bled for us when we ourselves were warring against the Father he loves. Paul, following this radical countercultural pattern of enemy-love (and no stranger to the world's brutality himself), commands blessing to the persecutor, peaceable living with all, a ban on vengeance, food for the hungry enemy, and goodness to overcome evil.[12] It is significant that neither Jesus nor Paul nor any Spirit-inspired author commands us to love, bless, make peace with, or feed either the Devil or the sin-drives in our own hearts.

When pondering war, therefore, the Christian must ask: Is the object of my warfare the flesh or the Devil? If yes, then fight on. If, however, the church feels assaulted by a militant culture, we need to postpone our natural fight-or-flight response long enough to ponder the unnatural command of Jesus and Paul to meet the force of hatred with the force of love. And we must pray for the supernatural infusion of love necessary to live such an impossible and countercultural command.

2. *Culture war misses the biblical distinction between combatants and captives, mistaking a mission of liberation for one of extermination.* A Christian culture warrior may object, "Yes, the Bible does call us to war against Satan. But as 'the ruler of this world,'[13] Satan enlists human soldiers to carry out his diabolical orders. Therefore, you can't engage in spiritual warfare without simultaneously waging a culture war." I agree with this objection insofar as I believe, with Scripture, that there is more than mere human evil at work in culture. I do not believe satanic forces were distant and uninterested spectators to the slave plantations or concentration camps.

But arguing to a war-on-culture from a war-on-Satan overlooks another important biblical distinction. Consider Paul's words: "The Lord's servant must not be quarrelsome but kind to everyone, able to teach, patiently enduring evil, correcting his opponents with gentleness. God may perhaps grant them repentance leading to a knowledge of the truth, and they may come to their senses and escape from the snare of the devil, after being captured by him to do his will."[14]

Paul does not picture his human opponents as soldiers in Satan's army to be met with lethal force. Rather, they are described as snared captives who must be met with kindness, gentle correction, and a hopefulness that works not toward their extermination but their liberation.[15] Peter summarized Jesus's ministry to the world not as smiting Satan's soldiers but as "doing good and healing all who were oppressed by the devil."[16]

Soldiers make war. Paul calls us to "live peaceably with all."[17] A soldier sheds his opponent's blood; Paul sheds tears for his.[18] A soldier becomes cold-hearted toward the enemy; Paul had "unceasing anguish in [his] heart" for those who opposed him.[19] A soldier puts a higher premium on his own survival than that of his enemies; Paul wished to be "accursed and cut off from Christ" for the sake of his unbelieving brothers.[20] Paul was imprisoned, impoverished, battered half to death, and finally decapitated by Nero's executioners. And this was all to carry out his mission, not to put *x*'s on his enemies' eyes but "to open their eyes, so that they may turn from darkness to light and from the power of Satan to God, that they may receive forgiveness of sins."[21]

From these biblical distinctions, it follows that war-on-Satan does not entail war-on-culture. Our aggressive acts of war against the Devil must be matched by empathetic acts of abolition for our neighbors who remain trapped in the oppressive grip of history's oldest human trafficker.

The Metaphors Matter

Am I arguing that a postculture-war Christian no longer offers meaningful critiques of hurtful and dehumanizing ideologies that shape culture, no longer cares about politics, no longer challenges and converses with those beyond his own spiritual tribe? Of course not. The call of Jesus was never that of a cult leader to coax us from society, to buy guns and gold, and to move to a secluded mountain compound where we all drink Kool-Aid and bid farewell to the world's problems. Jesus commissions us to go into the world. What I am arguing is that the culture war metaphor has a profound, often subconscious effect on how we go about obeying Jesus's Commission. Are we going more as disciple makers or enemy slayers? Is culture more of a field to plentifully harvest or an army to be vanquished? Are we more like abolitionists on a mission to liberate people in chains or a SEAL team on a search-and-destroy mission? How shall we then live in the "post-Christian age," like a jarhead or like Jesus, trying to kill or willing to die for our enemies?

The metaphors matter.

Appendix F

Fragility and Antifragility

There is a principle that rings just as true in the doctor's office, as it does in the preschool, as it does in the bedroom, as it does in the world of social justice: if you don't understand the nature of something or someone, then your best efforts to help will almost always end up harming that something or someone. Often the more energetically we pursue the good of that misunderstood something or someone, the more swiftly we bring about their demise. And the better our intentions, the worse the damage, because our deep-seated belief that we're doing something noble and virtuous will blind us to the harm of our "helping." Add to that misunderstood nature, that energetic action, and those noble intentions a fourth factor—a whole lot of people doing the same thing under the sway of some ideology—and we have a recipe for creating hell on earth.

Jonathan Haidt offers a telling example with peanut allergies. Once extremely rare—seen in one in five thousand people in the 1980s—peanut allergies began skyrocketing in the 2000s. The cause? A misunderstanding of human nature, plus energetic action to fix a problem, plus a deep-seated belief in our best intentions, plus a whole lot of people doing the same thing equals a 5,000 percent increase in peanut allergy sufferers.

In his bestseller *Antifragile*, Nassim Nicholas Taleb draws an important distinction between fragility and antifragility. A wine glass is fragile. Handle it with extreme care, or it will shatter and become a useless heap of shards. Other things exhibit the curious property of antifragility. If you break your muscles down by subjecting them to heavy strain, you don't turn into a pathetic ball of flab. Instead, your antifragile muscles become stronger every time you break them down with exercise. In a sense, the more traumatized they are, by long hours at the gym, the more gloriously they bulge into what they were designed to be. So the question is, is the human spirit fragile or antifragile?

It is clear which way Social Justice B answers that question. Don't subject our minds to perspectives we find offensive. We need more safe spaces. Which way does the Bible answer the question? Consider what God has to say about whether he designed us as fragile or antifragile:

Count it all joy, my brothers, when you meet trials of various kinds, for you know that the testing of your faith produces steadfastness. And let steadfastness have its full effect, that you may be perfect and complete, lacking in nothing.[1]

We rejoice in our sufferings, knowing that suffering produces endurance, and endurance produces character, and character produces hope, and hope does not put us to shame, because God's love has been poured into our hearts through the Holy Spirit who has been given to us.[2]

Since we are surrounded by so great a cloud of witnesses, let us also lay aside every weight, and sin which clings so closely, and let us run with endurance the race that is set before us, looking to Jesus, the founder and perfecter of our faith, who for the joy that was set before him endured the cross, despising the shame, and is seated at the right hand of the throne of God.[3]

Do not lose heart. Though our outer self is wasting away, our inner self is being renewed day by day. For this light momentary affliction is preparing for us an eternal weight of glory beyond all comparison.[4]

It has been granted to you that for the sake of Christ you should not only believe in him but also suffer for his sake.[5]

In this you rejoice, though now for a little while, if necessary, you have been grieved by various trials, so that the tested genuineness of your faith—more precious than gold that perishes though it is tested by fire—may be found to result in praise and glory and honor at the revelation of Jesus Christ.[6]

Brothers and sisters, we are not fragile. Let us pursue justice together as the antifragile image-bearers God designed us to be.

Appendix G

"Good News to the Poor"

L uke 4 is a favorite passage of many who champion social justice. It is one of my favorite passages too. Jesus launches his public ministry by standing in a synagogue, unrolling the Isaiah scroll, and reading:

> The Spirit of the Lord is upon me,
>> because He has anointed me
>> to preach good news to the poor.
> He has sent me to proclaim freedom to captives,
>> recover of sight to the blind,
>> to set at liberty those who are oppressed,
> to proclaim the acceptable year of the Lord.[1]

There you have it, straight from the red letters. The gospel according to Jesus is about good news for the poor, freedom for slaves, and liberation for the oppressed. Edit social justice out of the gospel, and instead of the gospel Jesus announced, you are left with a "truncated" or "incomplete" gospel at best and a Gnostic, individualistic, white supremacist gospel at worst. Those are the charges. Here are six helpful questions we should ask about such an interpretation of Luke 4.

1. *Is it important to avoid reading our personal politics and perspectives into Scripture?* American slaveowners twisted the Bible's original meanings about the curse of Ham, Paul's charge to Philemon, words like *doulos*, and more, all in a self-serving effort to justify treating Africans like property instead of divine image-bearers. God's Word was co-opted to justify white supremacy. As has been noted throughout church history, the Bible can be easily turned into

"a nose of wax,"[2] a nose that can be fashioned to fit the profiles of some ugly ideologies. Should we be careful to let the context of a passage determine its meaning more than a given political or personal ideology? Of course.

2. *Is it possible to take this particular Scripture—Jesus's words in Luke 4—out of context in a way that hurts the poor and oppressed?* Take the prosperity gospel, the televangelists' doctrine that God promises health and wealth. Luke 4 is one of the televangelists' favorite passages. "See, it's right there in the text. The gospel is 'good news to the poor' and restoring 'sight to the blind.' If you edit financial blessing and physical healing out of the gospel, then you have an incomplete gospel. Jesus does not just want your soul to float off to heaven; he wants health and wealth for the sick and poor *now*!"

The stakes are high with such textual twisting. Over the course of my career, I have received hundreds of letters from poor people around the world who have been exploited by the false gospel of Benny Hinn, Kenneth Copeland, Fred Price, Creflo Dollar, and other religious con men. The letters are tear-jerking, and the impact of the false health and wealth gospel is nothing short of catastrophic, especially for the sickest and poorest among us.

We need to be extremely careful not to read into Jesus's words something he did not intend. Otherwise we will end up with what Paul calls "a different gospel."[3] As Sam Chan puts it, "In Romans 1:1, the apostle Paul tells us that the gospel is 'the gospel of God'; it is God's gospel. This means that the story belongs to God; it is not our story to invent, modify, or embellish."[4]

Do we believe it's possible to twist not only Scripture in general but this passage in particular to turn the gospel into a false ideology that hurts people and that we must, therefore, take the context seriously to avoid doing so? Hopefully we can all agree.

3. *If Luke 4 means that the gospel is about confronting social injustice, then what social injustices did Jesus confront that day?* Let's look at the immediate context. Right after reading from the Isaiah scroll, Jesus says, "Today this Scripture has been fulfilled."[5] Jesus goes on to set people free from sickness and demonic oppression. If justice is not merely an implication of a gospel-transformed life but intrinsic to the gospel itself, then we may ask, "What, if anything, resembling what people today call 'social justice,' did Jesus do *that day?* There was no shortage of social injustice when Jesus read from the Isaiah scroll—systems of infanticide, slavery, and misogyny, to name a few. If we believe social justice is the gospel or part of the gospel, then we must conclude that Jesus himself preached a truncated gospel that day.

Does this mean justice is *optional* for Christians, that we can shrug our shoulders when we encounter injustices like infanticide, slavery, or misogyny? Of course not. "Do justice" is a command, not a suggestion, of Scripture. I am simply arguing from the text that keeping the biblical command to "do justice" is not the same as the gospel any more than telling the truth, staying faithful to your spouse, loving your neighbor, or carrying out any other divine command is the gospel.

4. *What does Jesus actually preach to the poor?* When Jesus declares his mission to "preach the good news to the poor," he tells us a *community* he intended to bless with good news, not the *content* of the good news itself. This would be like CEO Frank saying, "I came to give good news to the board," Professor Jill saying, "I came to give good news to the students," or Coach Bill saying, "I came to give good news to the team." We haven't learned much about the content of their messages. The CEO's boardroom briefing could be about a huge profit boost or a failing competitor. The professor's lecture could be about an extra credit opportunity or the health benefits of green beans. The pep talk could be about rising to first place or an injury of the other team's star player. Knowing who the *audience* is does not constitute knowing what the *announcement* is.

The phrase "good news to the poor" doesn't spell out precisely what the good news is. We must be careful not to use Jesus's words—"good news to the poor"—like a Rorschach inkblot to project our own meaning. Again, for the televangelists, the good news to the poor is that by believing hard enough (and proving that belief with large donations to the televangelists' ministries) the poor can experience a hundredfold financial blessing.

Thankfully, we don't have to dump our own definitions into Jesus's good news. The New Testament records Jesus's actual preaching to the poor. In Mark 1:14–15 we read that "Jesus came into Galilee, proclaiming the gospel of God, and saying, 'The time is fulfilled, and the kingdom of God is at hand; repent and believe in the gospel.'" Two verses later Jesus calls his first disciples with the invitation, "Follow me." Those words held tremendous force in first-century Judaism. To become a disciple of a rabbi was a long and arduous task. Candidates for discipleship often had to shadow rabbis for years, proving their merit and moral fitness. And maybe, just maybe, if they proved themselves worthy, they would hear the rabbi utter, "Follow me." Jesus flips that whole system on its head, launching his entire ministry with an act of grace that spoke those cherished words to men who had done nothing to prove themselves.

Later in Mark, Jesus makes his famous statement that a camel has an easier time fitting through the eye of a needle than the rich do entering God's kingdom. His disciples are shocked and ask, "'Then who can be saved?' Jesus looked at them and said, 'With man it is impossible, but not with God. For all things are possible with God'" (10:26–27). Several verses later Jesus defines his mission on earth to "give his life as a ransom for many" (10:45). After his resurrection, Jesus commands his disciples to "go into all the world and declare the gospel to the whole creation. Whoever believes and is baptized will be saved, but whoever does not believe will be condemned" (16:15–16).

In Luke, we find the famous parable of the prodigal son, in which Jesus makes it clear that God runs to us, embraces us, and showers us with blessings as a divine act of free, ill-deserved grace. Then in Luke 18:13–14, it is not the Pharisee flaunting his own righteousness and giving to the poor, but the tax collector beating his breast crying, "God, be merciful to me, a sinner!" who goes home justified before God. At the first Lord's Supper, Jesus speaks of his death, saying "This cup that is poured out for you is the new covenant in my blood" (22:20). Read up on the "new covenant" from the Old to the New Testament and you will see the good news of salvation by grace alone throughout. Later Jesus tells the poor thief on the cross, "Truly, I say to you, today you will be with me in paradise,"[6] though the thief had no time before his final breath to do any good works.

In the book of John, Jesus addresses the poor on the shores of Capernaum. After Jesus brings up eternal life, the crowd asks, "What must we do, to be doing the works of God?" (6:28). Jesus did not say, "Go reform unjust systems." Instead, "Jesus answered them, 'This is the work of God, that you believe in him whom he has sent'" (6:29). At Lazarus's tomb Jesus declares, "I am the resurrection and the life. Whoever believes in me, though he die, yet shall he live, and everyone who lives and believes in me shall never die" (11:25–26). In sum, there is no shortage of red letters to help us discern what Jesus actually preached to the poor.

Salvation by God's grace alone through Christ is good news for the poor for several reasons. Oppressive governments and societies send a loud and clear message to the poor: *Your life has no worth!* I have listened to many dear oppressed brothers and sisters around the world. They have shared with me just how liberating the good news is, how subversive and revolutionary it is for them to hear that even as society treats them like garbage, the sovereign Creator of the universe deems them worthy enough to die for. If society treats you like subhuman scum, then it is profoundly good news to hear that God—whose perspective is infinitely more authoritative than politicians or their minions— declares you his beloved.

If, however, the "good news" includes social activism, then where, we may ask, does Jesus preach such news to the poor anywhere in the red letters of the

four gospels? Nowhere. This is not to say working toward justice is unimport-
ant or unbiblical; it is simply saying that such work is not equivalent to the "the
good news" as Jesus defined in Luke 4 or anywhere else in the New Testament.

5. *How is the gospel defined in the rest of Scripture?* The good news Jesus
preaches to the poor fits other New Testament passages that explicitly define
the gospel for us. In 1 Corinthians 15 Paul says, "Now I would remind you,
brothers, of the gospel I preached to you.... For I delivered to you as of first
importance what I also received: that Christ died for our sins in accordance
with the Scriptures, that he was buried, that he was raised on the third day in
accordance with the Scriptures."[7]

Notice that "the gospel" is "of first importance." And what is that gospel?
It is the good news of free salvation by trusting in the sin-atoning death and
bodily resurrection of Jesus. It shouldn't surprise us that Paul understands the
gospel this way, since he received it directly from Jesus.[8] Unlike toppling social
and economic systems through social activism, this good news of salvation by
grace through faith in Christ is what Jesus proclaims to poor in the red letters. It is what the earliest missionaries declare with astonishing saving results
throughout the book of Acts. It is the same good news declared throughout the
New Testament epistles. Ask your friends who include social justice in their
definition of the gospel: *How does the New Testament's consistent message of
salvation by God's grace alone fit into your definition of the gospel?*

If social justice is not the gospel, then some may ask, "Why should we give a
rip about the poor?" For the same reason we should care about telling the truth,
being faithful to our spouses, and not stealing. Because God commands us to,
and such obedience is evidence that we have truly been saved by grace. If God
is willing to go to the great lengths of the incarnation and bloody crucifixion
to prove his love for the poor, then certainly we should be willing to go to
great lengths to dignify those whom culture treats as worthless. Such love for
the poor is not the gospel, but it is something that ought to flow from our
hearts (and wallets and purses) if we recognize just how spiritually bankrupt
we were when God sovereignly decided to make us rich through the death and
resurrection of Jesus.

6. *Is it possible that redefining "the gospel" to include our own visions of social
justice can prove harmful?* Most of my friends and colleagues who see a gospel
of social justice in Luke 4 link their understanding of social justice to specific
political and economic systems. This is where things can get particularly dicey.

Let us not forget Chile in the early 1970s. Many socially concerned

Christians rallied behind Salvador Allende's presidential candidacy. They believed his socialist policies would expand the kingdom of God, bringing good news to the poor by combatting income inequality. Allende's "social-ism . . . offers a possibility for the development of the country for the benefit of all, especially the most neglected." They believed his "socialism generate[s] new values which make possible the emergence of a society of greater solidarity and brotherhood." "The profound reason for this commitment is our faith in Jesus Christ."[9]

With Christian support, Allende won. In the name of helping the poor, he instituted socialist policies. He collectivized land and agriculture. Inflation skyrocketed 600 percent. Poverty rates jumped by 50 percent. Even more people were forced into the sad ranks of the neglected. Let us learn the lessons of history: conflating Jesus's gospel with political visions of social justice turns good news into bad news for the poor. Instead of misinterpreting Luke 4 as a proof text for our highly fallible political ideologies, let us "contend for the faith that was once for all delivered to the saints."[10]

Notes

What Is "Social Justice"?

1. Jeremiah 22:3.
2. Micah 6:8.
3. Isaiah 58:6.
4. Isaiah 58:8, 10. See also See Psalm 41:1.
5. Jeremiah 22:16.
6. Isaiah 1:15–17.
7. Isaiah 1:17.
8. Jeremiah 7:5, emphasis added.
9. 1 Thessalonians 5:21; Romans 12:9.
10. Luke 4:18, citing Isaiah 61:1.
11. Isaiah 11:3–4.
12. John 7:24.
13. Philippians 1:9.
14. Romans 12:2.
15. 2 Corinthians 10:5.
16. Jonah Goldberg, "The Problem with 'Social Justice,'" *Columbia Daily Tribune*, February 6, 2019, https://www.columbiatribune.com/news/20190206/problem-with-social-justice.Old Testament theologian John Goldingay adds,

   > The notion of social justice is a hazy one. It resembles words such as community, intimacy, and relational, warm words whose meaning may seem self-evident and which we assume are obviously biblical categories, when actually they are rather undefined and culture relative.... The meaning of the phrase social justice has become opaque over the years as it has become a buzz expression (*Old Testament Theology Vol. 3: Israel's Life* [Downers Grove, IL: IVP Academic, 2016], 500).

17. "What We Believe," Black Lives Matter, https://blacklivesmatter.com/what-we-believe/.
18. For a wide range of readings advancing Social Justice B, see *Race, Class, and Gender: An Anthology, 9th Edition*, eds. Margaret Anderson and Patricia Hill Collins (Boston, MA: Cengage Learning, 2015).
19. Jude 3 NIV

20. "Love is a Weapon of Choice," *Flight of the Conchords*, Season 2, Episode 6, Written by James Bobin, Jemaine Clement, and Bret McKenzie. Directed James Bobin. HBO, Febraury 22, 2009.

21. Martin Luther King Jr., "Letter from a Birmingham Jail," April 16, 1963, https://www.africa.upenn.edu/Articles_Gen/Letter_Birmingham.html

22. As renowned Sovietologist Harry Schaffer sums up, "Socialists and Communists of all shades and leanings believe in the perfectibility of all mankind. Man is basically good and capable of being master of his own destiny. Only the economic, social, and political environment (with the stress on "economic") has prevented man from realizing the utmost limits of his capabilities both as a productive and social being" (*The Soviet System on Theory and Practice* [New York: Appleton-Century-Crofts, 1965], 30).

    This communist view of human nature yields very different results from a Christian anthropology. Where a biblical worldview built orphanages and hospitals to help the marginalized and broken, communism gave us the killing fields of the Khmer Rouge. Where the gospel led to the abolishing of the human dumps of the Roman Empire and brought society's unwanted into loving community, communism endorsed the systematic termination of society's unwanted. Where biblical Christianity set slaves free, communism sent millions to the gulags. Where Christianity inspired the Oxfords and Cambridges into existence to pursue knowledge to the glory of God, communism inspired thought policing. Where Jesus transformed deep racial tensions into a new, beautiful, reconciled community, communism helped spawn identity politics and all the divisiveness that goes with it.

23. Cathy Newman, "Jordan Peterson Debate on the Gender Pay Gap, Campus Protests and Postmodernism," Channel 4 News, January 6, 2018, YouTube video, 29:55, https://www.youtube.com/watch?v=aMcjxSThD54.

24. Aaron Lynch, *Thought Contagion: How Belief Spreads Through Society* (New York: BasicBooks, 1996), 208. Lynch's analysis focused on memes or "thought contagions" primarily in terms of ideas themselves, how, for example, ideas like "Socialism is good/bad," "We should/shouldn't follow our hearts," or "Wealth is/isn't a worthy life goal" spread through generations. I'm getting at something deeper. Yes, ideas themselves can become memes or "thought contagions," but so can our idea-forming attitudes, our epistemic tendencies, the way we process and interpret life itself. That is what the Newman effect is, not just this or that specific idea about feminism or the pay gap or whatever, but the deeper habit of how we form our beliefs—namely, assuming the worst of those who disagree with us to self-righteously validate our own perspectives and story of reality. That habit itself has become a meme in our social media age, regardless of the side of the political spectrum one inhabits.

25. Francis Schaeffer, *The God Who is There* (Chicago: Inter-Varsity Press, 1968), 127.

26. Philippians 3:18.

27. Matthew 9:36; Luke 19:41–44

Part 1: Jehovah or Jezebel?

1. Katherine Timpf, "University Policy Allows for Expulsion for 'Mean' Facial Expressions," *National Review*, December 10, 2018, https://www.nationalreview .com/2018/12/university-policy-allows-expulsion-for-mean-expressions.

2. Cited in Daron Acemoglu and James A. Robinson's *Why Nations Fail: The Origins of Power, Prosperity, and Poverty* (New York: Crown, 2012), 7–44.

3. *Encomendia* made its way through Nicaragua where Spanish "lords" made "the whole of the native population . . . labor night and day in his own interests, without any rest whatsoever." The Spanish brought *encomendia* to Colombia and Peru, where a conquistador named Pizarro enslaved the inhabitants. For a superb historical treatment of *encomendia* and its lingering effects today, see chapter 1 of Acemoglu and Robinson, *Why Nations Fail*, 7–44.

Chapter 1: The God Question

1. Romans 1:28–29.

2. Jacques Maritain, "Chapter 15: A Faith to Live By," *The Range of Reason,* The Jacques Maritain Center, https://maritain.nd.edu/jmc/etext/range15.htm, accessed July 12, 2020.

3. Romans 3:10. See Psalm 14:1–3 for Paul's source.

4. Romans 1:20.

5. Michael Horton clarifies: "This refusal [in Romans 1:20–21] is not, therefore, simply an intellectual problem, but is rooted in an ethical rebellion that is willfully perpetuated. As Paul goes on to relate in that passage, the biblical term for this pursuit of autonomous metaphysics is *idolatry*." (*The Christian Faith: A Systematic Theology for Pilgrims on the Way* [Grand Rapids: Zondervan, 2011], 57, emphasis in original).

6. Romans 1:21.

7. Romans 1:25.

8. Romans 1:29.

9. Romans 1:23.

Chapter 2: The Imago Question

1. As James K. A. Smith defines the immanent frame in his helpful pop distillation of Taylor's thought, it is the "constructed social space that frames our lives entirely within a natural (rather than supernatural) order" (*How (Not) to be Secular: Reading Charles Taylor* [Grand Rapids: Eerdmans, 2014], 141).

2. In other words, we inhabit what the great sociologist Peter Berger would call a "plausibility structure" in which it is "plausible" (i.e., you won't be laughed out of the classroom or have a mob campaigning for your firing) if you talk about the economic or political roots of justice. You may even be invited to do a TED Talk. But appeal to anything or anyone beyond our "immanent frame" and you had better duck and cover.

3. Found in the tract *In epistulam Ioannis ad Parthos* (*Tractatus* VII, 8), the passage reads: "Once for all, then, a short precept is given unto you: Love God, and

do what you will: whether you hold your peace, through love hold your peace; whether you cry out, through love cry out; whether you correct, through love correct; whether you spare, through love do you spare: In all things, let the root of love be within, for of this root can nothing spring but what is good."

4. See Jean-Paul Sartre, *Existentialism and Human Emotions* (Secaucus, NJ: Citadel, 1957), 21–23; Arthur Allen Leff, "Unspeakable Ethics, Unnatural Law," *Duke Law Journal* 6 (December 1979): 1229–49; and Alex Rosenberg, *The Atheist's Guide to Reality: Enjoying Life without Illusions* (New York: W. W. Norton, 2012).

5. In Charles Darwin's words,

> At some future period, not very distant measured by centuries, the civilized races of man will almost certainly exterminate and replace throughout the world the savage races. At the same time the anthropomorphous apes... will no doubt be exterminated. The break will then be rendered wider, for it will intervene between man in a more civilised state, as we may hope, than the Caucasian, and some ape as low as a baboon, instead of as at present between the negro or Australian and the gorilla (*The Descent of Man* [New York: D. Appleton and Company, 1871), 193).

6. David Garcia, *Strategies of Segregation: Race, Residence, and the Struggle for Educational Equality* (Oakland, CA: University of California Press, 2018), 35.

7. Cited in Garcia, *Strategies of Segregation*, 35. I confirmed this story, with its gut-wrenching details, over burgers and root beer with Grandma Tony, February 9, 2020.

8. 1 Thessalonians 3:12.

Chapter 3: The Idolatry Question

1. And when we consider that our hearts aren't idol sanctuaries, where a single god is worshiped, but idol factories with ever-rolling conveyor belts churning out a multiplicity of worship objects, you could build a strong case that there are even more gods in the West than there are Westerners.

2. I owe this insight to Russell Moore.

3. I owe this insight to Matthew Smethurst.

4. Camille Paglia, "Feminism: In Conversation with Camille Paglia," interview with Claire Fox, Institute for Ideas, November 4, 2016, YouTube video, 47:50–48:30, https://www.youtube.com/watch?v=4y3-KIesYRE.

5. Andrew Sullivan, "America Wasn't Built for Humans," *New York Magazine*, September 18, 2017, https://nymag.com/intelligencer/2017/09/can-democracy-survive-tribalism.html.

6. Elizabeth Corey, "First Church of Intersectionality," *First Things*, August 2017, https://www.firstthings.com/article/2017/08/first-church-of-intersectionality

7. Francis Schaeffer, *A Christian Manifesto* (Wheaton, IL: Crossway, 2005), 17.

8. Schaeffer, *A Christian Manifesto*, 17.

9. Alexander Solzhenitsyn, "A World Split Apart," Commencement Speech at Harvard (1978).

10. Abraham Kuyper, *Lectures on Calvinism* (Grand Rapids: Eerdmans, 1999), 11, emphasis in original.

11. David Kinnaman and Gabe Lyons, *Good Faith: Being Christian When Society Thinks You're Irrelevant and Extreme* (Ada, MI: Baker, 2016).

12. Paul Hiebert, *Transforming Worldviews: An Anthropological Understanding of How People Change* (Ada, MI: Baker Academic, 2008), 170.

13. Cady Lang, "Ru Paul on Why Identity Shouldn't Be Taken Seriously, But Loving Yourself Should," *Time*, April 20, 2017, https://time.com/4746895/rupaul-time -100-video/ Retrieved July 13, 2020.

14. Thaddeus J. Williams, *Reflect: Becoming Yourself by Mirroring the Greatest Person in History* (Bellingham, WA: Lexham, 2017), 73. For careful documentation of these unnerving facts, see David G. Myers, *The American Paradox* (New Haven, CT: Yale University Press, 2000). I am not arguing that shifting the weight of self-making from the Creator to the creature's shoulders is the exclusive factor in these unnerving statistics. But if we take seriously Paul's Romans 1 argument about the disarray that ensues from creation-worship, then we would be missing something profound if we limited ourselves to a sociological (at the exclusion of a spiritual) account of our present brokenness.

15. G. K. Chesterton, *Christendom in Dublin*, in *G. K. Chesterton: Collected Works*, vol. 20 (San Francisco: Ignatius, 2001), 57.

16. 1 John 2:1–2.

17. See Williams, *Reflect*, 77–78.

18. I discuss this further in 2.1 of *Love, Freedom, and Evil* (Leiden: Brill, 2011).

19. David French, "When Christians Are Too Afraid to Hear Ben Shapiro Speak" *National Review*, February 4, 2019, https://www.nationalreview.com/2019/02 /ben-shapiro-speaking-ban-when-christians-are-too-afraid/.

20. See "How to Meet Your Future Self," in *Reflect*.

21. Fulton Sheen, "Ways of Killing Freedom," *The Daily Standard*, March 12, 1966, 3.

22. See Matthew 10:22.

23. See James 4:4.

24. Quoted in Ewald Plass, ed., *What Luther Says* (St. Louis: Concordia, 1959), 1107–08.

25. Quoted in Roland Bainton, *Here I Stand: A Life of Martin Luther* (Nashville: Abingdon, 1950), 144.

26. Cited in Bainton, *Here I Stand,* 144.

Part 2: Unity or Uproar?

1. Melissa August et al., "The Hundred Worst Ideas of the Century," *Time*, June 14, 1999, http://content.time.com/time/magazine/article/0,9171,991230,00.html.

1. Conor Barnes, "Sad Radicals," *Quillette*, December 11, 2018, https://quillette.com /2018/12/11/sad-radicals/.

2. Robert Putnam, *Bowling Alone: The Collapse and Revival of American Community* (New York: Simon & Schuster, 2000), 331.

3. Lisa Berkman and Leonard Syme, "Social Networks, Host Resistance, and Mortality:

A Nine-Year Follow-up Study of Alameda County Residents," *American Journal of Epidemiology*, Vol. 109 (1979): 186-204.

4. Genesis 2:18.

5. See Williams, "Love," chap. 4 in *Reflect*.

Chapter 4: The Collective Question

1. "A Reformed White Nationalist Speaks Out on Charlottesville," August 13, 2017, https://www.npr.org/2017/08/13/543259499/a-reformed-white-nationalist -speaks-out-on-charlottesville.

2. "A Reformed White Nationalist Speaks Out on Charlottesville."

3. Barnes, "Sad Radicals."

4. Romans 3:23.

5. Of course our different nurturing—the families, communities, and cultures in which we came of age—can teach us how to be better or worse at lying, which false gods to worship, the preferred methods for pushing others down, etc. Some cultures are more effective than others at cultivating laziness, others better at cultivating greed, others at inspiring self-righteousness, and still others are adept at inspiring sexual recklessness. But the truth is that underneath all the seductive and corrupting forces outside us, there is still something already twisted and bent toward the wrong inside us. We aren't born blank slates. There's something in each of us that's highly responsive to the temptations of our given cultures. If the cultures we are born into are like one pole of a giant magnet, then our hearts aren't like rocks in our chests but like poled magnets that are easily drawn to the particular sin attractions that surround us in our given cultures.

6. These words come from the *Book of Common Prayer* and they, or some approximation of them, are repeated weekly around the world.

7. Jean-Jacques Rousseau, *il n'y a point de perversité originelle dans le cœur humain Émile ou De l'éducation/Édition 1852/Livre II*; *Letters to Malesherbes*, in *The Collected Writings of Rousseau*, vol. 5, eds. Christopher Kelly, Roger D. Masters, and Peter G. Stillman, trans. Christopher Kelly (Hanover, NH: University Press of New England, 1995), 575; *Oeuvres Complètes*, vol. I, eds. Bernard Gagnebin and Marcel Raymond (Paris: Gallimard, Bibliothèque de la Pléiade, 1959–1995), 1136.

8. I argue this point more expansively in *Reflect*, 75–82.

9. Romans 3:9.

10. Romans 3:10–12.

11. Romans 3:22–23.

12. Galatians 3:26–28.

13. Ephesians 2:13–14.

14. Romans 3:26.

15. Romans 8:1.

16. Romans 8:33–34.

17. James Cone, *God of the Oppressed* (Maryknoll, NY: Orbis, 1997), 222.

18. On Cone's view of oppression as a white phenomenon, see *God of the Oppressed* and *A Black Theology of Liberation* (Maryknoll, NY: Orbis, 2010).

19. Cone, *Black Theology of Liberation*, 61.
20. Philippians 3:7–9.
21. Colossians 3:11.
22. Philippians 3:8.
23. Colossians 3:11.

Chapter 5: The Splintering Question

1. Tom Segev, *Soldiers of Evil: The Commandments of Nazi Concentration Camps*, trans. Haim Watzman (New York: McGraw-Hill, 1987), 80.
2. RTLM stands for Radio Télévision Libre des Mille Collines, a media outlet during the Rwandan genocide that broadcast dehumanizing propaganda that turned neighbor against neighbor.
3. Thomas Sowell, *Black Rednecks and White Liberals* (New York: Encounter, 2006), 112.
4. Sowell, *Black Rednecks and White Liberals*, 112.
5. Sowell, *Black Rednecks and White Liberals*, 113, 116.
6. Sowell, *Black Rednecks and White Liberals*, 117–123, 132.
7. Sowell, *Black Rednecks and White Liberals*, 117.
8. Sowell, *Black Rednecks and White Liberals*, 116, 126.
9. Sowell, *Black Rednecks and White Liberals*, 116.
10. Suzanna Danuta Walters, "Why Can't We Hate Men?" *Washington Post*, June 8, 2018, https://www.washingtonpost.com/opinions/why-cant-we-hate-men/2018/06/08/f1a3a8e0-6451-11e8-a69c-b944de66d9e7_story.html.
11. Ekow Yankah, "Can My Children Be Friends with White People?" *New York Times*, November 11, 2017, https://www.nytimes.com/2017/11/11/opinion/sunday/interracial-friendship-donald-trump.html.
12. Michael Harriot, "White People Are Cowards," The Root, June 19, 2018, https://www.theroot.com/white-people-are-cowards-1826958780. Harriot argues, "*Some* white people will speak out *sometimes*, just like *some* fish can fly and *some* bears can ride bicycles. But if a biologist were lecturing on the mobility of aquatic animals or grizzlies, it would be idiotic to interrupt with the rare cases of flying fish or bears that ride Huffys. Fish swim. Bears walk. And white people are cowards."
13. Barnes, "Sad Radicals."
14. An expanded and revised edition of that book is being republished with Lexham Press in 2021 under the new title *God Reforms Hearts: Rethinking the Problem of Evil in Light of God's Love-Generating Power*.

Chapter 6: The Fruit Question

1. 1 Corinthians 1:10.
2. Corrie ten Boom, "Corrie ten Boom on Forgiveness," *Guideposts*, November 1972, https://www.guideposts.org/better-living/positive-living/guideposts-classics-corrie-ten-boom-on-forgiveness.
3. Elahe Izadi, "The Powerful Words of Forgiveness Delivered to Dylann Roof by Victims' Relatives," *Washington Post*, June 19, 2015, https://www.washingtonpost

.com/news/post-nation/wp/2015/06/19/hate-wont-win-the-powerful-words
-delivered-to-dylann-roof-by-victims-relatives/.

4. Izadi, "The Powerful Words of Forgiveness."

5. Izadi, "The Powerful Words of Forgiveness."

6. Izadi, "The Powerful Words of Forgiveness."

7. Bell hooks, "A Killing Rage," https://sjugenderstudies.files.wordpress.com/2013
/09/killingrage-bell-hooks.pdf, 2, retrieved August 29, 2019.

8. See Matthew 5:43–48.

9. Ephesians 4:31–32.

10. Romans 12:17–21.

11. hooks, "A Killing Rage," 3, 4.

12. hooks, "A Killing Rage," 2–3.

13. See Galatians 5:22–23.

14. Neil Shenvi and Patrick Sawyer make an important observation about Social Justice B:

> The primacy of the duty of liberation can be seen in the relative lack
> of emphasis on (or even the complete absence of) any other moral
> imperatives in modern progressive discourse. For example, it is very rare
> for proponents of critical theory to affirm and promote moral norms like
> chastity, fidelity, honesty, patience, or self-control. In fact, some of these
> terms are problematized as being fraught with power implications that
> reify oppression and patriarchy. These perspectives flow out of an ideology
> which places 'oppression of subordinate groups' at the center of our moral
> concern. This does not mean there aren't proponents of critical theory
> who are honest, patient, promoters of fidelity, or self-disciplined in ways
> that are consistent with normative understandings of these terms. Of
> course there are. It just means that these attributes are present because of
> beliefs outside of critical theory's core concerns. (Neil Shenvi and Patrick
> Sawyer, "Understanding Critical Theory and Christian Apologetics"
> The Aquila Report, March 12, 2019, https://www.theaquilareport.com
> /understanding-critical-theory-and-christian-apologetics/).

15. I argue that outrage can be a Christlike emotion. See *Reflect: Becoming Yourself by
Mirroring the Greatest Person in History* (Bellingham, WA: Lexham, 2017), 54–6.

Part 3: Sinners or Systems?

1. Psalm 94:20.

Chapter 7: The Disparity Question

1. Felix Richter, "Women Vastly Underrepresented In Silicon Valley Tech Jobs,"
Statista, August 14, 2014, https://www.statista.com/chart/2582/female-employ
ment-in-tech-companies/.

2. David Kocieniewski, "Study Suggests Racial Gap in Speeding in New Jersey,"
The New York Times, March 21, 2002, https://www.nytimes.com/2002/03/21
/nyregion/study-suggests-racial-gap-in-speeding-in-new-jersey.html.

3. Cited in Thomas Sowell, *Discrimination and Disparities* (New York: Basic, 2019), 88–89.

4. See, for example, Acts 6:1–7; Galatians 3:27–28; and James 2:1–13.

5. Ibram X. Kendi, *Stamped from the Beginning: The Definitive History of Racist Ideas in America* (New York: Nation, 2016), 11.

6. "'When I See Racial Disparities I see Racism.' Discussing Race, Gender, and Mobility," *New York Times*, March 27, 2018, https://www.nytimes.com/interactive /2018/03/27/upshot/reader-questions-about-race-gender-and-mobility.html.

7. Kocieniewski, "Study Suggests Racial Gap in Speeding in New Jersey."

8. Sowell echoes, "Younger people are more prone to speeding, and groups with a younger median age tend to have a higher proportion of their population in age brackets where speeding is more common" (*Discrimination and Disparities* [New York: Basic, 2019], 96).

9. Sowell, *Discrimination and Disparities*, 88–89.

10. Sowell, *Discrimination and Disparities*, 89.

11. Sowell expands,

> Such data seldom, if ever, saw the light of day in most newspapers or on most television news programs, for which the black-white difference was enough to convince journalists that racial bias was the reason. . . . One of the very few media outlets to even consider alterative explanations for the black-white statistical difference was the *Atlanta Journal-Constitution,* which showed that 52 percent of blacks had credit scores so low that they would qualify only for the less desirable subprime mortgages, as did 16 percent of whites. . . . But such statistics, so damaging to the prevailing preconception that intergroup differences in outcomes showed racial bias, were almost never mentioned in most of the mass media (*Discrimination and Disparities*, 89).

12. On the power of something as undamning as geography to generate inequalities, see Sowell, *Discrimination and Disparities*, 18–23.

13. Sowell, *Discrimination and Disparities*, 24.

14. Michael Rand, "The Intersection of Malcolm Gladwell, the Wild and the NHL Draft," *StarTribune*, July 13, 2017, https://www.startribune.com/the-intersection -of-malcolm-gladwell-the-wild-and-the-nhl-draft/434329063/.

15. Sowell, *Discrimination and Disparities*, 11.

16. Sowell concludes, "The idea that the world *would* be a level playing field, if it were not for . . . discrimination, is a preconception in defiance of both facts and logic" (*Discrimination and Disparities*, 18).

17. Proverbs 10:4.

18. Proverbs 14:23.

19. Proverbs 20:4.

20. 2 Thessalonians 3:10.

21. Proverbs 24:3–4.

22. Proverbs 24:30–34.

23. Neil Shenvi, "A Long Review of Kendi's Stamped from the Beginning: Part 3,"

https://shenviapologetics.com/a-long-review-of-kendis-stamped-from-the
-beginning-part-3/, accessed August 2, 2019.

24. See Lisa Keister, "Religion and Wealth: The Role of Religious Affiliation and Participation in Early Adult Asset Accumulation," *Social Forces* 82:1 (2003): 175–207, and "Conservative Protestants and Wealth: How Religion Perpetuates Asset Poverty," *American Journal of Sociology* 113:5 (2008): 1237–71.

25. C. S. Lewis, "Forgiveness," chap. 7 in *Mere Christianity*.

26. Lewis, "Forgiveness," chap. 7 in *Mere Christianity*.

27. Sowell, *Discrimination and Disparities*, 218.

28. See Ephesians 6:11–12.

Chapter 8: The Color Question

1. Hank Johnson, "Rep Johnson Rips Congress Over Inaction to Police Shootings," RepHankJohnson, April 13, 2015, 2:10, YouTube video, https://www.youtube.com/watch?v=hlQNW5LFN1g&feature=emb_logo.

2. *Washington Post*, Fatal Force database, www.washingtonpost.com, accessed May 13, 2019.

3. John McWhorter, "Police Kill Too Many People—White and Black," *Time*, July 4, 2016, https://time.com/4404987/police-violence/.

4. McWhorter, "Police Kill Too Many People—White and Black."

5. *Washington Post*, Fatal Force database, www.washingtonpost.com, accessed July 16, 2020.

6. Peter Kirsanow, "Dissenting Statement of Commissioner Peter Kirsanow," in *Police Use of Force: An Examination of Modern Policing Practices*, U.S., Commission on Civil Rights, Briefing Report, November 2018, 197–216, https://www.usccr.gov/pubs/2018/11-15-Police-Force.pdf

7. Roland Fryer, "An Empirical Analysis of Racial Differences in Police Use of Force," revised January 2018, https://www.nber.org/papers/w22399.

8. Lois James, Stephen James, and Bryan Vila, "The Reverse Racism Effect: Are Cops More Hesitant to Shoot Black than White Suspects?" *Criminology and Public Policy*, January 14, 2016, https://onlinelibrary.wiley.com/doi/full/10.1111/1745-9133.12187.

9. See Heather MacDonald, *The War on Cops: How the New Attack on Law and Order Makes Everyone Less Safe*; Thomas Sowell, *Black Rednecks and White Liberals*, 53–54, 284–285; Walter Williams, *Race and Economics: How Much Can Be Blamed on Discrimination?*; Shelby Steele, *White Guilt: How Blacks and Whites Together Destroyed the Promise of the Civil Rights Era* and *A Dream Deferred: The Second Betrayal of Black Freedom in America*; and John McWhorter, *Winning the Race: Beyond the Crisis in Black America*.

10. See Devah Pager, Bruce Western, and Bart Bonikowski, "Discrimination in a Low-Wage Labor Market: A Field Experiment," *American Sociological Review* 74 (October 2009): 777–99.

11. See Michael Emerson, George Yancey, and Karen Chai, "Does Race Matter in Residential Segregation? Exploring the Preferences of White Americans," *American Sociological Review* 66 (December 2001): 922–35; George Galster and

Erin Godfrey, "By Words and Deeds: Racial Steering By Real Estate Agents in the U.S. in 2000," *Journal of American Planning Association* 71:3 (Summer 2005): 251–68. For discrimination in criminal justice systems, see Allen Beck and Alfred Blumstein's "Racial Disproportionality in U.S. State Prison," *J Quant Criminol* 34 (June 9, 2017): 854–83; and "Demographic Differences in Sentencing," United States Sentencing Commission, November 14, 2017, https://www.ussc.gov /research/research-reports/demographic-differences-sentencing.

12. Jessica L. Semega, Kayla R. Fontenot, and Melissa A. Kollar, "Income and Poverty in the United States: 2016," US Department of Commerce, United States Census Bureau, Issued September 2017, https://www.census.gov/content/dam/Census /library/publications/2017/demo/P60-259.pdf. See also Lisa J. Dettling et al., "Recent Trends in Wealth-Holding by Race and Ethnicity: Evidence from the Survey of Consumer Finances," Federal Reserve, September 27, 2017, https://www .federalreserve.gov/econres/notes/feds-notes/recent-trends-in-wealth-holding-by -race-and-ethnicity-evidence-from-the-survey-of-consumer-finances-20170927.htm.

13. See Mehrsa Baradaran, *The Color of Money: Black Blanks and the Racial Wealth Gap*, Richard Rothstein's *The Color of Law: A Forgotten History of How Our Government Segregated America*; Ta-Nehisi Coates, "The Case for Reparations," *The Atlantic* (June 2014), https://www.theatlantic.com/magazine /archive/2014/06/the-case-for-reparations/361631/; and Jemar Tisby, *The Color of Compromise: The Truth about the American Church's Complicity in Racism* (Grand Rapids: Zondervan, 2019), 198. Sociologist William Julius Wilson places the blame for economic disparities on "the enduring effects of slavery, Jim Crow segregation, public school segregation, legalized discrimination, residential segregation, the FHA's redlining of black neighborhoods in the 1940s and '50s, the construction of public housing projects in poor black neighborhoods, employer discrimination, and other racial acts and processes" (*More Than Just Race: Being Poor and Black in the Inner City* [New York: W.W. Norton, 2009], 152–53).

14. "2018 Median Household Income in the United States," United States Census Bureau, September 26, 2019, https://www.census.gov/library/visualizations /interactive/2018-median-household-income.html.

15. "Births: Final Data for 2017," Joyce A. Martin et. al., Centers for Disease Control and Prevention, *National Vital Statistics Reports* 67:8, (November 7, 2018): 12, 25, https://www.cdc.gov/nchs/data/nvsr/nvsr67/nvsr67_08-508.pdf.

16. "Births: Final Data for 2017," 12, 25,

17. Drawing on data from the US Census Bereau, Zerintha Prince adds, "While 74.3 percent of all White children below the age of 18 live with both parents, only 38.7 percent of African American minors can say the same" "Census Bureau: Higher Percentage of Black Children Live with Single Mothers," *Afro News*, December 31, 2016, https://afro.com/census-bureau-higher-percentage-black-children-live-single-mothers/.

18. "Barriers to Black Progress: Structural, Cultural, or Both?" Manhattan Institute, February 11, 2019, https://www.manhattan-institute.org/html/barriers-black -progress-structural-cultural-or-both-11751.html.

19. Ron Haskins, "Three Simple Rules Poor Teens Should Follow to Join the Middle

Class," The Brookings Institute, March 13, 2013, https://www.brookings.edu /opinions/three-simple-rules-poor-teens-should-follow-to-join-the-middle-class/.

20. Sowell, *Discrimination and Disparities*, 116. In light of these facts, Sowell asks, if the continuing effects of past evils such as slavery play a major *causal* role today, were the ancestors of today's black married couples exempt from slavery and other injustices.

21. "Barriers to Black Progress: Structural, Cultural, or Both?"

22. "On Views of Race and Inequality, Blacks and Whites are Worlds Apart," Pew Research Center, June 27, 2016, http://www.pewsocialtrends.org/2016/06/27 /on-views-of-race-and-inequality-blacks-and-whites-are-worlds-apart/. This same study from Pew Research has found that blacks are more likely than whites to say a lack of motivation to work hard may be holding blacks back: 43 percent of black adults and 30 percent of whites say this is a major reason blacks are having a harder time getting ahead than whites. This study also reveals the sad fact that a majority of blacks (71 percent) say they have experienced discrimination or been treated unfairly because of their race or ethnicity. Roughly one in ten (11 percent) say this happens to them on a regular basis, while 60 percent say they have experienced this rarely or from time to time.

23. Robert Jones and Daniel Cox, "Attitudes on Child and Family Wellbeing: National and Southeast/Southwest Perspectives," PRRI Kid's Wellbeing Survey, September 18, 2017, https://www.prri.org/research/poll-child-welfare-poverty -race-relations-government-trust-policy/.

24. "Talking About Race," The National Museum of African American History and Culture, Smithsonian, https://nmaahc.si.edu/learn/talking-about-race/topics /whiteness, retrieved July 23, 2020.

25. Judith Katz, "Some Aspects and Assumptions of White Culture in the United States," 1990, http://www.cascadia.edu/discover/about/diversity/documents /Some%20Aspects%20and%20Assumptions%20of%20White%20Culture%20 in%20the%20United%20States.pdf

26. Peggy McIntosh, "White Privilege: Unpacking the Invisible Knapsack," in Understanding Prejudice and Discrimination, ed. S. Plous (New York: McGraw-Hill, 2003), 191–196.

27. See Robin DiAngelo, *White Fragility* (Boston, MA: Beacon, 2018).

28. The addition of power to the definition of racism was first put in print in 1970 by Patricia Bidol-Padva, as "prejudice plus institutional power." A. Sivanandan, *Communities of Resistance: Writings on Black Struggles for Socialism* (London: Verso, 1990), 99.

29. Musa al-Gharbi, "Who Gets to Define What's 'Racist'?" Contexts: Sociology for the Public, May 15, 2020, https://contexts.org/blog/who-gets-to-define-whats -racist/, emphasis in original.

30. "Barriers to Black Progress."

31. Proverbs 18:15, 17.

32. By Thomas Sowell, I recommend *Discrimination and Disparities, Black Rednecks and White Liberals, The Quest for Cosmic Justice,* and *Race and Intellectuals*.

See also Walter Williams, *Race and Economics: How Much Can Be Blamed on Discrimination?*; Shelby Stele, *White Guilt: How Blacks and Whites Together Destroyed the Promise of the Civil Rights Era*; Shelby Stele, *A Dream Deferred: The Second Betrayal of Black Freedom in America*; John McWhorter, *Winning the Race: Beyond the Crisis in Black America*; and Heather MacDonald, *The Diversity Delusion: How Race and Gender Pandering Corrupt the University and Undermine Our Culture*.

33. For helpful articles, read Walter Williams, "Disparities Do Not Prove Discrimination," *Times News*, November 7, 2019, https://www.thetimesnews.com/opinion/20191107/walter-williams-disparities-do-not-prove-discrimination; Glenn Loury, "Why Do Racial Disparities Persist? Culture, Causation, and Responsibility," The Manhattan Institute, May 7, 2019, https://www.manhattan-institute.org/racial-inequality-in-america-post-jim-crow-segregation; and Coleman Hughes, "The Racism Treadmill," *Quillette*, May 14, 2018, https://quillette.com/2018/05/14/the-racism-treadmill/.

34. See Jean Halley, Amy Eshelman, and Ramya Mahadevan, *Seeing White: An Introduction to White Privilege and Race*; Dalton Conley, *Being Black, Living in the Red: Race, Wealth, and Social Policy in America*; Michelle Alexander, *The New Jim Crow: Mass Incarceration in the Age of Colorblindness*; Beverly Tatum, *Why Are All the Black Kids Sitting Together in the Cafeteria? And Other Conversations about Race*; and Robin DiAngelo, *White Fragility: Why It's So Hard for White People to Talk about Racism*.

35. See John 17.

36. "Dallas Conference On-Stage Interview with Ekimini Uwan," sistamatictheology, April 7, 2019, 33:15, YouTube video, https://www.youtube.com/watch?v=G9J Qntpn71I. In the book *Can White People Be Saved?* (Downers Grove, IL: IVP Academic, 2018), Willie James Jennings of Yale Divinity School explains whiteness in less charged terms than Uwan, but the identification of a color with an evil superiority complex remains:

> Whiteness is a way of imagining the world moving around you, flowing around your body with you being at the center. Whiteness is a way of imagining the true, the good, and the beautiful configured around white bodies. Whiteness is a way of imagining oneself as the central facilitating reality of the world, the reality that makes sense of the world, that interprets, organizes, and narrates the world, and whiteness is having the power to realize and sustain that imagination ("The Fuller Difference: To Be a Christian Intellectual").

See also Richard Delgado and Jean Stefancic, *Critical Race Theory: An Introduction* (New York: Critical America/NYU Press, 2017), 85.

37. We don't have to speculate which thinkers helped inspire Uwan's understanding of whiteness. At the end of her Sparrow Conference message, she recommended Nell Irving Painter, *The History of White People (New York:* W. W. Norton & Company, 2011); David R. Roediger, *Working Toward Whiteness: How America's*

Immigrants Became White: The Strange Journey from Ellis Island to the Suburbs (New York, NY: Basic Books, 2006)*; Robin DiAngelo, *White Fragility* (Boston, MA: Beacon, 2018)*; and Noel Ignatiev, *How the Irish Became White* (New York: Routledge, 1995). "Dallas Conference On-Stage Interview with Ekimini Uwan," April 7, 2019,

38. "Dallas Conference On-Stage Interview with Ekimini Uwan," April 7, 2019,

39. Jean-Jacques Rousseau, *il n'y a point de perversité originelle dans le cœur humain* Émile ou De l'éducation/Édition 1852/Livre II; *Letters to Malesherbes*, in *The Collected Writings of Rousseau*, vol. 5, eds. Christopher Kelly, Roger D. Masters, and Peter G. Stillman, trans. Christopher Kelly (Hanover, NH: University Press of New England, 1995), 575; *Oeuvres Complètes*, vol. 1, eds. Bernard Gagnebin and Marcel Raymond (Paris: Gallimard, Bibliothèque de la Pléiade, 1959–1995), 1136.

40. Nancy Mathews, *Paul Gauguin: An Erotic Life* (New Haven, CT: Yale University Press, 2001), 157–67.

41. "Noble Savage," https://www.britannica.com/art/noble-savage, accessed August 1, 2019.

42. Thomas Sowell, *Black Rednecks and White Liberals* (New York: Encounter, 2005), 112. Sowell is referring to the historical scholarship of Robert Davis, *Christian Slaves, Muslim Masters: White Slavery in the Mediteranean, the Barbary, and Italy, 1500–1800* (New York: Palgrave Macmillan, 2003), 23.

43. Sowell, *Black Rednecks and White Liberals*, 113. Sowell is referring to Davis's research again in *Christian Slaves, Muslim Masters*, 59.

44. Sowell, *Black Rednecks and White Liberals*, 113.

45. Sowell, *Black Rednecks and White Liberals*, 120.

46. Sowell, *Black Rednecks and White Liberals*, 136.

47. Sowell, *Black Rednecks and White Liberals*, 121.

48. Sowell, *Black Rednecks and White Liberals*, 112.

49. Sowell, *Black Rednecks and White Liberals*, 112.

50. Sowell, *Black Rednecks and White Liberals*, 112.

51. Sowell, *Black Rednecks and White Liberals*, 166.

52. Sowell, *Black Rednecks and White Liberals*, 169.

53. "Executive Summary," Global Slavery Index, Menderoo Foundation, https://www .globalslaveryindex.org/2018/findings/executive-summary/, retrieved July 12, 2020. For facts on modern day slavery and strategies for fighting it, see Kevin Bales, *Disposable People: New Slavery in the Global Economy*, 3rd ed. (Berkeley, CA: University of California Press, 2012).

54. "2018 Global Findings," Global Slavery Index, Menderoo Foundation, https:// www.globalslaveryindex.org/2018/findings/global-findings/ retrieved July 12, 2020.

55. "2018 Global Findings," Global Slavery Index, Menderoo Foundation, https:// www.globalslaveryindex.org/2018/findings/global-findings/ retrieved July 12, 2020.

56. Romans 3:23.

57. Sowell, *Black Rednecks and White Liberals*, 168.

58. Sowell, *Black Rednecks and White Liberals*, 138–39.

59. Sowell, *Black Rednecks and White*, 131.

60. Sowell, *Black Rednecks and White Liberals*, 129.

61. Sowell, *Black Rednecks and White Liberals*, 116.

62. Neil Shenvi, "An Anti-Racism Glossary: Whiteness," https://shenviapologetics .com/an-antiracism-glossary-Whiteness/, accessed August 1, 2019.

63. Jeremiah 31:30.

64. 2 Corinthians 5:10.

65. Deuteronomy 24:16.

66. Ezekiel 18:20.

67. Ephesians 4:3.

68. Zechariah 8:16.

Chapter 9: The Gospel Question

1. C. S. Lewis, "First and Second Things," in *God in the Dock: Essays on Theology and Ethics* (Grand Rapids: Eerdmans, 1994), 280.

2. 1 Corinthians 15:1, 3–4, emphasis added.

3. Jeremiah 22:3.

4. Luke 4:18, quoting Isaiah 61:1.

5. Isaiah 1:17.

6. For a parallel analysis of the claim that social justice is a gospel issue, see D. A. Carson, "What Are Gospel Issues?" *Themelios* 39:2 (July 2014). See also Kevin DeYoung's helpful articles "A Modest Proposal," Gospel Coalition, January 12, 2010, https://www.thegospelcoalition.org/blogs/kevin-deyoung/a-modest -proposal/ and "Is Social Justice a Gospel Issue?" Gospel Coalition, September 11, 2018, https://www.thegospelcoalition.org/blogs/kevin-deyoung/social-justice -gospel-issue/.

7. The original impetus for the argument I unfolded previously was an excellent piece by apologist Neil Shenvi entitled "A Crucial Question about Social Justice," https://shenviapologetics.wordpress.com/a-crucial-question-about-social-justice/, accessed November 6, 2018.

8. Galatians 1:9.

9. This problem is even worse for those who would identify or include Social Justice B with the gospel. Given the doctrine that inequality equals injustice, there is literally an infinite amount of "injustices" to exert our energies to oppose: the lack of Asian representation in Hollywood, the lack of female representation in the STEM field, the lack of gay representation in politics, the lack of [fill in the blank]. This view of social justice, the view that envisions any inequality as an injustice, leads to a definition of social justice that quickly becomes exhausting. In a Christian context, instead of circumcision and dietary restrictions being added to the gospel, one is now saddled with literally an infinite set of "social justice" actions that must be acted upon.

10. *The Good Place*, season 3, episode 11, "Chidi Sees the Time-Knife," originally aired January 17, 2019, on NBC.

11. *The Good Place*, season 3, episode 10, "The Book of Dougs," originally aired January 10, 2019, on NBC.
12. Quoted in Conor Barnes, "Sad Radicals," *Quillette*, December 11, 2018, https://quillette.com/2018/12/11/sad-radicals/.
13. Ozlem Sensoy and Robin DiAngelo, *Is Everyone Really Equal: An Introduction to Key Concepts in Social Justice Education* (New York: Teachers College Press, 2017), 203.
14. Conor Barnes, "Sad Radicals," *Quillette*, December 11, 2018, https://quillette.com/2018/12/11/sad-radicals/.
15. See Williams, *Reflect*, 75–79.
16. Elizabeth Nolan Brown, "Moral Outrage Is Self-Serving, Say Psychologists," Reason, March 1, 2017, https://reason.com/2017/03/01/moral-outrage-is-self-serving/.
17. Roland Bainton, *Here I Stand: A Life of Martin Luther* (Nashville: Abingdon, 1950), 50.
18. Cited in Bainton, *Here I Stand*, 30.
19. Romans 1:16–17.
20. Cited in Bainton, *Here I Stand*, 49.
21. Psalm 103:8–10.
22. Luther, *The Bondage of the Will*, tr. J. I. Packer and O. R. Johnston (Westwood, NJ: Revell, 1957), 153.
23. Cited by John Calvin, *Institutes of the Christian Religion*, vol. 20, ed. John T. McNeill (Louisville, KY: Westminster John Knox Press, 1960), 357.
24. Romans 8:1.
25. Margaret Killingray, "The Bible, Slavery, and Onesimus," *ANVIL* 24:2 (2007):85–96, 89.
26. Acts 2:45.
27. The gospel is the good news of Jesus's death and resurrection. In the death and resurrection of Jesus, we can find a new identity, our deepest identity as sons and daughters of God, through no virtue or performance of our own. It's a gift, a free gift, grace. Grace has been defined as undeserved favor. But a better definition is ill-deserved favor. If I'm walking down the street and a stranger drives by and hands me a thousand dollars, that is an undeserved favor. If I'm sticking a knife into the stranger's tires and he hands me a thousand dollars, that is an ill-deserved favor. In one case, I don't deserve the money. In the next case, I deserve the opposite of the money.

There is implication of salvation as ill-deserved favor that ought to be obvious but took me too long to realize. It means that I have no grounds whatsoever for thinking I'm better than someone else.

This is why racism is not just wrong, though it is certainly that. It is fundamentally, undeniably, egregiously antigospel. It is a way of feeling superior over others. The racist doesn't want to be justified by the death and resurrection of Jesus. He wants to be justified by the melanin levels in his skin cells. It is a way of achieving status as "good" apart from and antithetical to the finished work of Jesus. We are saved not by our "in Christ" spiritual identity but by our ethnic group identity. And that, my friends, is a damnable false gospel.

28. Doing justice is an existential implication of the gospel, yes. But this makes it sound like it is something that comes after the gospel. There is another sense in which doing justice comes not after but before the gospel, an antecedent not an implication of the good news. Think of truth-telling as a parallel. If I'm known as a pathological liar, then people will hardly take me seriously if I tell the truth about the death and resurrection of Jesus. My credibility is shot. This of course does not mean telling the truth, keeping the seventh commandment, is essential to my salvation. Then we would be back in the false gospel of how can I ever know if I've been honest enough to be saved. So there is a difference between gospel content and gospel credibility. When we describe justice as a "gospel issue," this distinction gets lost. Gospel credibility is a biblical category. In John 17, Jesus prays that the world would know Jesus is who he said he is because of the depth and authenticity of Christian love. This doesn't mean Christians loving well is the gospel. Jesus is the gospel. It just means that for the good news of Jesus to be taken seriously, the church must be marked by love.

29. See Acts 8:26–40.

30. Excellent books that help us pursue social justice without losing the gospel include Ronald Nash, *Social Justice and the Christian Church* (2002) and Cal Beisner, *Social Justice: How Good Intentions Undermine Justice and the Gospel* (rev. ed. 2018).

Chapter 10: The Tunnel Vision Question

1. Abraham Kuyper, *Lectures on Calvinism* (Grand Rapids: Eerdmans, 1999), 113.

2. Jacob Bogage, "Dodgeball is a Tool of 'Oppression' Used to 'Dehumanize' Others, Researchers Argue," June 7, 2019, *Washington Post,* https://www.washingtonpost .com/sports/2019/06/07/dodgeball-is-tool-oppression-used-dehumanize-others -researchers-argue/.

3. For deeper insight into concept creep, see Nick Haslam, "Concept Creep: Psychology's Expanding Concepts of Harm and Pathology," *Psychological Inquiry* 27:1 (2016): 1–17.

4. As Brian Brooks points out, "When a Nazi-affiliated publisher attempted to publish his works in Germany, he asked whether the author was of 'Aryan' descent. Tolkien, a noted cultural anthropologist, first dismantled the fictitious 'Aryan' label, then gave this brilliant reply: 'But if I am to understand that you are enquiring whether I am of *Jewish* origin, I can only reply that I regret that I appear to have *no* ancestors of that gifted people. . . . I cannot, however, forbear to comment that if impertinent and irrelevant inquiries of this sort are to become the rule in matters of literature, then the time is not far distant when a German name ["Tolkien" was of Germanic origin] will no longer be a source of pride.'" "Give Stories the Benefit of the Doubt: The 'Lord of the Rings' Orc Controversy Reveals a Disturbing Trend in Our Attitudes Toward Stories," *Chimes,* December 14, 2018, https://chimesnewspaper.com/43275/opinions/give-stories-the -benefit-of-the-doubt/. See Katherine Timpf, "Lord of the Rings Slammed for Perpetuating Racism through Depiction of Orcs," *National Review,* November 27,

2018, https://www.nationalreview.com/2018/11/lord-of-the-rings-slammed-for
-perpetuating-racism-through-depiction-of-orcs/.

5. E. Melanie Dupuis, *Nature's Perfect Food: How Milk Became America's Drink* (New York: New York University Press, 2002), 11.

6. A third-party digital forensics firm corroborated the authenticity of the videos exposing PP's abortion practices, unlike the firm PP itself hired that, predictably, ruled the videos fraudulent. Not only has Planned Parenthood's 3 percent claim been proved a fiction, Planned Parenthood—by its president's own admission—does not provide mammograms. Moreover, women's health clinics with full range services including mammograms outnumber PP centers by a ratio of 20:1 and could easily absorb PP's clientele. Many try to push an ultimatum in which we must either defund PP or care about women's health. But it is not a simple either-or. It can be a beautiful both-and. As policy analyst Sarah Torre puts it, we could "put the funds to more effective use by redirecting them to the thousands of health centers across the country that provide women's health care that is not entangled with abortion or questionable handling of baby body parts." "Congress Should Have Ended Federal Funding to Planned Parentood and Redirected It Toward Other Health Care Options," *The Heritage Foundation*, September 22, 2016, https://www.heritage.org/health-care-reform/report/congress-should-end
-federal-funding-planned-parenthood-and-redirect-it.

7. Vincent Rue et al., "Induced Abortions and Traumatic Stress: A Comparison of Russian and American Women," *Medical Science Monitor* 10:10 (2004): 5–16.

8. Priscilla Coleman, "Abortion and Mental Health: A Quantitative Synthesis and Analysis of Research Published, 1995–2009," *British Journal of Psychiatry* 99:3 (September 2011): 180–86.

9. See, for example, Sarah Owens, "I Went to Planned Parenthood for Birth Control, but They Pushed Abortion," *Federalist*, September 28, 2015, https://thefederalist
.com/2015/09/28/i-went-to-planned-parenthood-for-birth-control-but-they
-pushed-abortion/.

10. See Micaiah Bilger, "Abortion Was the Leading Cause of Death Worldwide in 2018, Killing 42 Million People," Life News, December 31, 2018, https://www
.lifenews.com/2018/12/31/abortion-was-the-leading-cause-of-death-worldwide-in
-2018-killing-42-million-people/.

11. On the methods used to dismember tiny image-bearers, see Francis Beckwith, *Defending Life: A Moral and Legal Case Against Abortion Choice* (Cambridge: Cambridge University Press, 2007), 83–92.

12. Clarence Thomas, "Box v. Planned Parenthood of Indiana and Kentucky, Inc." Justice Thomas cites George Will, "The Down Syndrome Genocide," *Washington Post*, March 15, 2018, A23, col. 1.

13. Caroline Mansfield, Suellen Hopfer, and Theresa Marteau, "Termination Rates after Prenatal Diagnosis of Down Syndrome, Spina Bifida, Anencephaly, and Turner and Klinefelter Syndromes: A Systematic Literature Review," *Prenatal Diagnosis* 19:9 (1999): 808–12.

14. Clarence Thomas, "Box v. Planned Parenthood of Indiana and Kentucky, Inc."

Justice Thomas cites Mara Hvistendahl, *Unnatural Selection: Choosing Boys Over Girls, and the Consequences of a World Full of Men* (Philadelphia: Perseus, 2011).

15. With data from a 2013 NYC report, Lauren Caruba reports, "Black women accounted for 29,007 terminated pregnancies, representing almost 42 percent of all abortions in the city. That same year, black women in the city gave birth to 24,108 babies. With abortions surpassing live births by nearly 5,000, African American women in the city clearly terminated pregnancies more often that they carried babies to term." "Cynthia Meyer Says More Black Babies Are Aborted in New York City than Born," Politifact, November 25, 2015, https://www.politifact.com/factchecks/2015/nov/25/cynthia -meyer/cynthia-meyer-says-more-black-babies-are-aborted-n/.

16. "What We Believe," Black Lives Matter, https://blacklivesmatter.com/what-we -believe/, accessed July 10, 2019.

17. "Births: Final Data for 2017," Joyce A. Martin et al., Centers for Disease Control and Prevention, *National Vital Statistics Reports* 67:8 (November 7, 2018): 12, 25, https://www.cdc.gov/nchs/data/nvsr/nvsr67/nvsr67_08-508.pdf.

18. "Things Are Looking Up in America's Porn Industry," NBC News, January 20, 2015, https://www.nbcnews.com/business/business-news/things-are-looking -americas-porn-industry-n289431.

19. "Can You Guess 2018's Most Viewed Categories On the Largest Porn Site?," July 9, 2019, https://fightthenewdrug.org/pornhub-visitors-in-2018-and-review-of-top -searches/?_ga=2.91985818.183373559.1595796982-473482071.1595796982.

20. "Pornography & Public Health: Research Summary," National Center on Sexual Exploitation, August 2, 2017, https://endsexualexploitation.org/publichealth/.

21. Cristina Maza, "Christian Persecution and Genocide Is Worse Now Than 'Any Time in History,' Report Says," *Newsweek*, January 4, 2018, https://www.news week.com/christian-persecution-genocide-worse-ever-770462.

22. "What Is Christian Persecution," Open Door USA, https://www.opendoorsusa .org/what-is-persecution/, accessed July 9, 2019.

23. Jean-Louis Panne et al., *The Black Book of Communism: Crimes, Terror, Repression* (Cambridge, MA: Harvard University Press, 1999).

24. "Generation Perceptions: Victims of Communism Memorial Foundation Report on U.S. Perceptions Toward Socialism," October 2016, 3–5, http://arielsheen .com/wp-content/uploads/2017/11/VOC-Report-101316.pdf

25. Being selective about which groups make the cut frees us from having to face our own forms of privilege and, thereby, secures our position on the virtuous-victim side of the equation rather than the vicious-victimizer side of the equation.

26. "Almost Half of Practicing Christian Millennials Say Evangelism Is Wrong," Barna, February 5, 2019, https://www.barna.com/research/millennials-oppose -evangelism/.

Chapter 11: The Suffering Question

1. James 1:19.
2. Galatians 6:2.
3. Romans 12:15.

4. For Shai Linne's full story, see "George Floyd and Me," Gospel Coalition, June 8, 2020, https://www.thegospelcoalition.org/article/george-floyd-and-me/.

5. Exodus 3:7.

6. Exodus 22:23, 27.

7. Jeffrey Schwartz and Rebecca Gladding, *You Are Not Your Brain* (New York: Avery, 2011), 124.

8. Conor Barnes, "Sad Radicals," *Quillette*, December 11, 2018, https://quillette.com/2018/12/11/sad-radicals/.

9. Barnes, "Sad Radicals."

10. Neuroscientists talk about Hebb's Law. Neurons that *fire* together *wire* together. Schwartz explains: "When groups of nerve cells (or brain regions) are repeatedly activated at the same time, they form a circuit and are essentially 'locked in' together." Schwartz and Gladding, *You Are Not Your Brain*, 96. Think of how Tribes thinking, then, could literally restructure a human brain.

11. Musa al-Gharbi, "Who Gets to Define What's 'Racist'?" Contexts, May 15, 2020, https://contexts.org/blog/who-gets-to-define-whats-racist/, emphasis in original.

12. Ozlem Sensoy and Robin DiAngelo, *Is Everyone Really Equal: An Introduction to Key Concepts in Social Justice Education* (New York: Teachers College Press, 2017), 203.

13. Shay-Akil McLean, "The People's Science: A Call for Justice Based Ethics for the March for Science & Beyond," Decolonize All the Science, March 2, 2017, https://decolonizeallthescience.com/2017/03/02/the-peoples-science-a-call-for-justice-based-ethics-for-the-march-for-science-beyond/#more-54.

14. Judith Katz, "Some Aspects and Assumptions of White Culture in the United States," 1990, http://www.cascadia.edu/discover/about/diversity/documents/Some%20Aspects%20and%20Assumptions%20of%20White%20Culture%20in%20the%20United%20States.pdf. One could point out that it wasn't science but pseudoscience that was used to justify racism throughout history.

15. Nora Berenstain, "Epistemic Exploitation," *Ergo* 3:22 (2016), http://dx.doi.org/10.3998/ergo.12405314.0003.022.

16. Charles R. Lawrence III, "The Word and the River: Pedagogy as Scholarship as Struggle," *CRT*, 338. See also the standpoint feminism of Patricia Hill Collins.

17. Jonathan Haidt, "Two Incompatible Sacred Values in American Universities: Hayek Lecture Series," Duke University Department of Political Science, October 15, 2016, 1:06:55, YouTube video, https://www.youtube.com/watch?v=Gatn5ameRr8&feature=emb_logo.

18. Quoted in Gustavo Gutierrez, *A Theology of Liberation* (Maryknoll, NY: Orbis, 1986), 112.

19. Quoted in Gutierrez, *A Theology of Liberation*, 113.

20. Quoted in Gutierrez, *A Theology of Liberation*, 113.

21. Happily, Chile has risen from the dark days of the early 1970s to become one of the most prosperous countries in South America. Why? Because it reversed course from Allende's socialist policies. Compare Chile with Venezuela, which was once Latin America's richest nation. Since Allende's rule ended in the early 70s

and Venezuela has continued its path toward the socialist's dream of fighting the unjust economic inequality, a lot of interesting things have happened. The average annual Gross Domestic Product per capita rose 230 percent in Chile. It dropped 20 percent in Venezuela. In 1974, Venezuelans, on average, outlived Chileans by one year. In 2015 the average Chilean lived eight years longer than the average Venezuelan. Chileans are now 51 percent richer than Venezuelans. Unemployment in Chile stands at 6 percent. In Venezuela it stands at 17 percent. Chile's inflation is 3 percent and Venezuela's 487 percent. In 2016 the Chilean economy grew by 2.7 percent. It shrunk by 10 percent in Venezuela. Chile's debt is 17 percent of its GDP. Venezuela's is 50 percent. See Marian L. Tupy, "Chile Is Thriving—So Why Is Socialism Rising?" Fee, December 12, 2016, https://fee.org/articles/chile-is-thriving-so-why-is-socialism-rising.
22. Romans 12:15.

Chapter 12: The Standpoint Question

1. Robin DiAngelo, *White Fragility* (Boston, MA: Beacon Press, 2018), 117.
2. Thaddeus Williams, "Post-Postmodernism," *The Journal of Christian Legal Thought* 6:1 (Fall 2016): 1–4.
3. Margaret L. Andersen and Patricia Hill Collins, "Reconstructing Knowledge," in *Race, Class, and Gender: An Anthology* (Belmont, CA: Wadsworth, 2012), 4–5.
4. Cited in Tyler Tsay, "What Happens Behind Closed Doors: Calling on Faculty and Administration to Dismantle Violent Structures," Williams Record, February 20, 2019, https://williamsrecord.com/2019/02/what-happens-behind-closed-doors-calling-on-faculty-and-administration-to-dismantle-violent-structures/, emphasis added.
5. These words were spoken by an Evergreen State College professor of media studies named Naima Lowe to professor Bret Weinstein. See "The Evergreen State College: Part Two: Teaching to Transgress," Mike Nayna, published March 6, 2019, YouTube video, beginning at 2:45, https://www.youtube.com/watch?v=A0W9QbkX8Cs.
6. John 18:37. See Williams, "Reason," chap. 1 in *Reflect*, for a deeper look at Jesus's use of logic and evidence.
7. Sowell, *Discrimination and Disparities*, 25–26.
8. James Cone, *Black Theology of Liberation* (Maryknoll, NY: Orbis, 2010), 61. Elsewhere Cone adds that "The white vision of reality is too distorted and renders whites incapable of talking to the oppressed about their shortcomings" (51). Notice that color is determinative for Cone in who can and who cannot access truth.
9. The only exception to the list I provided before is Thurgood Marshall, who served on the Supreme Court during the 1973 *Roe v. Wade* decision.
10. Charles Camosy adds, "We should reject taking any direction that would shut certain voices out of the debate based merely on their lack of personal experience. One does not need to have experienced something in order to make a valid claim about it. I believe, for instance, that fast-food corporations ought to pay all of their employees a living wage. Surely, I should reject a claim made by one of their finance

officers who might reply, 'Since you aren't a business owner, and you don't know what it's like to run a business, you need to stay out of the minimum wage debate. Only those with experience running a business get to be part of the argument over just wages.' So could those running child sex-trafficking rings." *Beyond the Abortion Wars: A Way Forward for a New Generation* (Grand Rapids: Eerdmans, 2015), 111.

11. Ron Sider, "An Evangelical Theology of Liberation," in *Perspectives on Evangelical Theology*, eds. Kenneth Kantzer and Stanley Gundry (Grand Rapids: Baker, 1980), 117.
12. Proverbs 14:31 and 19:17.
13. See Psalm 140:12 and Hosea 12:7.
14. See Exodus 22:22–23 and James 1:27.
15. Nicolas Wolterstorff, "Why Care About Justice?" *The Reformed Journal* 36:8 (August 1986): 9.
16. Liberationists argue that "the reader of the Bible must deliberately choose his eyeglasses before he begins reading, and that the 'preferential option for the poor' means just that—a deliberate bias or perspective. Without this, the true meaning cannot be known. We must discard our North Atlantic lenses, we are told, and put on Third World ones—we must lay aside the eyeglasses of the rich to use those of the poor." W. Dayton Roberts, "Liberation Theologies," *Christianity Today* (May 17, 1985): 15.
17. Romans 3:23.
18. Luke 5:20.
19. 2 Peter 3:9.
20. Exodus 23:3.
21. Deuteronomy 19:1–2 and 1 Timothy 5:19.
22. Anthony T. Evans, *Biblical Theology and the Black Experience* (Dallas: Black Evangelistic Enterprise, 1977), 19.
23. Tom Skinner, *If Christ Is the Answer, What Are the Questions?* (Grand Rapids: Zondervan, 1975), 112–13.
24. See Luke 5:32; 7:22; 10:1–9.
25. Isaiah 11:3–4.
26. John 7:24.

Epilogue: 12 Differences Between Social Justice A and B

1. Exodus 20:3.
2. Galatians 3:28.
3. Ephesians 2:14.
4. Romans 12:18. See also Hebrews 12:14 and 1 Peter 3:11.
5. 2 Timothy 2:24.
6. Ephesians 4:1–6.
7. Romans 3:23–24.
8. Acts 3:19.
9. 1 John 1:9.

10. Matthew 22:37.
11. Exodus 23:3.
12. James 2:1.
13. John 7:24.
14. Jude 3.
15. T. S. Eliot, "Thoughts After Lambeth" in *Selected Essays* (London: Faber, 1972), 342. Perhaps Solzhenitsyn said it even better in the closing lines of his Harvard speech: "No one on earth has any other way left but upward. . . . We will be a moral and Christ-loving people, or we will cease to be a people." "A World Split Apart," Harvard Commencement, 1978.

Appendix A: Abortion and the Right to Life

1. The credit for much of this appendix belongs to my friend and colleague Dr. Francis Beckwith, whom I consider the world's leading ethicist on the question of abortion. The primary arguments and examples from this appendix are heavily indebted to his articles "Abortion Rights (Part 1): The Appeal to Pity," *Christian Research Journal* (Fall 1990), March 26, 2009, http://www.equip.org/PDF/DA020-1.pdf and "Abortion Rights (Part 2): Arguments from Pity, Tolerance, and Ad Hominem," *Christian Research Journal* (Winter 1991), March 26, 2009, http://www.equip.org/PDF/DA020-2.pdf. For an updated and expanded version of his arguments, see his book *Defending Life: A Moral and Legal Case Against Abortion Choice* (Cambridge: Cambridge University Press, 2007).
2. See Micaiah Bilger, "Abortion Was the Leading Cause of Death Worldwide in 2018, Killing 42 Million People," Life News, December 31, 2018, https://www.lifenews.com/2018/12/31/abortion-was-the-leading-cause-of-death-worldwide-in-2018-killing-42-million-people/.
3. Clarence Thomas, "Box v. Planned Parenthood of Indiana and Kentucky, Inc." Justice Thomas cites George Will, "The Down Syndrome Genocide," *Washington Post*, March 15, 2018, p. A23, col. 1.
4. Caroline Mansfield, Suellen Hopfer, and Theresa Marteau, "Termination Rates after Prenatal Diagnosis of Down Syndrome, Spina Bifida, Anencephaly, and Turner and Klinefelter Syndromes: A Systematic Literature Review," *Prenatal Diagnosis* 19:9 (1999): 808–12.
5. Tessa Longbons, "Abortion Reporting: New York City (2016)," Charlotte Lozier Institute, December 19, 2018, https://lozierinstitute.org/abortion-reporting-new-york-city-2016/.
6. Clarence Thomas, "Box v. Planned Parenthood of Indiana and Kentucky, Inc." Justice Thomas cites Mara Hvistendahl, *Unnatural Selection: Choosing Boys Over Girls, and the Consequences of a World Full of Men* (Philadelphia: Perseus, 2011).
7. Mary Calderone, "Illegal Abortion as a Public Health Problem," *American Journal of Health* 50 (July 1960): 949.
8. U.S. Bureau of Vital Statistics Center for Disease Control, cited in J. C. Wilke, *Abortion: Questions and Answers* (Cincinnati, OH: Hayes, 1988), 101–2.
9. Bernard Nathanson, MD, *Aborting America* (New York: Doubleday, 1979), 193.

10. Mary Anne Warren, "On the Moral and Legal Status of Abortion," in *The Problem of Abortion*, 2nd ed., ed. Joel Feinberg (Belmont, CA: Wadsworth, 1984), 103.
11. Elaine Duckett, Glynn Verdon, and Caryl Hodges, "Letter to the Editor," *London Daily Telegraph*, December 8, 1962.
12. C. Everett Koop, *The Right to Live: The Right to Die* (Wheaton, IL: Tyndale, 1976), 51–52.
13. Stephen Krason, *Abortion: Politics, Morality, and the Constitution* (Lanham, MD: University Press of America, 1984), 301–10.
14. George Will, "The Killing Will Not Stop," *Washington Post*, April 22, 1982.
15. Francis Beckwith, "Answering Arguments for Abortion Rights (Part One): The Appeal to Pity," 6.
16. Scott Rae, *Moral Choices: An Introduction to Ethics* (Grand Rapids: Zondervan, 2000), 135.
17. Baruch Brody, *Abortion and the Sanctity of Human Life: A Philosophical View* (Cambridge, MA: M.I.T. Press, 1975), 36–37.
18. Lawrence B. Finer et al., "Reasons U.S. Women Have Abortions: Quantitative and Qualitative Perspectives," Guttmacher Institute (September 2005), https://www.guttmacher.org/journals/psrh/2005/reasons-us-women-have-abortions-quantitative-and-qualitative-perspectives.
19. Rae, *Moral Choices*, 136.
20. Charles Camosy, *Beyond the Abortion Wars: A Way Forward for a New Generation* (Grand Rapids: Eerdmans, 2015), 44.
21. Vincent Rue et al., "Induced Abortions and Traumatic Stress: A Comparison of Russian and American Women," *Medical Science Monitor* 10:10 (2004): 5–16.
22. Priscilla Coleman, "Abortion and Mental Health: A Quantitative Synthesis and Analysis of Research Published, 1995–2009," *British Journal of Psychiatry* 99:3 (September 2011): 180–86.
23. Peter Singer and Helen Kuhse, "On Letting Handicapped Infants Die," in *The Right Thing to Do: Basic Readings in Moral Philosophy*, ed. James Rachels (New York: Random House, 1989), 146.
24. Cardinal Roger Mahoney, "Creating a Culture of Life," November 12, 1998, https://www.priestsforlife.org/magisterium/mahonyelectionltr.htm.
25. Jerome LeJeune, "Subcommittee on Separation of Powers, Report to Senate Judiciary Committee S-158," 97th Congress, 1st session, 1981.

Appendix B: Black and White

1. Proverbs 30:5; John 4:24.
2. John 14:6; 18:37–38.
3. John 8:32.
4. John 14:17.
5. Psalm 86:11; Ephesians 4:15; 1 Corinthians 13:6; 3 John 3–4.
6. 1 Timothy 3:15.
7. "Bigot," Merriam-Webster, https://www.merriam-webster.com/dictionary/bigot, retrieved July 20, 2020.

8. Thomas Sowell, *Discrimination and Disparities* (New York: Basic, 2019), 148.

9. The addition of power to the definition of racism was first put in print in 1970 by Patricia Bidol-Padva, as "prejudice plus institutional power." A. Sivanandan, *Communities of Resistance: Writings on Black Struggles for Socialism* (London: Verso, 1990), 99.

10. *Dear White People*, written and directed by Justin Simien, independent, released 2014.

11. Franchesca Ramsey, "5 Things You Should Know About Racism | Decoded | MTV News," MTV Impact, August 12, 2015, 6:17, YouTube video, https://www.youtube.com/watch?v=8eTWZ80z9EE.

12. Michael Eric Dyson, "Michael Eric Dyson Shares Why 'Black People Can't Be Racist' Backstage at Don't Sleep!" BETNetworks, October 4, 2012, YouTube video, https://www.youtube.com/watch?v=bZ0QfLkjujY&feature=youtu.be.

13. In the words of Jemar Tisby,

> What do we mean when we talk about *racism?* Beverly Daniel Tatum provides a shorthand definition: racism is a system of oppression based on race. Notice Tatum's emphasis on systemic oppression. Racism can operate through impersonal systems and not simply through the malicious words and actions of individuals. Another definition explains racism as *prejudice plus power*. It is not only personal bigotry toward someone of a different race that constitutes racism, racism includes the imposition of bigoted ideas on groups of people. In light of these definitions it is accurate to say that many white people have been complicit with racism. . . . White complicity with racism isn't a matter of melanin, it's a matter of power. . . . In the United States, power runs along color lines, and white people have the most influence (Jemar Tisby, *The Color of Compromise: The Truth about the American Church's Complicity in Racism* [Grand Rapids: Zondervan, 2019], 16).

> See also *Can White People Be Saved? Triangulating Race, Theology, and Mission*, eds. Love L. Sechrest, Johnny Ramirez-Johnson, and Amos Young, eds., (Downers Grove, IL: IVP Academic, 2018). This redefinition is also the starting point for discussing race on such popular podcasts as *Pass the Mic* by The Witness: A Black Christian Collective and *Truth's Table* by Michelle Higgins, Christina Edmondson, and Ekemini Uwan.

14. Farrakhan made these racist remarks at a speech in Chicago on February 25, 2018. See Sophie Tatum, "Nation of Islam Leader Farrakhan Delivers anti-Semitic Speech" CNN, February 28, 2018, https://www.cnn.com/2018/02/28/politics/louis-farrakhan-speech/index.html.

15. Lisa Feldman Barrett, "When Is Speech Violence?" *New York Times*, July 14, 2017, https://www.nytimes.com/2017/07/14/opinion/sunday/when-is-speech-violence.html.

16. Romans 8:1.

17. See Thomas Sowell, *Black Rednecks and White Liberals* (New York: Encounter, 2005), chapters 1–3.

18. Sowell, *Black Rednecks and White Liberals*, 111.

19. Romans 2:11.

20. That is not white supremacy speaking; the universal call to repentance from sin that you may know and enjoy your Creator is a repeated call of Scripture, which were not authored by white Western males.

Appendix C: Capitalism and Socialism

1. Mary Meehan, "The Next Generation: What Matters to Gen We," *Forbes*, August 11, 2016, https://www.forbes.com/sites/marymeehan/2016/08/11/the-next -generation-what-matters-to-gen-we/#34531f1d7350

2. Meehan, "The Next Generation: What Matters to Gen We."

3. Yet for all this self-reported altruism, there is also an alarming rise in narcissism among the millennial generation. According to Joel Stein, "The incidence of narcissistic personality disorder is nearly three times as high for people in their 20s as for the generation that's now 65 or older, according to the National Institutes of Health; 58 percent more college students scored higher on a narcissism scale in 2009 than in 1982" "Millennials: The Me Me Me Generation," *Time*, May 20, 2013, https://time.com/247/millennials-the-me-me-me-generation/.

4. Meehan, "The Next Generation: What Matters to Gen We."

5. John Stuart Mill, *On Liberty and Other Writings*, ed. Stefan Collini (Cambridge: Cambridge University Press, 1989), 38.

6. "Generation Perceptions: Victims of Communism Memorial Foundation Report on U.S. Perceptions Toward Socialism," October 2016, 5, http://arielsheen.com /wp-content/uploads/2017/11/VOC-Report-101316.pdf

7. "Generation Perceptions: Victims of Communism Memorial Foundation Report on U.S. Perceptions Toward Socialism," 3.

8. "The Holocaust Knowledge and Awareness Study," The Conference on Jewish Material Claims Against Germany, Schoen Consulting, 2018, 3–4, http://www .claimscon.org/wp-content/uploads/2018/04/Holocaust-Knowledge-Awareness -Study_Executive-Summary-2018.pdf.

9. "The Holocaust Knowledge and Awareness Study," 2.

10. Cited in Joel Stein, "Millennials: The Me Me Me Generation," *Time*, May 20, 2013, https://time.com/247/millennials-the-me-me-me-generation/.

11. Proverbs 19:2.

12. *BLUE*, directed by Jeffrey D. King (Broken Hints Media, 2014), 24–29:30. My purpose here is not to enter into the ecological debates regarding the effects of the logging industry or environmental legislation about the northern spotted owl. My point is illustrative to approach the deeper anthropological point that legislation that fails to adequately understand the nature of those it is intended to help will achieve ironic results.

13. Is capitalism unbiblical? The argument goes that the Bible bans the accumulation of wealth since (1) the OT year of Jubilee, the Sabbatical Year, gleaning, and land redemption are designed to keep people from inordinately hoarding wealth, (2) poverty is a virtue, and richness a vice (Luke 6:20; Matthew 19:16–26), and (3) the early church shared all their goods (Acts 2:42–47).

The OT practices were not aimed at the redistribution of wealth to prevent inequality per se, but rather the redistribution of wealth-gaining opportunities. In addition, the practices of the early church in Acts 2 were voluntary acts of charity, which are a far cry from socialism and government-forced redistribution of wealth.

14. Is Capitalism oppressive? Capitalism, the argument goes, unjustly concentrates wealth in a few hands, causes global inequalities in resource use, and makes the First World rich at the price of Third World poverty.

This argument makes the false assumption that the global supply of goods is a zero-sum game (i.e., there's only so much pie to go around. If America gets a big slice, the rest of the world will starve on slivers). Capitalism is the only economic system that is capable of making the pie bigger by creating new wealth and distributing it. Moreover, capitalism is our best prospect for an economic system when it comes to relieving poverty. The "Asian tigers," Singapore, South Korea, Taiwan, and Japan, have been prosperous despite a lack of natural resources, while resource rich Russia and Brazil are poor because of noncapitalist systems that discourage creativity and risk-taking (e.g., impoverished North Korea versus prosperous South Korea). Bad government policy, not capitalism, shoulders the blame for Third World poverty.

What, then, is the church's role? To intentionally sacrifice luxuries to meet Third World needs (e.g., World Vision child sponsoring). That is, we must consciously use our wealth to obey the biblical mandates to care for the poor (Isa. 58:6–7; 61:1–2; Luke 4:18–19; Jer. 22:1–6; Prov. 19:7).

15. Is capitalism greedy? I highly recommend the work of economist and theologian Deirdre McCloskey to see the other side of this argument, to see how love and service to the community can be and often are motivating factors in free marks. See especially "Avarice, Prudence, and the Bourgeois Virtues," in *Having: Property and Possession in Religious and Social Life*, eds. Williams Schweiker and Charles Matthewes (Grand Rapids: Eerdmans, 2004).

Since greed is a real problem in our capitalist society, the church must take an active role in countering it. How? Greed goes hand in hand with a lack of community. We live in a culture of rugged individualism in which people pursue their own agendas of accumulation and end up living not only profoundly luxurious but also profoundly lonely lives. Jesus prayer in John 17 that Christians would impact the world by showing not lonely individualism but loving, unified Trinity-mirroring community. Church can thereby become a place where people get deprogrammed from the me, me, me mentality and learn to live a more others-centered lifestyle that in turn can have a broader cultural-economic influence of countering the excesses of greedy capitalism.

16. Is capitalism soul-sucking? The charge is that capitalism generates a spiritually void culture of consumerism, a culture flooded with an absurd array of superfluous (e.g., eight hundred brands of sport shoe) and often socially destructive products (e.g., pornography). How might we respond to such charges? First, there is a measure of truth to it. However, the influx of such products is a small price to pay when juxtaposed with the value of economic freedom. Over-consumption says

something about people's character (or lack thereof) more than it speaks to the shortcomings of capitalism. Responsible use of wealth is a matter of the heart and not of an economic system. Materialism can occur in any system.

What should the church's role be in all this? We must resist the urge to conform to consumer culture, the urge to make our churches microcosms of that soul-stifling culture by elevating comfort and egocentric satisfaction. Consumerism gets people preoccupied on superficialities. Churches must reawaken in people a love for the deep things. Consumerism gets people obsessed with meeting their own felt needs. Churches must winsomely mirror to people others-centered, Christ-imitating service. Consumerism makes people relationally shallow. The church must exhibit Trinity-mirroring relational depth.

17. 2 Corinthians 9:7.
18. Deuteronomy 15:10, 11.
19. Hebrews 13:16; Galatians 2:10; and Romans 12:13.
20. "Competing Worldviews Influence Today's Christians," Barna Research Group, May 9, 2017, https://www.barna.com/research/competing-worldviews-influence -todays-christians/.
21. "Three Reasons to Have Hope about Global Poverty," Barna Research Group, April 26, 2018, https://www.barna.com/research/3-reasons-hope-global-poverty/.
22. David O'Reilly, "A Study Asks: What's the Churches Economic Worth?" *Philadelphia Inquirer*, February 1, 2011, https://www.inquirer.com/philly/news /religion/20110201_A_study_asks__What_s_a_church_s_economic_worth_.html.
23. Alexander Hamilton, "The World's Poorest Are Getting Richer Faster Than Anyone Else," *Foundation for Economic Education*, October 27, 2017, https://fee .org/articles/the-worlds-poorest-people-are-getting-richer-faster-than-anyone-else/.
24. McCloskey, "Avarice, Prudence, and Bourgeois Virtue," in *Having*, 330.
25. This scenario comes from Ronald Nash's *Social Justice and the Christian Church* (Lima, OH: Academic Renewal Press, 2002), 104–105.
26. For further insight on how to love the poor well from a Christian worldview perspective, I highly recommend Ronald Nash's *Social Justice and the Christian Church*, Steve Corbett and Brian Fikkert, *When Helping Hurts: How to Alleviate Poverty without Hurting the Poor . . . and Yourself* (Chicago: Moody, 2012); Brian Fikkert and Russell Mask, *From Dependence to Dignity: How to Alleviate Poverty Through Church-Centered Microfinance* (Grand Rapids: Zondervan, 2015); and *Poverty Cure*, a six-part DVD series hosted by Michael Matheson Miller, produced by Acton Media, 2012.
27. In their book *When Helping Hurts*, Steve Corbett and Brian Fikkert helpfully expose another false assumption about human nature behind bad economic ideologies. *If we assume that we are most fundamentally material beings, then we define poverty purely in material terms, which actually makes poverty worse.* The standard socialist story sees people as primarily material beings, poverty as primarily a matter of material lack. The solution, therefore, must be primarily material—that is, the redistribution of material wealth. Corbett and Fikkert argue that this represents a seriously impoverished view of poverty itself. In a biblical

worldview we are material and economic beings, but there is a lot more to us as image-bearers. We are created for relationship with God, with ourselves, with others, and the rest of creation. Poverty can stretch to all these relational domains. "Poverty," Corbett and Fikkert note, "is the result of relationships that do not work, that are not just, that are not for life, that are not harmonious or enjoyable." *When Helping Hurts*, 59.

In other words, a more robust and biblical view of human nature leads us to a more robust definition of poverty, which, in turn, leads to a more holistic approach to poverty alleviation. As we seek to help the poor as Scripture commands (not suggests), we will not focus narrowly on material poverty as socialism has done historically, often meeting material needs in ways that only serve to increase people's spiritual and relational poverty (what Corbett and Fikkert call our "poverty of being"). We will be able to work toward true human flourishing as we allow our view of humans, and therefore, our view of poverty and poverty alleviation to break free from the straightjacket of modern worldviews (from which socialism comes). We are then able to truly love our neighbors more truly as Scripture requires. Taking the Bible's view of human nature more seriously, we will not be swept unknowingly into a false gospel of economic equality and parody of Christ's kingdom that promises shalom but brings only further oppression.

28. G. K. Chesterton, *Christendom in Dublin* in *G. K. Chesterton: Collected Works*, vol. 20 (San Francisco: Ignatius, 2001), 57.

29. Roger Trigg, *Equality, Freedom, and Religion* (Oxford: Oxford University Press, 2012), 29.

30. Harry G. Shaffer, *The Soviet System in Theory and Practice* (New York: Appleton-Century-Crofts, 1965), 30). For theological analysis on this point, see Thaddeus Williams, *Love, Freedom, and Evil: Does Authentic Love Require Free Will?* (Amsterdam: Rodopi, 2011), 77–81.

31. Darrell Cosden, *The Heavenly Good of Earthly Work* (Grand Rapids: Baker Academic, 2006), 108.

Appendix D: Defining Sexuality

1. Marshall Kirk and Erastes Pill (a pseudonym for Hunter Madsen, "The Overhauling of Straight America," November 1987, http://library.gayhomeland.org/0018/EN/EN_Overhauling_Straight.htm.

2. Kirk and Madsen, "The Overhauling of Straight America."

3. Kirk and Madsen, "The Overhauling of Straight America."

4. Kirk and Madsen, "The Overhauling of Straight America."

5. Kirk and Madsen, "The Overhauling of Straight America."

6. Kirk and Madsen, "The Overhauling of Straight America."

7. Kirk and Madsen, "The Overhauling of Straight America."

8. Kirk and Madsen, "The Overhauling of Straight America."

9. See Romans 1:18–32. For theological insight on this passage, see Peter Jones, *God of Sex: How Spirituality Defines Your Sexuality* (Escondido, CA: Main Entry Editions, 2006).

10. Phillip Yancey, *Rumors of Another World: What on Earth Are We Missing* (Grand Rapids: Zondervan, 2003), 88.

11. Chris Hinkle, "More than a Matter of Conscience: Homosexuality and Religious Freedom," *American Academy of Religion* (2000), 112.

12. Quoted in William B. Rubenstein, "Since When is Marriage a Path to Liberation?" in *Lesbians, Gay Men, and the Law* (New York: New Press, 1993), 398, 400.

13. See Romans 1:18–32.

14. Yancey, *Rumors of Another World,* 77.

15. Abraham Kuyper, *Lectures in Calvinism* (Grand Rapids: Eerdmans, 2009), 132.

16. Kuyper, *Lectures in Calvinism,* 54.

17. Jeremiah 17:9; Ecclesiastes 9:3; and Ephesians 2:1.

18. Kuyper, *Lectures in Calvinism*, 132.

19. Kuyper, *Lectures in Calvinism*, 132.

20. Morris Dickstein, *Gates of Eden: American Culture in the Sixties* (New York: Liveright, 1977), 81.

21. C. S. Lewis made a similar point when he said, "Everyone who believes in God at all believes that He knows what you and I are going to do tomorrow." *Mere Christianity* (New York: HarperOne, 2001), 170.

22. Yes, God is so vast and transcendent that there are truths about him we cannot and will never realize. But the minute God reveals a certain truth about who he is, and the minute we brazenly reject that truth, is the minute we reject the God who actually *is*.

23. This has everything to do with what theologians call the simplicity of God. God is simple not in the sense of being easy for us to understand, as in the sum of two and two is simply four. Rather, God is simple as in he is not a sum of parts. The opposite of "simple," theologically, is not "hard to understand" but rather "the sum of different parts." We don't take love then add grace then throw in a bit of omniscience, do some theological arithmetic, and it all adds up to God. No. God is, always has been, and always will be everything he is as a fully actualized being. He is not a composite of more fundamental attributes that, when hammered and nailed together in the right configuration, form a deity. God is, in other words, unbuilt. We, by contrast, are built. We aren't simple in the way God is simple, nor are we authoritative in the way God is authoritative. Someone can deny something we believe to be true of ourselves without trying to cancel our existence.

24. Colin Campbell quoted by Craig M. Gay in "Sensualists Without Heart: Contemporary Consumerism in Light of the Modern Project," in *The Consuming Passion*, ed. Rodney Clapp (Downers Grove, IL: InterVarsity, 1998), 28.

25. See Thaddeus Williams, *Revere* (Bellingham, WA: Lexham, forthcoming 2021), chap. 1 and 4.

26. C. S. Lewis, *The Abolition of Man* in *The Complete Lewis Signature Classics* (New York: HarperCollins, 2007), 710.

27. Around the turn of the new millennium, a new value made its way into children's entertainment. Disney shows like *Hannah Montana* featured plotline after plotline in which grown-ups had zero wisdom worth passing on. Instead, they

were all easy to dupe dimwits and curmudgeons, or, best-case scenario, the feckless cheerleaders of their kids' dreams of superstardom.

28. Matthew 18:6.
29. J. I. Packer, *Evangelism and the Sovereignty of God* (Downers Grove, IL: InterVarsity, 2008), 61.

Appendix E: Ending the Culture War

1. Ephesians 6:10–20.
2. John Calvin, *John Calvin's Bible Commentaries on St. Paul's First Epistle to the Corinthians, Vol. 2,* tr. William Pringle (North Charleston, SC: CreateSpace, 2017), 194.
3. 1 Peter 2:11. See also James 4:1.
4. Romans 7:23.
5. Romans 13:12, 14.
6. Romans 8:13 and Galatians 5:16–24.
7. Matthew 28:19.
8. Romans 12:2; James 1:27; and Philippians 2:15.
9. See Galatians 4:9; 6:14; James 4:2–4; and 1 John 2:16–17.
10. See John 15:18–19 and Matthew 10:22, 25.
11. Luke 6:27, 35.
12. Romans 12:14–21.
13. John 14:30.
14. 2 Timothy 2:24–26.
15. See Luke 4:5–6 and Ephesians 2:2.
16. Acts 10:38.
17. Romans 12:18. See also Hebrews 12:14 and 1 Peter 3:11.
18. Philippians 3:18.
19. Romans 9:2.
20. Romans 9:3.
21. Acts 26:18.

Appendix F: Fragility and Antifragility

1. James 1:2–4.
2. Romans 5:3–5.
3. Hebrews 12:1–2.
4. 2 Corinthians 4:16–17.
5. Philippians 1:29.
6. 1 Peter 1:6–7.

Appendix G: "Good News to the Poor"

1. Luke 4:18–19.
2. Alain of Lille used this phrase to describe the abuse of Scripture in the twelfth century, as did Johann Geiler von Kaisersberg in the fifteenth and Albert Pighius in the sixteenth centuries.

3. See Galatians 1:6–10.

4. Sam Chan, *Evangelism in a Skeptical World: How to Make the Unbelievable News about Jesus More Believable* (Grand Rapids: Zondervan, 2018), 18.

5. Luke 4:21.

6. Luke 23:43. In Luke 18:9–14, Jesus confronts those "who trusted in themselves that they were righteous." He tells them a story in which a Pharisee prays self-righteously, "Thank you that I am not like other men, extortioners, unjust, adulterers or even like this tax collector." Then a tax collector—an oppressor who perpetrated social injustice against the poor—"beat his breast, saying, 'God, be merciful to me, a sinner.' The second man 'went down to his house justified.'" (Note his justification was by grace through faith. It wasn't contingent on him righting the social wrongs he had done, though such just action would be an expected aftereffect of his justification, as in the case of Zacchaeus.)

7. 1 Corinthians 15:1, 3–4.

8. See Galatians 1:11–18. On the unity between Paul's understanding of the gospel as Jesus's gospel as laid out in Matthew, Mark, Luke, and John, see Simon Gathercole, "The Gospel of Paul and the Gospel of the Kingdom," in *God's Power to Save*, ed. Chris Green (Nottingham, England: Inter-Varsity Press, 2006), 138–54, https://media.thegospelcoalition.org/static-blogs/justin-taylor/files/2012/05/Gathercole-GODS-POWER-TO-SAVE-p138-154.pdf.

9. Quoted in Gustavo Gutierrez, *A Theology of Liberation* (Maryknoll, NY: Orbis, 1986), 112–13.

10. Jude 3.

General Index

CPSIA information can be obtained
at www.ICGtesting.com
Printed in the USA
LVHW050136110221
678976LV00002B/2